LOCAL DJ

A Rock 'n Roll History

Peter C.
Cavanaugh

Pioneering the Evolution of
Rock 'n' Roll Radio

Launching the Careers of Bob Seger,
Ted Nugent, Alice Cooper
and Dozens More

13337-CAVA

Library of Congress Number:		2001119892
ISBN #:	Hardcover	1-4010-4164-7
	Softcover	1-4010-4163-9

This book was printed in the United States of America.

To order additional copies of this book, contact:
Xlibris Corporation
1-888-7-XLIBRIS
www.Xlibris.com
Orders@Xlibris.com

To All My Special Ladies:

Mother Isabelle

Wife Eileen

Daughters Laurie, Colleen, Candace and Susan

Granddaughters Katherine, Elise and Riley

And These Gentlemen of Highest Esteem:

Father Donald

Uncle Vincent

Sons-In-Law Paul, Lindsey, Jeff and Rich

Grandsons William, Cooper, Josh and Owen

13337-CAVA

"I'M GONNA WRITE A LITTLE LETTER

GONNA MAIL IT TO MY LOCAL DJ.

IT'S A JUMPIN' LITTLE RECORD

I WANT MY JOCKEY TO PLAY"

Chuck Berry

"Roll Over Beethoven"

(1956)

FOREWORD

From my earliest memories, I had always wanted to be "on the air." That was all I ever had in mind. This was true even before my father died on the radio when I was six years old. Donald J. Cavanaugh was working for the Veteran's Administration as Assistant-Chief in Syracuse by the summer of 1948.

Having always achieved the highest possible scores in Civil Service Examinations, he may well have attained higher organizational distinction were it not for several dedicated Irish predispositions, heavy consumption of alcoholic beverages not being the least impactive. The "Holy Water" had cost him a number of years of unemployment, but he had not taken a drink in over six months when he entered WNDR's studios to narrate a program called, "News for Veterans" on Thursday morning, July 29. It was a long, thirty minute script. Halfway through, he paused for breath. He began gasping. There was a problem. He slumped back in his chair. It was a massive coronary.

He was dead at 52, an age I have amazingly surpassed. A transcription was made of the broadcast. At my mother's wish, it was destroyed. I was not allowed to attend the funeral, being "too young." I stayed at home. With my radio.

13337-CAVA

CHAPTER ONE

MEET THE BEATLES

Rock 'n Roll Radio. It's all that you need to be free.

This raging Irish son, condemned to the finest of educations for childhood sins, first grew to have faith in nothing at all.

Except acceptance.

Before the Internet or satellites or television, our country had just won the greatest war in the history of Earth. Communication no longer required press or paper. For the first time in human history, we had become easily linked by electrons.

Invisible radio beams were everywhere, sent and received. Yet there was disparity. "Broadcasting" was a one-way channel by definition and design. All could hear, but few might speak. For every individual station waited 200,000 minds. It seemed a terribly sacred thing, such magic never known before— thoughts connecting over vast distance at the very speed of light, unified and controlled in each instance by a single transmitting source. I was powerfully drawn by inexorable and instinctive inclination.

Then came new music through this gateway. Memory brings it present.

The Beatles are virtually inaudible even 20 feet away. They could be singing: "This Is the Way We Wash Our Clothes" for all we know, but it's **THE BEATLES**.

Imagine the exact center of your psychic universe only enticing inches away. Past commandments and catechisms, contradictions and confusions; beyond sin and salvation, you are delivered. Unequivocal validation stretches distant into the future.

Here come Stones and Who. Zeppelin too.
Nugent and Seger. Bare women quite eager.
Alice and KISS. Grand Funk couldn't miss.
Jimi needs coke. MC5's not a joke.
Sergeant Pepper arrives as a war shatters lives.
The power rolls in, sacramental with sin.
A lifeweb spin

The Beatles perform for a full 25 minutes. As captured on early radio station cassette recorders, the entire program from start to finish is one enormous, ear-shattering, mind-rattling, caterwauling shrrieeeeeeeeeeeeeeek as thousands of females, most barely pubescent, give birth to the most primal roar ever witnessed before or since. These young creatures are now in their early fifties, perhaps less joyously astride the baby boom's cresting wave, even those occasionally graced with rare moments of physical sex orgasmically approaching the intensity of that prolonged, collective, vocal climax so many autumns ago.

For me, it flashed with sudden, inexplicable, wordless anointing, having come so curiously about.

In August of 1963, Philadelphia's Swan Records was singularly unsuccessful in promoting the first American release of a totally unknown British band blithely named after insects. "She Loves You" died without fanfare at the bottom of the charts. Radio airplay in major cities had been limited, if not completely lacking. Contact had failed.

"Beatles?" "Spiders?" Why not "Cockroaches?" "We could call them "The Cocks," snickered industry "experts" although preserving their repartée from even minimal public consumption. This would have been completely unthinkable and potentially career-ending in such restricted times. There were many more secrets then. Eventually we would learn about The Beatles ingesting happy little European picker-uppers during their earliest sets together, a discovery far outshadowed by prior headlined revelations of marijuana and LSD usage. There would also come news about John and Paul both marrying relatively strange women. Far more important than such minor matters would be a master-shift in world music less than three short years away. All these things were absent from thoughts that September day. Mere presence of The Beatles as they were, before lasting fame, brought all one could possibly hold.

I had sensed from the start they were special, playing "She Loves You" as a disc-jockey on WNDR in Syracuse only months before as a "Peter C. Hitbound Discovery." The song was pulled by station management from airplay after one week's chance in August of '63. They remained essentially unknown. Then came Sullivan.

Ed Sullivan was the most powerful reigning figure in national television entertainment. "The Ed Sullivan Show" was watched by millions on CBS every Sunday night. Mr. Sullivan, a mumbling, dour-faced New York newspaper columnist catapulted to fame and power by "radio with pictures," was demonstrably devoid of any performance skills himself, nor did he ever make pretense of possessing any significant attributes other than the ability to "spot talent," and book virtually anything or anyone he wanted on his "variety show." This went a very long way. Ed featured all the "A" list singers, bands, groups, actors, and dancers of the day on his top-rated program, and even made time for counting horses, singing dogs and talking mice. You just never knew who or what might show up, from when or where. In the 'Fifties, he'd launched Elvis.

It was at Heathrow Airport in London when Sullivan, bound for New York after a brief European jaunt, noticed substantial turmoil and clamor greeting the arrival of four "long-haired" musicians arriving home off a British Airways flight from Germany. Interest aroused, he did some checking. The "Beatles" had just become the United Kingdom's top-selling recording group and offered what we now call a "unique selling proposition" for lack of clearer verbiage in declaring the indescribable. There was not the slightest hesitation. Sullivan offered The Beatles $50,000 for three appearances on his show. The first would be in February. Word quickly spread. Everyone knew Sullivan had "the feel." Capitol Records signed the group, then planned and executed a massive promotional assault. The hype was historic with a product perfect. Media coverage was unrelenting. Everything detonated at once.

Even before the Beatles appeared on Sullivan, I outrageously went all the way, being in a brand new city starting a whole new life. There was nothing to lose but loss. The sudden death of a President had severed former professional ties and fated me to Flint. Hundreds of thousands of strangers now joined me each night over WTAC, "The Michigan Monster," top-rated in Flint, Bay City, Saginaw, Midland and twenty surrounding counties. The agenda seemed predetermined. My message was the music. Every other cut played on WTAC's " Peter C. Show" was by The Beatles.

Local record shop tracking echoed a coast to coast chain reaction of unfathomable proportion. After just a few short weeks, The Beatles vaulted from borderline obscurity in the States to enjoy an unparalleled top five slots on the Billboard Magazine singles chart ("Can't Buy Me Love," "Twist and Shout," "She Loves You," "I Want To Hold Your Hand," and "Please Please Me"), while seven other singles were moving up with bullets in the Top 100. In contesting for "WTAC Beatles' Books", 10,000 of which had been ordered "betting on the boys", 20,000 pieces of mail were received each day. I'd call out several names a few times an hour, and those mentioned would phone to win. Michigan Bell equipment regularly overloaded, and the phone company seriously threatened to pull our lines.

By summer, "A Hard Day's Night," the first Beatles' film, debuted at the Palace Theater in downtown Flint. WTAC had set up a live remote broadcast and I was mobbed— a phenomenon sadly not to be experienced again upon any subsequent occasion. Teenage girls clutched at my clothing, wrestled with my wristwatch and grabbed at my groin. I escaped minus tie, shirt, shoes and socks. Every man should experience such attentive passion at least once in his lifetime. Then it was announced that the Beatles would appear at 2 P.M. on September 6th at Olympia Stadium in Detroit; utter pandemonium broke loose.

Aware that security would be massive, much time was spent in thought and strategic planning. Although WTAC's Program Director and I had obtained two tickets for the instantly sold-out performance through Capitol Records, we had been told there would be no radio interviews, nor radio folk allowed backstage. The only ones who could meet briefly with the Beatles were television representatives and a few reporters from the Detroit Newspapers. We were asked to understand that the Beatles, certainly, had nothing against radio people. Indeed, they felt quite to the contrary. It was simply a matter of controlling logistics.

Sure.

Our theory was that the Beatles probably thought all the rest of us were like "Murray the K," a New York personality who had clung to them like a leech once they hit our golden shores and even had the audacity to run around proclaiming himself "the Fifth Beatle." He seemed a complete asshole with a bad toupée. Who could blame those Beatles? Clear challenge presented itself as a test of cultural and personal integrity.

Bending rules had become a practiced art for my emerging generation. It was far easier gaining forgiveness than permission, and usually unnecessary after the fact. Opportunity was only limited by soft imagination, or reticence to explore edges and boundaries beyond the given. Acceptance of the Olympia prohibition was unthinkable and never discussed.

An official looking "Michigan State Police Beatle Security Pass" was designed, which a printer accomplice set to type with several colors featuring the Michigan State Seal. If officials in Lansing might ever protest appropriation of their implied authority, it would be a "baby bust" in the context of the exercise and provide plentiful publicity. Thus, even arrest offered a strong second best.

That enchanted Sunday we drove to Olympia and parked adjacent to the stage entrance. Leaving our also self-constructed "State Police Beatles' Parking Permit" prominently displayed on the dashboard. We casually strolled inside. At each of three perimeter security points, we were ushered right through. Part of the secret was that we had practiced at length assuming a very "we belong" demeanor, a delicate mixture of congenial arrogance and condescending patience. This was the unspoken message:

"We know you have to look at these things. We are obviously well-connected people, so make it snappy. If provoked, we may quickly do serious injury to your station in life as a minimal consequence of boorish behavior."

We naturally went right down front on the floor and were less than 20 feet away as The Beatles hit the stage. Recorders rolling, minutes passed like seconds. And then the moment was at hand. Would our Beatles passes work with their own English security squad? We approached a side stage entrance with energetic élan and were greeted with a very British , "Of course, Gentlemen. Right this way, please."

Goddamn. A Grand Slam Home Run.

We were backstage at Olympia. The television and newspaper contingent had yet to be admitted. The Beatles were sitting at a large, uncovered banquet table. We told them who we were and how and why we made up the passes. We also explained that "Murray the K" was a jerk and the "K" stood for "queer" since he couldn't spell worth a shit. John found this particularly amusing and observed, "Brian (their manager) seems fond of him." With their consent, we quickly interviewed all four.

Frothy questions and answers were standard for the era. Yes, The Beatles loved playing "The States," thought Michigan girls were attractive and were pleased with their sudden success. No, they weren't breaking up, getting married or changing record companies. Possibly, they'd come back to Detroit, make a new movie, or tour Europe next winter. They hesitated at doing "station promos," since there'd been "trouble before" from competing facilities and Capitol had asked them to "pleasantly refrain." We then boldly asked to have our pictures taken with them, apologizing for being uninvited intruders. The Beatles seemed to be entertained by our audacity and the cameras clicked.

All in all, the Beatles were quite nice, reflecting a delicate mixture of congenial arrogance and condescending patience. Lennon and McCartney seemed particularly bright. Paul privately asked us to convey to our listeners back home an important single thought: "Tell 'em ta quit trowin' 'em fookin' jelly beans!"

We returned to Flint and spent the entire night in the studio producing "WTAC Meets The Beatles," which combined all of our floor taping and band interviews. It became an hour-long program that reasonably captured the adventure. It ran every other hour for a day-and-a-half. Ratings skyrocketed. I could almost hear roaring applause from old men gathered in a whirling Irish bar

13337-CAVA

CHAPTER TWO

OCCASIONS OF SIN

It certainly all began in a fine, traditional way.

"My name is MacNamara. I'm the leader of the band."

Although I was barely two, and could hardly walk (a condition I have since chronically experienced in similar surroundings through subsequent times for reasons other than infancy), my father would stand me up on the bar to entertain his cronies with a fairly impressive ensemble of various Irish ballads, dirges and chants, which I mastered even as I learned to speak. They would give me pennies and shot glasses of beer for my trouble. To this day, it seems like more than a fair exchange as I recall the laughter and the love.

Ed Murphy played nothing but Irish music every Saint Patrick's Day on WSYR radio in Syracuse, a departure from his usual mix of selections from "The Hit Parade." He had the most popular morning show in town. One of his sponsors was "Old Spice After Shave." I use it to this day. Ed came on at 7 A.M. right after my real hero left the air. "The Deacon" would finish broadcasting from his "old wired-woodshed, Uptown and Down City" with the sound of a slamming gate. To be mentioned as climbing this gate for the program's close was a public honor and envied distinction. I sent in dozens of postcards 'til he finally said, "Whadyaknow, little Peter Cavanaugh's on board today, too!" It was my eighth birthday and friends and relatives were immeasurably impressed, even though the Deacon had started as a joke.

A young announcer named Bob Doubleday, exiled to reporting "Agricultural News" years earlier from five until seven each dawn back in the '40's, decided to do his reports "sounding like a farmer."

"Aye—yah. Bob Jones in Canastota's been up all night with a new colt. Henry Rogers out by Oneida got this fox in his front yard with one shot. Jim Taylor's wife over in Weedsport sent some jelly in and she sure didn't have to do that, but it was real, real nice."

Then, he'd hit his "player-piano" for a tune or two or, most often, engage in prolonged telephone calls with listeners, only his side of the dialogue being broadcast. He'd play scratchy barnyard sounds under his twangy recital of hog prices, and frequently offer several minutes of silence while he visited "the house out back." By the time his Program Director caught on, it was too late. "Deacon Doubleday" had the highest ratings on the station and held them for decades with an act begun in rebellion, ignoring all convention. His show pulled ages and lifestyles across the board, attracting even more listeners than the prior ratings champion for many a year: The Rosary, which was recited each weekday evening at six for a quarter-million Catholics residing within the Syracuse signal area. Whether they all listened or not, most faithfully reported they did so when questioned.

The Virgin Mary and I share the same birthday. Such a wondrous historical coincidence was brought to my attention shortly after starting parochial school at the age of 10 by Sister Stanislaus in the context of trying not to be a "bold, brazen thing." Cathedral Academy was "The Bishop's School." I, mixing with the offspring of prominent attorneys, doctors and other "professionals" usually several generations into the American experience, was economically deprived. One of but few admitted from "the area." Retrospectively, I suspect they had a ghetto quota. Our parish priest had intervened on my behalf when, as nine-year-old leader of a small gang of Irish boys seeking maxi-

13337-CAVA

mum fun with minimal funds, I became faced with the option of reform school or Catholic education following a highly unfortunate and absolutely accidental incendiary mishap.

The seven of us had a quarter. A new Tarzan film had opened at the neighborhood movie house. I bought a single ticket, then admitted my friends by opening a fire-door near the rear of the theater. I returned to the box office and announced that I had suddenly taken ill. I was in tears and obtained a refund. I was back in my seat within seconds through that fire door. We considered the movie surely a masterpiece. It was the first time we had seen Tarzan use "flaming arrows." Obviously, we would need to do the same.

The apparatus we assembled in my backyard was of the most basic construction, but proved to be functional when the arrow stuck near the very top of our neighbor's garage. It was quickly evident I had applied far too much lighter-fluid. There was an almost instantaneous wall of flames. The garage burned to the ground and was totally destroyed. A brand new '51 Dodge parked inside went with it. The police were called. Someone informed. Our doorbell rang. It was Catholic School or else.

Mickie Harlow was also from "the area." A dress code was rigidly enforced at Cathedral. On our first day of school, Mickie wore a paper tie displaying, in red-crayon, the words: "Times Are Tough." For such public admission of honest misfortune he was soundly slapped. The little Sister thought that Mickie was being provocative. He was merely wearing what his Mom had made. He had no tie of cloth. I was more fortunate, taking mental note of certain new realities.

Mrs. Harlow's failed expectations at surely invoking the sympathetic understandings of Christ's own bride notwithstanding, I was to spend eight years of my academic career at Cathedral. I graduated in 1959 as President of the Student Council with a New York State Regents' Scholarship. This would enable me to obtain four years of superb Jesuit training at LeMoyne College in Syracuse. In 1957, I began my dance with the devil.

"Have you lost your faith yet?" snarled Father Shannon. I had been unceremoniously released from an assignment and high honor which the good Father himself had arranged on my behalf at radio station WHEN. It was there I presented "Saints of the Week" as part of "The Catholic Hour." This gave me license to exit an ever more confining classroom three hours a week to hang around an actual radio station, while simultaneously earning what was then referred to as "major brownie points." I was asked to take my leave when WHEN's Program Director heard me on WNDR, the "Rock 'n Roll Station," playing "that music" with "those people."

Father Shannon had earlier been a big Syracuse "radio star" in his own right as a singer ("Smilin' Jackie Shannon") on WFBL and later on the CBS Radio Network. Around age 30, for reasons never given other than implied divine intervention, he left the business to enter the seminary. Following ordination, "Jackie" was eventually made "Director of Communications for the Diocese of Syracuse," stationed at the Cathedral, where all the hierarchical action was. I was sort of a "discovery" for him, I suppose. He had often discussed my potential as a candidate for the priesthood. He felt betrayed that Peter, an altar boy of highest standing, had become involved in "popular, common, vulgar entertainment." Far worse, it was "Negro" in origin, representing a new, clearly insidious invasion by forces undefined. It was surely Satanic in origin, consecrated to the decay and destruction of American youth.

Father Shannon wasn't impressed that the "Hound Dog" was a white guy. When I was in 8th grade, dealing with the vicious, soul-threatening, mind-reeling onslaught of puberty, several black friends told me about "The Hound." George Lorenz was well into his late forties; an old announcer with a brand new trick. He broadcast every night from seven 'til Midnight on 50,000 watt WKBW out of Buffalo at 1520 on the dial. He played nothing but "Rhythm and Blues" music and I was instantly hooked. He had this strange instrumental theme with which he'd open every show. It was a gut-bucket, honky-tonk rendition of "My Wild Irish Rose," his primary sponsor being "Wild Irish Rose Wine," alcoholically fortified for the financially challenged. My own familiarity with this fine product was limited to reading its name on the labels of empty bottles surrounding sleeping bums on park benches just down the block. I tried some once in later life, and came to believe it would make a fine after-shave itself.

George Lorenz rarely used his real name on the air. He'd force his powerful voice from deep in the chest and growl, "It's the Hound Dog, Mama! You got nothin' but the sounds of the Hound on KB-Buffalo. God, Almighty! I'm talkin' 'bout Love on the Loose! Dig it! James and 'Da Flames!" Lorenz struck a good fifteen years before "Wolfman Jack" and, when all is said and done, the "Wolfman" was just doing an imitation of "The Hound" all those years on Mexican radio and riding NBC's "Midnight Special." Jack hailed from Brooklyn, where "KB" came in loud and clear at night, and he even copied the Hound's trademark mustache and goatee. When Mama Willie Mae Thornton released "Hound Dog" in the early '50s, it was a salute to Lorenz. As Elvis made it truly famous, only the original faithful thought of George. But, it was "The Hound Dog" who introduced me to thoughts of "doin' the wang-dang doodle all night long." And "ballin' Annie in 'de fanny." And "squeezin' dat lemon 'til de juice runs down mah leg."

Christ. We had been told at Cathedral by Sister Cecilia that even listening to Don and Phil's "Wake Up Little Suzie" was a Mortal Sin since it implied that "a boy and girl were sleeping together without having partaken in the Sacrament of Marriage," an interpretation which had never remotely dawned on her students.

This era of Catholic education stressed a highly structured, excruciatingly well-defined philosophy regarding matters sexual in nature. Even the word "sex" was never openly uttered other than in extremely hushed tones and then only after the "boys" and "girls" had been separated for "frank discussion" of "certain private things." The tight confines went along these lines: To have brief "impure thoughts" was a venial sin. To willingly enjoy "impure thoughts," let alone engage in "impure acts," was a Mortal Sin.

Both sins could be forgiven if fully confessed to a priest who was empowered by God to grant penance and absolution. If you died with venial sins unforgiven, you'd need to spend a certain amount of time in a place called Purgatory before finally going to Heaven. Think of it as waiting at Detroit Metro in mid-January for a flight to Hawaii with a blinding blizzard delaying all planes. Every venial sin one carried would be six more inches of snow and another 12 hours in the terminal. A Mortal Sin, however, brought a far, far darker fate. Death's arrival with an unforgiven Mortal Sin damning the soul would mean burning in the raging, searing, blast-furnace, blow-torch fires of Hell for all Eternity.

There were the heavy spins.

"And how long is Eternity in which the soul and body burns forever?"

"If there was a giant steel ball the size of the planet earth suspended in space and if every 1,000,000 years a small, gentle dove flew past and the very tiniest tip of its feathery little wing just barely touched, a few itty-bitty molecules of steel completely invisible to the human eye being brushed away; by the time the ball was completely severed in two, Eternity will have just begun."

"And what part of the body burns the hottest in Hell?"

"The part you have sinned with!"

There was a finale.

"Is anything besides committing a sexually impure act a Mortal Sin?"

"Yes!"

"Wanting To!"

There I was being told "wanting to do it" was the same as "doing it" with an identical penalty. The punishment was, pardon the expression, Sister, a stiff one at that. I intellectually came to a painful realization that I was confronted with two mutually exclusive moral positions:

Either (a) I was condemned to be a Mortal Sinner throughout life with my only hope for Salvation being a friendly comet nailing me at light-speed velocity just seconds after leaving a Confessional or (b) I could avoid self-deception and explore my God-given conscience.

Uncle Vince was the one who helped me straighten it all out.

Vincent was my father's older brother and had studied for the priesthood. With my father's death, he had become my mentor. He and my Aunt Louella lived above us on Ashworth Place in Syracuse. He didn't have much money either.

Vincent had been noticed as a very young man by the nuns and had been educated in the finest schools at Church expense. While in Rome completing his education and just prior to ordination, Vincent felt obliged to enlist in the U.S. Army. World War One had started. He fought in the trenches of France and was gassed several times by German forces. It was a good thing he had that mask. He gave it to me on my seventh birthday.

When the war ended, Vincent decided that he didn't want to be ordained after all. Still, he owed the Church something. Debts must be paid. He spent many years teaching Greek and Latin at Mount Saint Mary near Baltimore, a major Catholic seminary where a significant number of Diocesan Priests in America received final training. He had instructed many of the Cathedral clerics and several of his students would become future Bishops. He had remained a single man into his early fifties.

Vincent would visit Syracuse on vacations and stay with his sister Molly. Aunt Molly was married to George Bassett. The Bassett family owned a farm near Syracuse where we would travel once in a while. They had owned the land since before the American Revolution. There was a farm girl named Louella who had been orphaned at a young age and adopted by the Bassetts. No one was quite sure who her father might have been or spoke of her mother.

Louella was in her late thirties and had been married briefly to a traveling salesman. He had abandoned her in Detroit, and she had obtained a divorce. She was not very polished. She had just managed to finish fourth grade and was barely literate, but could draw beautiful pictures. She was a Protestant. All these things were fine with Vince. They fell in love and were married. As expected, the powers-which-were went wild.

Having married a divorced-woman, Uncle Vince was bounced by the Church. He moved on to Cornell for six years, where he was a Professor of Philosophy. He came to the conclusion that he probably didn't know anything at all. He left teaching when he turned 65.

My Uncle Vince moved back to Syracuse and became a night desk-clerk at the old Howard Hotel in the very worst part of town. He told me he liked "hangin' out with the other bums." They didn't mind it if he said "ain't." He would bring me to the library all of the time and choose "important books." I read "Gone With the Wind" when I was eight and "Ulysses" before I was 10 (when I burned-down that garage). I would sneak out of my room in the middle of the night to study the stars with him through an old, dusty telescope he set up on his porch.

Vince's first-cousin was Dr. Joseph McGrath. He was Director of Music for the Diocese and played organ in the Syracuse Cathedral. For some reason I never knew, there was a bit of enmity between the two. "All he needs is a monkey," Vince would say. As I would ask him of life, Uncle Vince would answer all of my questions with questions. I later came to know he practiced the "Socratic Method" of instruction. He loved Socrates and would sign that name to many articles submitted to the Syracuse Herald-Journal and Post-Standard Editorial

Departments. He was published all the time incognito. He hated Republicans.

It was from Uncle Vince I learned of Ireland. He spoke of it incessantly. His only sorrow in life was that he would never visit the "Old Country." He said he was "too tired" and "too poor." He said that none of the Cavanaughs had ever "gone back." The only promise he ever asked of me was that I would "return" in memory of all who could not. He said, "All we dead Cavanaughs will go along for the ride, if you don't mind." He said it would be important to remember that. I assured him I would do so, but hoped he would live forever. There was sorrow in his eyes. He said that was not a problem.

When I questioned Uncle Vince about sex, he asked me where I thought all the priests and nuns who said it was sinful had come from. "Woolworth's?" he inquired.

Then when Buddy Holly, Richie Valens and The Big Bopper died in early '58, Sister Cecilia told us all that God had punished them. Yet WNDR's rating shares rose from 20's and 30's to 50's and 60's. Everybody seemed to be listening, including God. He heard everything.

WNDR's triumph marked the very birth of the "Rock era." It advanced in a vacuum despite the "traditional radio professionals" who shunned any aspect of the new phenomenon, which was a fusion of grass roots "Country and Western" (as it was then called) and Hound Dog style, black-based "Rhythm and Blues" (or "Nigger Music" as it was characterized by a majority of older whites.) I, and other young enthusiasts, was more than willing to step forward to grab the controls. We didn't have to wait for anyone to move out of our way. They weren't even there to begin with. Who would have thought?

My professional career started one April after riding my bike out to WNDR, which had moved to a swampy area just outside of town where the towers were located. Every spring there was a flood, so the last 50 feet were traveled by boat. I was answering phones on weekends for 50 cents an hour, a position obtained after many uninvited visits just "hangin' around."

My first efforts at WNDR were extended to include writing early morning news. I eventually cajoled my way into doing a few trial "newscasts" and then a regular weekend news schedule.

"If you see news happening, call WNDR Action Central at Gibson 6-1515. WNDR pays $10 for the Top News Tip of the Week!"

"WNDR Action Central News" was fully produced with hysterical hyperbole. Each newscast featured music beds, echo chambers, filter processing, sound effects, singing jingles and extreme editing. Fifty stories in four-and-a-half minutes were the minimum required. One time, I squeezed in seventy-two. Stapleton always had his stopwatch handy.

WNDR's News Director, Bud Stapleton, was a former Marine-tough and mean. Bud, a World War Two vet who spent several serious years "island hopping" in the South Pacific, considered his peaceful return to civilian life "a fuckin' pain in the ass." He was a certified American hero— it was Lt. Bernard J. Stapleton who raised the first American flag over Tokyo on September 3, 1945. I saw the picture. He was a short, wiry scrapper with laughing eyes, a sharp pug nose and the map of Eire stamped across his face.

Friday evenings brought Bud's spouse-approved "Night Out With The Boys." Bud's weekly trauma therefore occurred almost every Saturday morning, when he would rise for his weekend news shift from short and fitful sleep on an incredibly funky, sin-stained couch in our WNDR reception area. His booze-blistered eyes recoiled from the light, his psyche mangled in the torturing clutches of a heart-binding hangover. Bud would take the deepest breath his smoke encrusted lungs could endure, and shake the walls with mighty vocal magnificence.

We would be hanging around the studios, several rooms distant, and yet could still hear the two ritualistic screams, always faithfully delivered in exact sequence:

3337-CAVA

"Jesus, Mary and Joseph!"

"Where the fuck is it?"

At this point, we would helpfully and carefully join Bud in his anxious quest for "the gun."

"The gun" was Bud's beloved 38-caliber, Smith and Wesson "Police Special," for which he was fully licensed. Stapleton was also a duly sworn Deputy Sheriff, a distinction quite valuable during many "news investigations" he was prone to initiate at a second's notice, usually into the more sordid, squalid sectors of fair Syracuse.

"The gun" was always loaded, usually with safety released.

It would generally turn up in challengingly random spots, since Bud would have "hidden it from himself" as a "security precaution." Specifics as to its exact whereabouts would inevitably be obliterated in the misty shroud of an alcoholic blackout which Bud eloquently and poetically referred to as "The Dark Irish Night." The gun was usually somewhere in the building, although every so often it would turn up in his car.

The longest it was ever missing was half an hour. This was when Bud overlooked the fact he had comfortably slept with it shoved in his shorts. It was upon that occasion we heard Bud's tearful off-air lecture on the ravages of age "numbin' up your dick and balls." The thought that a fifth of Wild Turkey and a half-case of "Congress Beer" might have played a slight role in his accidental self-anesthetization was not offered.

WNDR "Action Central News" was Bud's wildly effective interpretation of Top 40 Tabloid Journalism, later reaching its highest plateau on such stations as WFUN in Miami, WKBW in Buffalo and the legendary CKLW in Detroit. It was quite popular with mass listenership.

Syracuse, New York, is also the home of Syracuse University and the celebrated Newhouse School of Communications. The Newhouse faculty regarded "WNDR Action Central News" as professionally falling somewhere between pig semen and rat vomit. They went out of their way to expound about the degrading, disgusting, depraving journalistic waste product available every hour on the hour at good old 1260 on their AM dial.

It was a classic case of unbridled mutual contempt.

Bud Stapleton charmingly categorized the Newhouse professors as "Candy-ass faggots who can suck my cock on the 6 O'Clock News." He made frequent reference to "shovin' their fuckin' ivory tower right up their baby-boy butts."

I tended to side with his position, albeit overstated.

Besides, Bud was the first person who ever shared with me the functional merits and outstanding benefits of "eatin' pussy." "If you eat that pussy, they'll fuck the livin' shit outta ya every goddamn time," Bud would quip. An important corollary from "Stapleton Sex Hints 101" was: "Show me a broad who ain't getting' her cunt chewed and I'll show you a bitch you can steal away from the stupid fucker who won't, if you will." This was an area of learning which Father Shannon had never addressed.

As inspiring as Bud was in both broadcast news and handling booze (he never actually lost that gun or shot off his pecker), I still considered news announcing a necessary evil. It was temporary dues-paying on the road to the Holiest of all possible Grails. Almost everyone knew the real radio stars were disc-jockeys.

Only the DJ's dealt Divinity. Along with "the Hound Dog," we kids had quickly come to worship the few who starting playing that "Rock 'n Roll" on Syracuse stations. Al Meltzer on WHEN (only three hours a day) and Bill Thorpe on WFBL (just four hours each afternoon on the "Top Forty Countdown") drew thousands to "record hops" sporadically held at area high schools and halls. WNDR was the first station destined to play the music 24 hours a day and, within weeks, was headed for the stratosphere.

After mounting a relentless, unyielding, non-stop campaign to land a real shot, management finally acquiesced. They would allow me a one-hour live on-air audition at Midnight the following Sunday, when the station would normally sign-off for "maintenance."

I wrote down every single word I would say; practiced each record introduction hundreds of times; sat in the control room for hours on end watching all the moves made; and memorized dozens of different "one-liners" to use if I needed, to, God forbid, "ad-lib." The adrenaline hit as soon as I sat down in "the chair." I went to open the microphone channel and my humble hand brushed against a "master-off" switch located directly beneath the intended target. I promptly plunged WNDR into 20 minutes of stone silence. The engineer on duty, fairly new to the business himself, took that long to determine the extent of my stupidity. After my "first hour" was finished, I assumed I was as well, the premiere performance also my last. By an astonishing stroke of fate or fortune, no one important heard my curious initiation. The engineer, whom I blamed for not discerning my dumbness more diligently, kept his mouth shut, as understood.

Soon I was pulling full "jock shifts" on weekends. During my senior year at Cathedral, I worked each evening from 7 'til Midnight. "Hooper Ratings," then the accepted standard in radio listening measurement, displayed a 58 percent total audience share during the time period—more than every other station combined. During my college years at LeMoyne, I covered a morning and afternoon slot. I became involved in the "Sock Hop" business, playing records at schools throughout Central New York. I started adding live bands to my presentations, and would also rent gyms and armories throughout the region to stage my own "Peter C. Rock 'n Roll Presentations." I had been inspired by WNDR Program Director "Dandy Dan" Leonard.

Dan had originally joined WNDR as News Director in pre-rock days when it was a failing Mutual Network affiliate with marginal listenership and major debts. Many stories were later told of collecting empty pop bottles and turning them in for deposit money on those days when paychecks bounced. As a teenager, Dan had hung out with Tony Curtis in New York when Tony was Bernie Schwartz and "Dandy" was Daniel Edelstein. They took their separate ways after Tony went to Hollywood and convinced millions that authentic medieval princes spoke with thick East Bronx accents. "Dandy Dan" headed for Upstate New York with visions of becoming another Walter Winchell, a famous radio commentator for "all the ships at sea." Such ambitions were cast aside without hesitation when the lights of Rock 'n Roll rose on the horizon. They flashed $$$$$!

Tossing aside his press cards and note pads, Leonard hit the Central New York airwaves as "Dandy Dan" and soon became the most highly identifiable figure on the facility. Imagine Howard Cosell on speed. Dan also made a fortune at the "Teen Canteen."

Three Rivers Inn was a nightclub just north of Syracuse in the fading days of the "Big Band" era. It also was rumored to have strong "family connections." Some of America's biggest stars would begin their tours with a "shakedown" week at Three Rivers Inn. The word "shakedown" in this context has nothing to do with Sicilians, although some irony may be construed in its usage connected with the fine establishment under discussion.

A "shakedown", in theatrical terms, is nothing more than a series of rehearsals in front of a live, yet relatively minor audience. You could "shake it down" in Syracuse without any deadly critics or major investors lurking about. Performers could work out the bugs, edit their lines and generally polish an act to perfection before hitting the stage in New York, Chicago or Detroit.

Regular performances would be held Wednesday through Sunday nights for the paying adult crowd. Dandy Dan's "WNDR Teen Canteen" was a Sunday Matinee. Attendance was normally well over 1000 teens. Admission was $1. The format was simple: playing some records; bringing on the act; appearing tremendously impressed with the entertainment; bringing off the act; and then closing with a few more recorded tunes.

3337-CAVA

Typical of the WNDR Teen Canteen were performances by The Four Seasons, Andy Williams, Johnny and the Hurricanes, Dion and the Belmonts, Santo and Johnny, Leslie Gore, the Tokens, Jay and the Americans, Gene Pitney, Brenda Lee, Bobby Sherman, Connie Francis, Bobby Darin, Paul Anka, Frankie Avalon, Link Wray and the Wraymen, Chubby Checker, Dee Dee Sharpe, the Ronnettes, Johnny Ray, Shelly Fabares, The Del-Vikings, Frankie Lymon and the Teenagers, Johnny Cash and dozens of others. I helped and appeared at all the "Canteens" and often escorted our "stars of the day" around the Syracuse area, even joining them in many an "after gig" drink or ten. We even had a little Jewish writer at one Canteen holding up a small Polaroid photo of his parents which he described as "actual size." It was funny. We laughed our asses off. "Woody" somebody. Barely eighteen, I was surrounded by fame.

Other Dandy Dan productions included annual appearances by all of Philadelphia's "American Bandstand" performers as the "Dick Clark Cavalcade of Stars" rocked and rolled into town. Dick didn't mind stopping in Syracuse for old times' sake, having been a student at Syracuse University. During that time he was the "Buckaroo Sandman" on station WOLF pushing Tex Ritter jams. We regularly traveled to WFIL-TV in Philadelphia with a busload of listeners to appear coast-to-coast on "Bandstand." Dan and Dick were tight. Some of our Italian girls from Syracuse would get into fistfights with their Philly counterparts, but the guys got along famously. We knew what the ladies were fighting about.

Another major Italian influence on early WNDR days arrived all the way from Buffalo in the Autumn of '61. All 300 pounds of Joseph Pinto were crammed into a highly weathered '56 Ford, which creaked from Mr. Pinto's insulting challenge to gravitational forces. Joseph easily became the most extraordinary entertainer on the station, combining dark visionary humor with an ever more self-destructive edge.

This latter quality peaked a year or so after his arrival when Pinto hand-constructed a large sign proclaiming, "Mickey Loves The Judge" and placed it over the entrance to Three Rivers Inn, where it greeted all attendees at a Sunday "Teen Canteen." "Mickey" was WNDR's 29 year-old red-headed receptionist, whom Mr. Pinto disliked for random reasons, while "The Judge" was 58 year-old Arthur C. Kyle, Jr., WNDR's sole owner. "Mickey" was bringing her 15 year-old niece to the "Canteen" to see Bobby Rydell, one of many teen idols of the time.

Rydell's main claim to fame was a #1 single called "Kissin' Time," appropriate in the context of Joseph's sign, since Mickey really did seem to love The Judge and their affair was rumored to have reached regular-romp status. Everyone was quite embarrassed, except Mr. Pinto, who was sent packing for Hartford as soon as The Judge caught word.

Pinto became legendary in the radio business, achieving monstrous ratings at dozens of stations. Sadly, success brought excess. There were years of alcohol and cocaine. But one can now eavesdrop every weekday night on New York's WOR-AM and a hundred affiliated stations as Mr. Pinto reigns supreme over his "night people," all of whom worship an infinitely slimmer, trimmer Buffalo native and know him by his air name through the years. "Joey Reynolds" again enjoys rarefied, hard-won status in the broadcast industry with a career revived and renewed. His show is more quiet. Try it. But I know Joey still misses those old "Armory Nights."

In the early 60's, Syracuse had no "Soul Stations", or "Urban Outlets" or anything remotely resembling "Afro-American" programming available on a regular basis to an ever-growing minority population, WNDR was pretty much it for all. The Jefferson Armory was in downtown Syracuse. One night, three trucks pulled up from Detroit as the first "Motown Review" completed a four-state tour. It was Choker Campbell and his Orchestra, with Smokey Robinson and the Miracles, Barrett Strong, The Marvelettes, a yet-unknown Marvin Gaye, The

Temptations and, headlining the show, the great Mary Wells with flaming red hair. She brought down the house, concluding her performance with a six minute version of "Bye Bye Baby." WNDR employees were the only white faces in the crowd. Along with me and Joey, one was a former competitor, lured over to the station when his "Dedication Show" on WOLF starting taking bites out of nighttime listenership. Lots of teeny-boppers loved Marv Albert.

In June of 1963, Uncle Vince was seventy-seven years old. Aunt Louella and he had been apart for a few years. She was in a mental institution. They said it was "nerves." Vince suspected she'd never recovered from that traveling salesman.

I was to receive my Bachelor of Science Degree in Social Sciences at the Syracuse War Memorial. Uncle Vince had made a point of arriving early to be certain of proper seating. He proudly waved at me from the front of the stands, holding a small Irish flag. I briefly saw him after the ceremony and we made plans to see each other the following weekend. I had parties to attend. He went home and died alone within hours.

He left me everything he had. His estate primarily consisted of over 3000 books covering every subject known to man. The volumes filled every room in his tiny apartment from ceiling to floor. Keeping the important ones, the rest went to the Jesuits at LeMoyne College. Although we had never discussed such disposition, I'm certain Vince is pleased. Knowledge only unifies as shared.

Five months later, in November of 1963, I took it upon myself to cancel several weekend dance appearances which I felt inappropriate to fulfill due to unanticipated circumstances. One of them involved an important station client, who was furious. Following a loud and fierce shouting match with our General Manager, I resigned from WNDR never to return. John F. Kennedy had been assassinated.

CHAPTER THREE

CITY OF FORBIDDEN FRUIT

After a few weeks, I departed Syracuse and traveled at night through a blinding snowstorm across Southern Ontario. Crossing the Blue Water Bridge at Sarnia and entering Michigan at Port Huron, I punched on the radio and heard my own voice promoting the arrival of "Peter C. Cavanaugh at the Home of the All-American Good Guys on Big Six Hundred— WEETAC Radio— W-T-A-C!"

WTAC's Program Director Bob Dell, an old Syracuse friend, had invited me to join him in Flint. I pulled into Bob's driveway some two hours later with another blizzard swirling about. This was an early Tuesday morning. Back home in Syracuse, the liveliest of the party people were in bed watching Jack Parr's new replacement, Johnny Carson.

Not even bothering to pull suitcases out of my trunk, I jumped into Bob's car and we drove several blocks, pulling into a jammed parking lot next to a large brown and white building housing "Contos' Lounge." A gigantic banner was strung across the entrance. Upon it an enormous message screamed in bold red lettering: "Welcome Peter C.!" We entered the bar and made our way through a wall-to-wall crowd. Bob grabbed a band microphone and introduced himself to thunderous applause. Ray Emmett and the Superiors, all dressed-up, sharp as hell in glittering gold show-jackets, followed my own well-received greeting to the throng by belting out a twenty-minute version of "What 'd I Say?" with their own delicately interpretive lyrics to the Ray Charles classic.

"See the girl with diamond stick? Give her a dime and she will suck your dick!"

The dance floor filled.

"My little girl has lots of class. She likes to take it right up her ass!"

Bouncing buttocks in tight blue-jeans writhed with the hint of forbidden fruit.

The last "revised line" was a real show-stopper and saved for the end of the set.

"See the girl all dressed in pink? She's the one who made my finger stink!"

Alright!

What'd Ah Say?

I felt welcomed.

After "last call," the entire band and a number of others returned with us to Bob's house. Around a quarter after five, the party ended. Bob went on the air at six. We were all back the following Sunday night to watch Ed Sullivan and witness the American television debut of The Beatles. Little did I know that a live interview with "The Fab Four" just a few months away would send me packing.

WTAC's owner, Thaddeus Murphy, was a big, ruddy Irishman in his late forties, almost 300 pounds of pure beef and blarney. He was Jackie Gleason without the June Taylor dancers. His love of the drink was prodigious and he displayed a dazzling intellect. He also had a deep, resonant, God-like voice, compared to which Rush Limbaugh sounds like Minnie Mouse. When much later in life I stood on the Hill of Tara, ancient home of the Irish High Kings, I thought of Thaddeus. How comfortable he would have been ruling all the land an eye can see from that sacred rise, cloaked in royal garments with wolfhounds at his side, surrounded by loyal soldiers ready to die in grateful sacrifice and serviced at will with comforts undenied by gentle maidens quickly attendant to every whispered wish.

Murphy, whose flair for spectacular promotion was as expanded as his girth, had lifted WTAC from an already successful position in the market to one of unparalleled pre-eminence. "WEETAC," an identifier he brought forth (one may safely assume) near the ass-end of a fifth of Chivas Regal (his beverage of preference), was bigger than life since he thought himself so. Anything or anyone Thaddeus felt opposition to or from was "dedicated to his destruction," a line he would use in dozens of masterful memos issued on a continual basis. Since Flint was the home of the famous '36 "Sit Down Strike" staged by autoworkers to gain General Motors recognition for their union, Flint was not only a big UAW town, but organized in virtually every other major manufacturing and service industry as well. WTAC was home to "The National Association of Broadcast Employees and Technicians," and membership was mandatory for all announcing and engineering personnel. The fact that all of the other Flint stations were unionized did not deter Thaddeus from feeling he had been personally singled out for particular foreign abuse. He consequently concluded that he had been selected by fate to single-handedly stave off the unwashed "socialist hordes" for the good of America, Motherhood, Democracy, and especially the Free Enterprise System.

A few days after "WTAC Meets The Beatles" aired, I was called into "The Office" by Thaddeus. He proclaimed, with characteristic skill, his "new dream." Mr. Murphy's inspiration was to move me to Des Moines, Iowa. I would become Program Director of KSO, a station he had just purchased and wished to turn into "another WTAC." His next move was to invite Bob Dell into the meeting. He had each of us stand at opposite ends of the room against the wall facing each other.

"Look! Look! Mirror images!"

"You're exactly alike!"

"Alike!"

Bob was then dismissed, hardly puzzled by the histrionics. Murphy was always pulling weird moves as a matter of course and would later explain, usually in private, the methods to his not infrequent madness. I resembled an Irish Buddy Holly at 6'1. Bob brought to mind an Italian Robert Goulet at 5'10. Facts were completely beside the point in "Murphy-speak."

"Peter!"

Having returned to my chair directly in front of "The Desk," I almost jumped three feet in the air. There was a long, unnerving pause.

"Peter, you are doing one hell of a job here for me. I want you to know that I know that you know that I know that."

Here it comes?

Thaddeus closed his eyes as though plunging into a mystic trance and then began the whiskey-rumblings, ascending with passionate crescendo into thundering, rolling, visionary exhortation. It was a majestic half-hour diatribe on how marvelous it would be if I would become his Program Director in Des Moines in the great State of Iowa. He wept a little in expressing his fondness for the fields, and hills, and valleys, and rivers, and streams, and all the little children of the Hawkeye State. He knew that nothing would make him more joyful than were I to accept his offer. He noted that nothing would make me happier either. His dream was so highly and mutually beneficial, it was clearly meant to be. But the choice was mine and mine alone. I could remain doing just what I was doing at WTAC. That would certainly be fine with him.

I cautiously asked Thaddeus if he was serious that I could stay at WTAC if I wanted, without in any way harming our warm relationship. Appearing somewhat offended that he wasn't being taken at his word, he offered his absolute assurance that I certainly could stay and indeed should not leave if there was any hesitation on my part toward extending complete commitment.

"A decision to accept a Program Directorship," said Thaddeus, "must be an individual one, made without any pressure or undue influence of any kind. Peter, you are making your first decision as a new Program Director!"

The last two words were uttered with reverence and awe the same way Sister Cecilia would bow her head, and softly pronounce the name "Jesus Christ" during religious instruction. I told Thaddeus I wanted to remain at WTAC. He seemed unusually gracious in his acceptance of my preference. I returned to the programming area. Within minutes, Murphy's secretary rustled in and posted a new announcing schedule permanently assigning me to the All Night Show, known amongst the staff as "Sound Siberia." My change of heart was instantaneous. The Prodigal Son was forgiven and showered with affection. I headed West once more, with my pregnant wife, to a brand new life.

Where did my pregnant wife come from? Three months after joining WTAC I had married Eileen Scaia.

Father David J. Norcott was the pastor of Saint Joseph's French Church in Syracuse, our family parish. It was Father Norcott who had gained me admittance to the hallowed halls of Cathedral Academy following accusations of pyromania in my early youth. Although just a few short blocks from the Cathedral itself, Saint Joseph's was in the "poor part of town." I had served there on the altar. Father Norcott asked for my assistance in establishing a chapter of the Catholic Youth Organization at Saint Joseph's following my sophomore year at Cathedral. The "C.Y.O." was a Diocesan outreach, aimed at providing a Catholic social environment for public school teens not graced with the blessings of religious supervision in after-hours activities. No nuns with binoculars? Well, now. I was elected President of our Saint Joseph's C.Y.O. and fifteen year-old Eileen Scaia was elected Secretary.

Eileen hated me and thought I was an overbearing, arrogant, conceited jerk. I made no efforts to alter her opinion, and she could never later say she didn't know what might wait ahead. Her last name actually should have been Brimley, that being her father's family name at birth. The Brimleys ran a resort hotel in England and hired a cook named Scaia. Mr. Brimley died unexpectedly, perhaps of food poisoning. Cook Scaia married the widow in short order. They changed baby Fred's last name to minimize immigration complications when they sailed to America. At my suggestion, Eileen would sign her last name as Brimley when writing to the Syracuse newspapers with inquiries as to who that "wonderful new disc-jockey named Peter Cavanaugh" was on WNDR.

Eileen was one of eleven children. Baby Fred had taken to serious procreation in his new nation. Eileen's mother had a little dog named "Pepper" who would viciously bark and nip at any strangers daring to intrude upon family property. Returning after our first date, while no one was looking, I kicked him in the balls.

On a dark, sultry August night in the summer of '57, we occupied the back seat of my light-blue '54 Dodge. The windows became so finally steamed from exhalations of ecstasy that beads of condensed moisture began creeping gently downward in soft, sweet flow. They seemed briefly transformed to the tender tears of my own Irish Mother, weeping wistfully over lost visions of eternal filial virginity. We've been married these last thirty-seven years, an achievement much more credited to Eileen's unending, unbending patience than my own mastery of marital arts.

We entered into the Sacrament of Matrimony at St. Joseph's on May 23, 1964. The following year, Bishop Walter J. Foery closed the church and sold the property at great financial gain to the Diocese. Due to expansive downtown development, it had become hot real estate. Besides, it was becoming a "Black Church." Certain things were expendable.

CHAPTER FOUR

STICKS AND STONES

KSO was one of the first stations to broadcast in the Midwest. It had fallen on rather hard times prior to Murphy's acquisition, going through a number of owners and formats. Once housed in a luxurious facility with multiple studios in the center of town, it had moved out to the sticks. I was greeted at KSO with an invasion of Timber Rattlers, which had established a number of nests beneath our new building. With the coming of winter, they started surfacing in various offices throughout the station. On a late Monday afternoon, one quickly came slithering across the sales room floor. Its appearance coincided with a visit by Mr. Murphy. He had come to town on one of his frequent visits and was in the middle of an inspired sales meeting. He was standing there, yelling something about how there were four different kinds of people in the world. The "people in the world" number would vary between two and five, depending on the subject at hand and his state of sobriety. His speech came to a dead halt between illustrations three and four. Thaddeus backed up at least two feet— the only time anyone had ever witnessed him in any form of retreat.

"What the fuck?????"

"It was only a snake, Thaddeus."

"What the fuck do you mean? Only a fucking **snake**?"

Sealing off the entire facility with plastic sheeting, the exterminators pumped cloud after cloud of concentrated cyanide

13337-CAVA

gas under the flooring and around everything else for three solid days. We were off the air during the entire period. I believe Thaddeus listed "power failure" on his insurance claim, snakes not being covered by any existing policy. In the final phase of the procedure, dead reptiles were individually retrieved by hook and hung across a cable conduit that ran out to our radio tower. There were 73 of them. There were big ones, thin ones, long and short. They were primarily Timber Rattlers, except for a few garter and grass snakes that suffered the sad misfortune of being in the vicinity.

Thaddeus was glad they were, in fact, rattle snakes. Anything less might have called into question certain aspects of ownership reaction at the initial moment of confrontation. Murphy pondered all such things at great length in his unyielding vigilance against potential destroyers, real or perceived. The station did climb a bit in the ratings through subsequent months, the snakes bringing luck in their absence for our Irish owner. And for Eileen and me as well. Our first daughter, Laurie, was born on February 17, 1965.

Along with programming responsibilities and an afternoon air-shift, my nights were again free to engage in personal promotion. I found these the source of both financial and professional satisfaction. I carted my sound system and record boxes through fields of corn and played from glen to glen, but down no mountainside. Iowa is as flat as Pam Anderson isn't. The main difference between "hops" in Iowa and Michigan was a generally increased level of social conservatism, evidenced by a heavily pronounced police presence, pulling armed chaperone duty at most teen functions. This was way before "Slipknot." I never felt any sense of intimidation and, in fact, was often assisted in gear-carrying by many a friendly badge on blue. There were Andy Griffiths everywhere, but they were not very amiable in early May.

Thaddeus Murphy made the front page of the morning paper, smiling and grinning with disingenuous glee. He grandly displayed his handcuffed wrists proudly before flashing cameras as though he was some kind of hostaged hero, rather than an uncommon man restrained by most common law. We executives had joined with Thaddeus for dinner at a Holiday Inn, where the station had a "trade agreement." This meant exchanging commercial air time for goods and services. Murphy stayed there while in Des Moines.

Though Thaddeus was surely well known in Flint for his love of liquid delights, his fondness expanded full-blown in Des Moines, where he had less concern for "union spies." He felt they might always be secretly watching in Flint behind potted-plants or in dimly-lit doorways, hoping to clandestinely gain (however slight) a negotiating edge at some distant point. Of even greater importance was the realization that Thaddeus's wife, Mary Murphy, was 500 sweet miles away.

With their youngest child having just started school, Mary was now "learning the business" with Thaddeus at WTAC. Her daily presence contributed significantly to the success of the operation, but sharply curtailed a number of previously enjoyed exploits and arrangements. Thaddeus was forced to exercise particular caution in entertaining clients over extended lunch-time periods of hedonistic bliss within the confines of his luxurious "WTAC Suite" at the Autorama Motel on South Dort Highway, the product of another "trade agreement." Thaddeus personally recorded commercials for the Autorama. According to him, South Dort Highway was "Flint's Golden Strip." Appropriately, it was there that the "WEETAC-Twins" were said to prance about in nude splendor. The whiskey flowed and Thaddeus bestowed. This particular set of twins were identical, flawlessly-configured sisters in their early twenties and were included on WTAC payroll ledgers as "promotional specialists." They certainly were special. Thaddeus was a master practitioner in the art of attending to client needs.

Without the "National Red Association of Socialist Broadcast Fellow-Traveling Employees and Communist Technicians" and Mary in evidence, Thaddeus was prepared to relax in Des Moines. "Dinner" started around 6:30 with eight or 10 rounds of drinks, then a bit of food. This was followed by another dozen or so beverages, with Thaddeus lifting us to new heights of cosmic camaraderie. His stories were of epic proportion and all dealt with fucking. Subjects included his start in the fucking business and everybody who tried to fuck him. We heard how he fucked them and how everybody (those present excluded) was still trying to fuck him. He expounded upon his first fucked-pussy, his last fucked-pussy, and all the fucking-pussies fucked in-be-fucking-tween.

Thaddeus was mirthfully reaching the end of a particularly engrossing tale involving a "married bitch with three nipples" when the clock behind the bar struck 11. In Michigan, this would have signaled three more hours of unrestrained frolic ahead. "Last call for alcohol" would have been politely issued a few minutes before two. In Iowa, it meant the night had ended.

The bartender was a plain, bored, sour-faced man, who may earlier have taken offense at Thaddeus's insistence upon affectionately and repeatedly calling him "Shithead." He strode up to the table and started hastily removing half-filled glasses. Mr. Murphy was initially simply wide-eyed with stunned surprise and undisguised disgust. Then, even sheets-to-the-wind under rudderless sail, the expert conciliator attempted reasonable resolution through the oldest, most time-honored method known to any. Grandly removing a crisp, new, one-hundred dollar bill from his wallet and weaving it in wandering arc toward the lowly lout who ignorantly knew not who he served, Thaddeus defined the terms.

"This says you keep pourin' and if so, there's to be another one like it in your pocket at the end of the night. Shithead."

"Keep it, Mister. Time to go. You've had enough."

The Holiday Inn bar, typical for the time, offered cheap Hawaiian motif. Within what seemed like a half an instant, Thaddeus leapt to his feet and started trashing. Each wall was stripped naked as a twin. There went the lovely leis, the volcano vases and the lava lights. Here came the chairs tossed through windows to the north, south and east. Westward, toward the bar itself and then behind, strode the raging behemoth. Out flashed the angry fist overturning shelf after shelf, shattering bottles by the bunch with now bloody blow, leaving none unseen, unstruck or unbroken.

"Is THIS enough? Is THIS ENOUGH? Is **THIS ENOUGH?"**

The barman was at first immobilized with understandable paralysis at such a fearsome sight. He was witness to 300 pounds of drunken havoc in a gold KSO radio station jacket. Thaddeus was a looped, leonine linguist displaying unsolicited definitions of "enough" with violent escalation, each new pronunciation of the word bringing yet more dedicated destruction. As Murphy finished breaking what remained, he glanced about the room with fresh, fierce fury and, spotting "Shithead," charged toward the cowering figure at full ramming speed. There were five of us and the best we could do was to slow him down. It turned out to be the final and best definition offered of "enough," for that was the amount of time afforded "Shithead" to race out of reach. Thaddeus became instantaneously and honestly remorseful, primarily because the only plentiful booze remaining was awash on the floor below.

He greeted the police upon their arrival with delicate grace and accepted the manacles with cheerful charm. Released from custody after proper payment with moneys successfully expended obtaining expeditious justice and apologies earnestly expressed to all, Thaddeus called a General Staff Meeting the following morning. Waving the newspaper headline which cried: "Radio Owner Arrested In Bar Disturbance," he proudly proclaimed. "I wanted to give you a real example of the dangers in drink. Don't make me do it again!" We all agreed to sin no more.

Shortly thereafter, a group of out-of-town investors brought a new English band into Des Moines who were heralded as a bunch of "dirty Beatles," sporting not only "long hair," but "street clothing," an "insolent attitude," "coarse language" and "rude behavior." I found the first two allegations to be true, but the last three were nothing more than flamboyant record company press agent drivel. Their first American release, an explosive remake of Buddy Holly's "Not Fade Away," had not been a smash hit, but had brought them to the public eye. Standing before the microphone in only a partially-filled auditorium with easily less than 800 in attendance, it was still clear the boys were very much on the ascent given the unusually enthusiastic welcome accorded by the crowd following my words of introduction.

"Ladies and Gentlemen. The Rolling Stones!!"

I found the Stones to be thoroughly polite, although quite tired. They were disappointed in the turn-out, but pleased to be playing in "The States", and quite confident that better things lay ahead. They were looking forward to spending some recording time in Chicago on their tour, and were particularly excited about a pending visit to Chess Records in the Windy City where Chuck Berry, Muddy Waters, Bo Diddley and other Black icons had put it "in the grooves." Judging from the title of their first million-seller, which came out of the Chess sessions, Mick and company certainly found playing within such sacrosanct studio walls the source of inspired "Satisfaction."

Other concerts by "The Searchers," "Gerry and the Pacemakers" and "The Kinks" drew a bit better, but I missed Flint considerably. Lying on my back on the cement bottom of our unfinished swimming pool in front of the station on a warm summer night, throwing empty beer cans at the full moon above, I was becoming ever more convinced that hot times and cold brew mixed more merrily in the "Auto City" than the "Hawkeye State."

In early August, Thaddeus blew into town with yet another "new dream." This was to drop rock "Top Forty" programming and convert the operation to a more "Adult-MOR" or "Middle-of-The Road" approach. This meant lots of Frank Sinatra, Ray Conniff, Andy Williams and Nat "King" Cole. And tons and tons of Tony Bennett. Goodbye Beatles, Beach Boys and Berry. I extended a full two week notice in advance of my resignation. I'd copped a very bad attitude on Tony Bennett after watching him whine on the Tonight Show about how his music wasn't getting the radio exposure it used to because of all the terrible conspiracies going around.

"You can't tell me they're not payin' somebody off, Johnny, 'cause the music stinks!"

Now he's hanging around with Flea, scarfing down Red Hot Chili Peppers for breakfast, lunch and his evening meal.

"These kids nowadays just love me!"

Yeah, well maybe 'cause they can't freely fuck without visions of HIV dancing through their heads instead of sugar plums at Christmas, you're the next best thing, Tony. Rock 'n Roll never forgets.

Thaddeus tried various ploys and promises for a few days, but eventually agreed that we had enjoyed a productive relationship and that he would be glad to draft an excellent letter of recommendation for me. I had been sending out tapes and resumes for several weeks and was hoping for a shot at WCFL in Chicago on a shift which eventually went to a different Barney, this one named Pip. He died in '94 at the age of 57, burning to death in his car. This Barney had fallen way down the ladder over the last few decades. He used to play a trumpet on the air and talk about turning people into "peanut butter." The broadcast trades offered minimal coverage or comment.

I decided to head back to Syracuse with my wife, Eileen, and our daughter, Laurie. We all spent a few months back home with my Mom and Brother Paul as I concentrated on landing a position with WIL in Saint Louis. Both the Program Director and General Manager of the facility were high on my audition tape, but had to put things on hold until an opening could be created. By December, I was tired of waiting and accepted a position as Morning Show host on WTLB in Utica. The station was just 50 miles to the east down the New York State Thruway.

Although Syracuse was relatively near, WNDR's signal didn't quite make the stretch. Consequently, WTLB reigned supreme in the Utica-Rome market, also enjoying extended listenership through much of the historic Mohawk Valley toward Albany. I had worked a bit at WTLB even while under the employment of WNDR a few years prior. The format was much looser in Utica and a young DJ could experiment with various techniques and approaches with almost unlimited license. There was substantial "artistic freedom" permitted since the station had no viable competitors playing Rock 'n Roll or "Top Forty" music. A chimp spinning the tunes would have enjoyed market dominance.

One Saturday night, I had segued two copies of Gary U.S. Bonds' "New Orleans" back to back non-stop for three consecutive hours on WTLB. It just seemed the right thing to do. Other times, it would be unscheduled hour-long blocks of Buddy Holly, Chuck Berry or Elvis. On a Sunday afternoon in late '63, just before leaving for Flint, I received a call from Annette Funicello, who was spending a few days in Utica visiting her family. I invited her out to the station and interviewed her on the air, interspersed with a few tunes, for two and a half hours. I mean, Jesus, it was the unfuckable Annette. Annette still exuded that untouchable, unknowable virginal innocence I've always associated with female Mouse-ka-teers and all Catholic High School girls.

"M-I-C"— "See ya real soon!"

"K-E-Y"— "Why? Because my body is the Temple of The Holy Ghost and/or Walt Disney and they won't share me."

"M-O-U-S-E"— "So go play with that one you've got down your pants."

While WTLB had been something of a personal playground in the past, things had tightened up considerably. I was still afforded ample liberty within reasonable parameters and "doing mornings" became quite entertaining to me and, judging from response levels, WTLB's audience.

Without "Program Director" duties, I could devote considerable time to show preparation and pre-production. I collected jokes and "one-liners" by the hundreds. I developed character-voices. I lined up limited interviews with rock performers and TV stars. I wrote little stories and set them to music, playing all parts myself. I collected sound-effects, sprinkling my show with whistles and bells and gongs. I even appeared at a major area race-track and participated in a "Figure-Eight-Demolition Derby." I was helmeted, padded and strapped inside an old tank-like '51 Hudson equipped with roll-bars. It was driven to victory. Mine was the last vehicle still running the field after savaging 11 opponents, bringing an automatic first-place finish. I still have the trophy. For purposes of important live music, however, I might as well have been in Rangoon.

Utica was chronically by-passed by most major tours, since its largest hall would seat only several thousand. Most interested Uticans were more than willing to drive to either Syracuse or Albany to attend concerts of consequence. The loonies from the boonies had the wheels for those deals.

"Put on yer shoes, boys, we're in the big city now!"

By the summer of '66, the music seemed to be gaining a strange power. So much fresh, new material seemed to be emerging from nowhere and everywhere. Major music. Master music. Mind music.

The Beatles went "farther out" with each new release. "Tomorrow Never Knows," the final cut on their "Revolver" album, brought the clearest clue as to what waited ahead.

"Aftermath" by the Rolling Stones became the #1 Album and "Paint It Black" the album's #1 single.

My two year old daughter Laurie stopped going "Yeah, Yeah, Yeah" like the Beatles and started imitating Mick Jagger's "Come-

On!" which sounded more like "Ka-Mow!." Her Irish grandmother asked me if she had been "exposed to Negroes."

Donovan's "Sunshine Superman" was a big hit in July. Then the Troggs went to #1 in August with "Wild Thing," a song I featured every 10 minutes one morning. This generated an irate phone call from the Program Director, who had risen before his normal waking time, much to my surprise. "Rules" called for a minimal one-hour separation between plays of even the most popular hits. He was quite correct in his chastisement, and I told him I just had foolishly gotten carried away, and would do it no more. At least not when he might be listening. That still left at least from 6 'til 7:15 or so for rule relaxation.

In September, The ever-wackier Beatles had a double-sided smash with "Yellow Submarine," backed by "Eleanor Rigby." In October, another baby daughter, Colleen Elizabeth, was born at Saint Luke's Hospital in New Hartford, just outside Utica. Eileen almost gave birth in the car. Colleen was a gorgeous little girl and, as is now true of all four daughters, remains lovelier than the other three.

In November, Thaddeus Murphy sold WTAC to Fuqua Industries, a Georgia-based conglomerate which would eventually become a multi-billion dollar corporation with most of their investment in non-broadcast related businesses.

Then, in December, Charlie called.

CHAPTER FIVE

PRINCE CHARLIE

Thaddeus Murphy's Vice-President and General Manager at WTAC, appointed in 1964 just before my departure for Des Moines, was Charles Speights. Charlie had originally grown up in Cleveland, Ohio, the single child of a prosperous shipping executive and his elegant wife. Understandably, the prominent couple had nothing in mind but the finest of educations and most fabulous business opportunities for their one and only son. Naturally, Charlie wanted to be a trumpet player. Completing college primarily to maintain parental subsidization of his musical interests, Charlie was a "Young Man with a Horn," somewhat like Kirk Douglas in that movie of the same name. By 21, handsome, blue-eyed, Aryan-child Charlie was hangin' out with the "heavies." He was wailin' "blues," smokin' "reefer," chasin' "gigs," blowin' "chops" and generally enjoying a wonderful life. He came along in time to catch the end of an era. He joined several multi-piece orchestras, traveling along from town to town with his wandering gypsy heart and carefree vagabond soul. He spent time with Ray Anthony, Jimmy Dorsey and Claude Thornhill. It was on such tours he met his Doris Day.

Her name was Nancy Clayton, a wondrous woman. Her striking physical beauty was possibly only exceeded by her keen intelligence and talented voice. She was, as in the movies, a "singer with the band." It was a wedding band of gold, not one

3337-CAVA

of brass and music, that Charlie placed upon her delicate, shaking hand. They were both as deeply and truly in love as love is ever thought to be. Both were leaving the "other bands" forever behind. It was not on the road that the two could settle down, with roots to establish and a family to raise. Nancy's hometown was Lapeer, Michigan, a small community twenty miles east of Flint. It was to Flint the newlyweds moved.

Charlie would have made an ideal candidate for executive grooming within the massive corporate confines of General Motors, which then employed more than two-thirds of those living in Flint and was exploding with unimagined profits and unbelievable opportunities for all. After contemplating what sort of "day-job" would bring maximum financial return and minimal personal pain, Charlie answered an ad in the Flint Journal soliciting "radio sales people." Naturally gifted in the art of conversation and persuasion, Charlie delightfully discovered that radio possessed a "show-biz" quality unique to itself and was, in his own words, "the next best thing to not having a real job."

Charlie sold well at WAMM and at WBBC and, at some precise point of predestined planetary alignment, met Thaddeus Murphy late one night in a dark Flint bar. A more perfect match cannot be conceived. Thaddeus instantly hired Charlie for WTAC Sales. Charlie quickly earned rapid advancement and promotion. They became almost inseparable personal and professional friends. The fact that Charlie happily survived this distinction offers no better testimony to his adroit skills and abilities,— especially in the art of "Thaddeus-handling." Charlie instinctively knew most of Murphy's buttons with keen intuition, and could effortlessly play them perfectly with polished precision. They served as each other's alter-egos.

Leader/Follower; Bully/Buddy; Orator/Audience; Fan/Musician; Starter/Finisher; Corpulent/Athletic; Aging Wisdom/Youthful Energy; Reigning King/Successor Prince. Really, quite a pair.

"Hey, Charlie, congratulations!"

"For what?"

"Murphy's memo says you're the new General Manager!"

"It does?"

"Should I ask you questions from now on or what?"

"How should I know? I'm only the General Manager. I guess. Wait 'til Thaddeus gets in. Where's the memo?"

Charlie was constantly called upon to navigate troubled waters churned to maelstrom magnificence by Murphy's fondness for things craved and captured.

"Jesus Christ, Peter C.! Mary must have seen the Riviera parked out front and she somehow got the room number. She's pounding on the door screaming, 'Thaddeus Murphy, I know goddamn well you're in there,' at the top of her lungs."

"Thaddeus is so fucking drunk he thinks it's funny.

I was lying in bed at four-thirty one afternoon listening to Dusty Rhodes, an old Syracuse friend, on CKLW in Detroit. I was remembering how much fun I'd had in Flint and how Des Moines hadn't really been a mistake, since I'd really had no choice in the matter anyway. Flint never sucked. I was thinking about our new copywriter with the great ass. Did she suck? Whom might she suck? Illicit love had been blooming at WTLB of late. Only two nights before, the station bookkeeper had chased our Chief Engineer around the building with an axe. He was trying to break-it-off. She was trying to chop-it-off, decades before Lorena. Both were married to others. His wife was a strict Italian-Catholic and wouldn't give him a blow-job or get naked with the lights on. The bookkeeper was French. Our phone rang. Eileen wasn't home. I answered it.

"Hey, Peter! It's Charlie!"

Charlie said that he and Bob Dell wanted to know if I'd be interested in returning to my old time slot on WTAC. The Communications Division of Fuqua Industries intended to be supportive of them in every way. As Thaddeus Murphy headed to sunny Fort Lauderdale with pocketed profits and was now completely out of the picture, Charlie was really Vice President and General Manager of WTAC and Bob was truly Program Director. Great times were ahead in Flint. And in Florida. Thaddeus would purchase a small AM Daytimer. There was this stupid little FM license which went along with it. He used this to build a station for his wife Mary to "have fun with." Under Murphy ownership, WSHE would eventually become the number one Rock 'n Roll station in Miami.

Charlie offered a very attractive financial package and Bob, who was doing his show, jumped in on the conversation between records to offer endorsement and encouragement. I told them I would call them back. When Eileen arrived home with Laurie and Colleen, we discussed Charlie's call. Eileen had never been particularly partial to Flint and, also a Syracuse native, had been glad when we returned to Central New York, with its rolling hills and sweeping scenery. By admitted comparison, Flint offered dull topographies and was the epitome of a factory town, although the richest on the planet.

I had returned to Syracuse for our wedding two years earlier. We spent our honeymoon night at Niagara Falls, which was conveniently en route back to WTAC. I proudly pulled into town via South Saginaw Street. Our temporary destination was the Skylark Motel, my happy home. The Skylark was in Grand Blanc, Michigan, and only a half-mile from the station. Mrs. Baker, the owner, also did all my laundry for a few extra pennies. She came in every day and cleaned my room, hung up my clothing and made cupcakes. Why leave? In addition to rent, the only thing Mrs. Baker had ever asked of me was to "not let Mr. Knight bring those young girls over anymore." Disc-jockey Terry Knight had "borrowed my room" upon several occasions while at WTAC and had left for WJBK in Detroit with several paternity suits trailing in his wake.

"I really wouldn't mind, Mr. Cavanaugh, but Mr. Knight's girlfriends seem awfully, awfully young!"

"Yes, Ma'am!"

My bride of one night took in Flint: smokestack after smokestack, and block after block of monolithic bricked and fenced factories. Their passage was broken only by a plenitude of coney-island restaurants, dozens of auto supply shops and score upon score of dingy bars, virtually all proclaiming, in flashing red neon, promises of "Whiskey!" "Liquor!" "Ice-Cold Beer!" One could only wish the Gates of Heaven welcomed sinners as well. Where I saw rapture, Eileen found repulsion.

"Honey, this is a dirty city!"

"Yes. Well. Now. Perhaps. Possibly. Maybe. I suppose some could think it so."

I had explained that what Eileen was seeing with troubled view was only part of Flint and that WTAC covered hundreds upon hundreds of gorgeous, unseen square miles. The beautiful waters of Lake Huron were to the east and the great, green forests of wooded Michigan waited to the north. The impressive State Capitol in Lansing, with its gleaming white dome, was to the west. The mighty metropolis Detroit, with its Lions and Tigers and parks and stores, was only minutes away to the south. Eyes can deceive.

I had spent Sunday night with Eileen at the Skylark and left for work early next day. By the time I arrived back at the motel, Eileen had found an apartment, purchased furniture, signed a lease, packed everything except immediate essentials, and announced a Tuesday move. Fine with me. Eileen could also clean, do laundry, pick up clothing and make cupcakes. A fine Irish wife. 'Bye, Mrs. Baker. Eileen had also come to know that if she had not seen everything Flint offered that fine May day in '63, the city had revealed its soul with dazzling illumination.

"Whiskey!" "Liquor!" "Ice-Cold Beer!"

Charlie's and Bob's extended invitation was thus not greeted with unquestioned enthusiasm by the mother of my daughters fair.

"Oh, Honey. I just don't know."

Rather than repeat the standard Chamber of Commerce speech, which had only marginal success 30 months earlier, I engaged a family finances/career trajectory/professional satisfaction approach. The salary was a full fifty percent more than WTLB was providing, and the union benefits even more valuable to our family of four. WTAC was much more in the mainstream of things. I had already established a large following in Michigan, which could fully be exploited upon our return. Charlie and Bob were trusted friends. Flint was our future. And as soon as we could swing it, she'd have her own car. They made lots of them there. She could even learn how to drive. Eileen's reluctant assent obtained, I phoned Charlie and accepted the position. I called Bob Dell and he was excited by the news.

"Man, it'll be just like before, only better; much better!"

CHAPTER SIX

CITY OF UNHIDDEN LOOT

My resignation at WTLB was received with a mixture of sincere sadness and warm congratulations. Program Director Bill Quinn was also starting to think about life outside Utica. The only exciting thing happening was that his friend Larry Santos was again writing for The Four Seasons. Utica Larry's first collaboration had done quite well and residuals were still coming in from "Candy Girl." I departed for Flint the day after Christmas '66, leaving Eileen and the girls with my family in Syracuse. Uncle Paul was pleased to have his two little nieces to spoil for a few days during the holiday season. Eileen was relieved to avoid the 500 mile car trip. She would fly with the daughters into Detroit Metro after the holidays. I stopped in the northern suburbs of Syracuse to pick up some Christmas gifts from Dell's family, which had been wrapped for the clan in Flint, then headed west again on the Thruway.

As expected, the weather took a wintry turn just past Rochester and became even nastier near Buffalo. Then came Niagara Falls with more snow. It was on to Saint Catherine's and still snowing. By Hamilton, I was down to forty miles-an-hour. Past Galt, make that thirty. At Kitchener, it wasn't as bad. Visibility became rough again near Ingersoll. At London, the roads were plowed. Mt. Brydges offered good traction toward Sarnia. It was clear sailing over The Blue Water

13337-CAVA

Bridge, through U.S. Customs to Port Huron. Lapeer and Davison shot by. I could see the lights.

Flint. Where the Cavanaugh family would remain for the next seventeen years.

Bob and Joannie, with sons Victor, Michael and Bobby, had moved into a much larger house in a brand new subdivision. They greeted me with affection, and I helped unload the presents from Syracuse. Then we had dinner, after which Bob and I sat down in the family room before a roaring fireplace to reminisce, plot and scheme.

"I'm the only fuckin' disc-jockey in the whole neighborhood," said Bob.

"There are doctors, dentists, stockbrokers and lawyers all over the goddamn place and I'm the only fuckin' disc-jockey in the neighborhood."

As we continued talking, it became clear that Bob was also the only fuckin' disc-jockey in the whole world presenting concerts at Mt. Holly. Mt. Holly was a popular ski area just south of Flint on the Dixie Highway. It featured a fairly large lodge, which had remained unused during the non-skiing season. It had been sitting there empty from April through October until Bob Dell tracked the owner down and suggested the empty building might be perfect for "record hops." Bob was an exceptional promoter and the essence of entrepreneurial hustle. He was always trying out different ideas and new venues all over WTAC Country. All he had to lose was his time. WTAC provided free broadcast announcements for all jock-related functions on the "WTAC D-J Datebook." A few "live plugs" for a given event were absolutely no sweat. In addition to shipment after shipment of promotional records piling up in the music library, "promo guys" lined up outside Bob's door each day with hats and hits in hand. They were glad to arrange live appearances by various artists for "exposure purposes," regardless of whether or not air-play was given. The consideration factor was enough. WTAC's listing of a song was enormous leverage, which could be used in obtaining potential Detroit chart action. The facility enjoyed unusual prestige as a consequence. The position of Program Director at WTAC offered a level of industry power far beyond the already valuable significance of station listenership. Mrs. Del Giorno had not raised a stupid son. Bob had seized the moment.

On a Friday night in late March of 1966, the first Mt. Holly experiment, featuring Bob with recorded music and several local Flint bands of marginal consequence, drew 400. Admission was $1. This was regarded as promising. Bob signed a contract for the remainder of the year until the snow flew and the slopes reopened. He would rent the facility for $100 a night. Concession profits from hot dog, candy and soft drink sales would be split evenly between him and the lodge owner. The next Friday night drew 750 attendees. By the end of the first month, as Dell added a few minor recording acts and talent from the University of Michigan scene in Ann Arbor to the mix, average turnout increased to 1000.

Sometimes amazing circumstances converge when everything comes together as though divinely preordained. Even human folly cannot impact the achievement of unqualified victory. Nothing begets success like success. Bob's phone at WTAC and home started ringing off the wall with calls from musicians, managers, bookers, promoters and other kindred spirits, all interested in becoming part of the action. In addition to the enviable distinction Bob enjoyed as WTAC Program Director and arbiter of music broadcast over the most important radio station in Michigan outside Detroit, now he personally controlled the hottest live-rock showplace in the state, including Detroit. Mt. Holly was 10 minutes south of Flint, 35 minutes northeast of Ann Arbor and only 50 minutes north of the Motor City. It was accessible to over a quarter-million emerging "boomers" in Southeast Michigan by foot, car or thumb. As the summer months arrived, Bob added Saturday nights and then Wednesdays to the Mt. Holly schedule as the beat went on. Record-playing was reduced to only a few minutes between live acts. The only challenge became selecting three or four groups a night from the dozens available, while simultaneously maintaining strong relationships with the more important labels and agents.

It was to the Mt. Holly stage that sixteen-year-old Bob Seger brought his "Last Herd" from Ann Arbor. 17-year-old Detroiter Ted Nugent grew long-hair and named his players "The Amboy Dukes" in his first appearance. Local Flint guitar player Mark Farner and drummer Donnie Brewer came together many a night at Mt. Holly in various temporary units, having recently left "The Pack" when lead-singer (and former WTAC jock) Terry Knight of Lapeer headed-off to New York to seek stardom. An Ann Arbor booking agent named Jeep Holland saw his "Rationals" and "Scott Richard Case" (later shortened to the initials "SRC") make their Mt. Holly debut. Dick Wagner and The Frost drove down from Saginaw and The Woolies pulled in from East Lansing for Mt. Holly sets.

Another assist in purchasing Bob's new house came from several Mexican-American musicians from Saginaw who had played Mt. Holly a few times and had recorded, under extremely limited technical conditions, a simple song using an organ as lead instrument. The recording session, if such an expression can even apply, was given to Bob on tape. He found the organ piece curious enough to air it occasionally in conjunction with another appearance by the band at Mt. Holly. They weren't even playing the main stage, just setting-up on an outside patio. The lead singer was this weird little dude with sunglasses who couldn't so much carry a tune as moan in the right key. Why take a chance?

Well, son-of-a-bitch. The request calls for the damn thing started pouring into WTAC. Bob first suspected band members and assorted friends and neighbors of the boys were jamming the lines. Experience gives one a feel for such contrivances, but soon it became certain that the dumb little ditty had that ever elusive "who-knows-what-the-fuck-it-takes-but-this-one's-got-it" quality. What to do? Bob got in touch with a friend at Cameo-Parkway records. He picked up the ball, bounced that baby down the court and took a shot from the center line. It went swiiiiiiiish to win the title. By summer's end, "96 Tears" by Question-Mark and The Mysterians was #1 almost everywhere in the world. It had sold 2.5 million copies. The group had been signed, sealed and secured. There was never any indication as to who had what piece of which, since Bob was being wisely discrete in such matters of sensitive specificity. Still, there was no question that Bob himself had hit the mark in a whole new way.

He enthusiastically regaled me with the narrative. As cold December winds howled and moaned across his expensive and extensive newly-purchased backyard, now hidden beneath several feet of freshly-fallen snow; perhaps it was the Scotch, but I felt a measure of displacement. It was, what? Envy or some other deadly sin taking hold? Not really, unless it was the Sin of Pride.

There I was, sitting in this wonderful new home with a very dear friend drinking excellent whiskey, chosen to once again become part of a very select and special universe. My decision to return to WTAC was evidently even more fortunate than I had originally imagined. WTAC had gone beyond merely playing and promoting the music. It was now selecting the music. Shaping the music. Creating the music. Bob was speaking with a new measure of confidence and assurance. His comments were statements. His questions were answers. His speculations rang prophetic. It was late that night or in the early morning hours of the following day that Bob sharply changed our focus from radio talk to things of more importance, shifting from idle conversation to serious contemplation.

"Man, this war is totally fucked!"

War? What war? Who's at war? Whose war?

"Johnson's really got his head up his ass."

The rock groups from Ann Arbor had brought with them to Mt. Holly more than the music which they played. They also shared, at first in private and then openly through their amplifiers, serious concerns about American involvement in Vietnam. They were much closer to the realities. Friends were being drafted. There was reasonable expectation that the numbers being summoned would increase proportionate to the extent of ever-increasing American involvement. There were those few who had been there and already returned. There was talk of dissension in the common ranks. There was disagreement on direction. Consensus was confused. With his own efforts profoundly productive and represented by significant worth, Bob Dell was hardly a screaming liberal. He was about as "pink" as a shamrock. This realization made his position of opposition all the more credible and, not in a small measure, persuasive. Basic assumptions were being questioned. Suppositions were becoming suspect. Values were under review. Back in Central New York, nobody appeared worried about the Viet Cong. Or the "conflict." Or governmental escalation. Or an increased enlistment quota. Or Selective Service.

Well, perhaps a few were concerned. Two Syracusans I knew well had become front page news for an outrageous act committed on the steps of the nation's Capitol Building. One: David Miller, who served on the altar with me at St. Joseph's French Church and later attended LeMoyne College. Two: of much more lasting memory for me, or anyone who ever crossed his path, was Father Daniel Berrigan of the Society of Jesus at LeMoyne College. He resembled an enchanted monkey.

One of the most fascinating aspects of instruction under the Jesuits was the wide spectrum of philosophical thought entertained within the walls of the institution. There was a balance carefully maintained in the overall curriculum, but individual professors were allowed wide latitude in expressing their own personal and particular viewpoints without fear of chastisement or censorship. The basic idea, truly excellent, was to expose students to a wide range of ideas and opinions from which one could draw one's own conclusions. Indeed, the idea of "thinking for yourself" seemed the primary objective of a Jesuit education. You had your conservative Jesuits, and your liberal Jesuits, and many who were strictly centrist in their views (not too hot and not too cold on any given issue). Then you had your Liberal Conservatives and your Conservative Liberals.

The Liberal Conservatives voted for Eisenhower, although they preferred Taft. They regarded Nixon with thinly veiled suspicion, and supported social legislation, which would provide the underclasses with initial wherewithal to begin pulling themselves up by the bootstraps, chinstraps or, in the case of black athletes, jockstraps.

The Conservative Liberals were all for sharing the world's wealth equally between nations, as well as citizens of any one given land. They advocated sweeping social reforms aimed at realizing this end, and yet maintained deep respect for, and insistence upon, individual effort and excellence. The reward for such conduct was collective joy in paradise, rather than self-indulgent happiness on earth. Father Berrigan was of this last breed.

LeMoyne College was named in honor of an early French Jesuit explorer and missionary to North America named Simon LeMoyne who concluded his priestly career at the wrong end of a tomahawk. There were many studying Theology and Philosophy under Berrigan at LeMoyne who would have preferred the quick, sudden termination experienced by our school's namesake to the slow, methodical, relentless, merciless pressures brought to bear by a true scholar who would suffer no fools, especially those entrusted to his care. Steel discipline was rigidly and evenly enforced in Berrigan's class, where he recruited "volunteers" to replace himself at the podium. All "volunteers" would be expected to complete the day's lecture in Berrigan's stead with material previously assigned. Not prepared? "Take a cut!" Total "cuts" in a single semester over double the number of course credit hours were grounds for automatic failure, "sick days" included. Passing Theology was mandatory for continued attendance at LeMoyne. No other instructor or professor would ever actually throw you out of class, especially since such action put you on the fast track to an "F," except Father Berrigan.

"This place smells like a rabbit hutch," Berrigan casually observed, floating into the lecture hall moments before a clattering ring of the starting bell.

Clang.

Round One!

Berrigan peered across seventy-five faces anxiously assembled, breathless in anticipation of "the selection."

"How's the disc-jockey today?"

Seventy-four sets of lungs found heavenly union in heaved sighs of unrestrained relief.

"The disc-jockey is fine, Father."

"Would the disc-jockey like to lead today's lesson on the first five chapters of St. Paul's Epistle to the Romans?"

"The disc-jockey would be pleased to do so, Father."

After awhile, he would stop me after class from time to time and be ever so charming. His success in radio certainly exceeded my own. Years before when he was in his late twenties, he had appeared in a program which became known as "The Jesuit Hour." It was then being carried in syndication Sunday mornings on over 500 stations across the country. He was quite the broadcast star in his own right. I would often drive him back to the Jesuit rectory after class, and always considered him a man set apart, especially among his fellow priests.

It was former Saint Joseph's French Church acolyte David Miller who set his draft card aflame on the Capitol steps in Washington in the summer of '65 and it was Daniel "Don't Call Me Danny Boy" Berrigan who put him up to it. When I read the story off our Associated Press Wire, I suddenly remembered the time that Berrigan had chained himself to a construction crane protesting some demolition work in one of Syracuse's poorer neighborhoods just after my graduation. I pretty much wrote these events off as typical Irish craziness, being comfortably familiar with the subject myself. I thought Berrigan might only have been weaving a strange Druidic spell with chains and cranes in place of clouds and shrouds. Who knew toward what end such magic might be directed? I knew Irish ritual in every form can be end enough in itself.

Most males of the Celtic race seemed to carry a perpetual attitudinal hard-on, erected consequential to centuries of oppression and economic enslavement. It was a matter of proud genetic entitlement. The ancient Celts had even gone into battle sporting visible physical erections with which to intimidate an enemy when they still came out on the winning side of things, as later depicted in Mel Gibson's "Brave Heart." I had always suspected that your typical Irish drunk, myself included, more often than not was attempting to dull this instinct. Berrigan, a thinking man, was not a drinking man. He was to later become most prominent in the growing anti-war movement, pouring blood on Selective Service files in Baltimore and being hunted for years as a Federal fugitive. He eventually was apprehended and served time in Lewisberg Penitentiary. His brother, Father Philip Berrigan, married a former nun. Philip spent time in Danbury Federal Prison, where he enjoyed friendly inmate chatter with Jimmy Hoffa.

Powerful thoughts were ricocheting through my mind. I had been temporarily stunned by Bob Dell's utterances regarding the "totally fucked" war and our President's head being stuck "up his ass," an orifice I still felt best left unviewed, let alone cranially visited. I was drifting. I was shifting. 1967 was but days away.

CHAPTER SEVEN

FILTH LOCKER

My assigned work schedule at the station was governed by our NABET contract, which required a full 40 hour work week, whether there was actually 40 hours of work to be done or not. There was also an unpaid "lunch hour" thrown in the middle, whether anyone wanted to have lunch or go hungry. The agreement was drafted exactly the same way for both announcers and engineers. In reality, it had been written by and for the technical employees, who had formed Local 46 years before. The announcing staff had originally just been invited along for the ride. The on-air radio disc-jockey "stars" and behind the scenes "button pushers" (as we arrogant jocks would label the engineers, especially to their faces) were treated with absolute parity in wages, benefits, scheduling and work rules. Solidarity required abandonment of prideful announcer egos. Not too far in the future, this arrangement would come back to haunt our technician brothers.

The logistics of broadcast operations involved an engineer in the "master control room" running all equipment. The single exception was two little 45 RPM turntables in a small "announcing booth," separated from "master control" by a sound-proof glass window. Communications between announcer and engineer were conducted via intercom or hand signals. "Confusions" arose from this setup, as a result of the vast generational gap between production partners on a number of levels.

The engineers were mostly veterans of World War Two. They had started in radio when Arthur Godfrey, Jack Benny, Fred Allen and Bob Hope had ruled the airwaves, and most programming was delivered over network lines. It was before television brought Milton Berle, Jackie Gleason and Sid Caesar into their living rooms at home and vastly increased engineering work-load back at the radio station.

In the "old days," an engineer would merely patch-in a network show and then wait a full twenty-eight minutes before any other move on their part was required. They could read magazines, check-out the newspaper, or even catch a brief nap between programs, as long as they theoretically monitored the signal to make sure things were still being broadcast. They also logged meter-readings off the transmitter every three hours or so. Any good technician worth his salt could peacefully fall asleep with his air monitor blasting away and wake in an instant if things suddenly became silent. With the advent of television's success, "long-form" network radio presentations had all but disappeared by the late '50s. Most local stations across the country had opted to fill the void with "music programming," ushering in the era of the "disc-jockey."

A gentleman named Todd Storz owned a radio station in Nebraska. He is credited with resting on a barstool one night in a neighborhood lounge just outside Omaha, watching as a waitress dropped nickel after nickel into a jukebox, playing the same song over and over and over again. It was Mr. Storz's revolutionary idea that if people wanted to hear their favorite records played over and over and over again with dependable repetition, why shouldn't music on his station be scheduled the same way? Why not figure out what, let's say, the forty most popular songs were every week and just play the hell out of them? Over and over and over again? This concept was completely original at the time. Mr. Storz's Omaha station soared to the top of the ratings, literally within weeks. KOIL was a killer. The other stations were playing half-hour blocks of Bing Crosby or Wayne

King or Guy Lombardo. "Big Band" or "Orchestral Mood Music" comprised the bulk of most station music libraries, with an occasional bow to "Country and Western," or maybe "Broadway Show Tunes" every so often. What was happening in Omaha started to spread.

An often unappreciated consequence of "Top Forty Radio" which proved to be of inestimable value and importance to the birth of "Rock 'n Roll" can be found in the single, objective criterion chosen for music selection: popularity. Since most of the "popular" music in the late 1950's tended to be fast, upbeat and energized, radio production surrounding the songs had to keep pace. Gone were the sonorous, deep, rich voices of baritone announcers, slowly measuring and intoning each and every spoken syllable with majestic style and infinite grace. Gone were programs with such nauseatingly obnoxious, pompously pretentious titles as "Melodies for a Soft Summer Eve" or "Musical Memories for Mother and Me." Gone were the five-minute stock market reports, ten-minute weather forecasts and fifteen-minute sports segments. In came the singing jingles, frenetic contests, echo chambers, wild promotions and frantic, shouting announcing teams with nary a breath taken between time and temp and titles of tunes. In came the "Secret Word of the Day" and the "Treasure Hunts" and the "Top Ten at Five." In came listeners by the drove, sponsors by the score, and money by the barrel. Our WTAC engineers were fucked.

The average age of the WTAC air staff was a full two decades younger than those who threw the switches and flooded the airwaves with the hits of the day. In terms of music appreciation, the two groups were light-years apart. If the older WTAC engineers hated anything worse than having to pay attention to their environment and hustle their butts almost every second of an eight hour shift, it was that GODDAMN MUSIC.

As a result of the work rules governed by "the contract" with NABET, announcing personnel would hang around the newsroom and production area three or four hours each day, with minimal responsibilities either before or after their actual "disc-jockey" shift. There would usually be at least two or three other announcers sharing "News and Production" assignments with me each day. A normal individual work-load might be recording two commercials and perhaps delivering a single 45 second sports summary in each four-hour time block, which theoretically included an hour for "lunch." Idle minds became Satan's playground.

The WTAC "Secret Archives" were housed in several large cardboard boxes which were stored by common consent in the transmitter room. The "Archives" contained the most extensive and thoroughly explored pornographic library anywhere east of Stockholm and the storage site was commonly referred to as our "Filth Locker." There was also an audio section. The primary content consisted of phone conversations recorded with "hot" participants sharing their most intimate, very personal secrets, wants, needs and desires with a WTAC disc-jockey who had asked his engineer to "run a tape off the phone line." The technicians were more than eager to oblige, interest in "primed pussy" being demographically universal in attraction.

One could score zillions of "bonus points" within the peer group by coming up with an exceptionally stimulating passage or two. The very best material in quantity and quality usually turned up during the late evening and early morning hours of our WTAC broadcast day. The true art was getting a caller to be very, very specific about her thoughts and promised actions. Delicious delight was taken in the delivery of details. Seductive, selective interrogation was sure to garner professional admiration and congratulation from all when productive. It was a matter of honor.

"Well now, Kathy. Your name is Kathy? What are you doing Kathy?"

"Ummmmmmmmmmmm. Nothin'. Talkin' to you. You make me hot!"

"How hot are you, Kathy?"

"I'm really hot. You know, just real horny!"

"How can you tell how hot you are, Kathy?"

"You know. Things happen!"

"No, I don't know, Kathy. What sort of things happen?"

"I can't tell you!"

"Of course you can tell me, Kathy. It's important you tell me. Friends tell each other special things. If you tell me a special thing, it'll mean you really want to be a special friend. A really, truly, special kind of friend."

"Well, when I'm hot, I get all wet."

"Where do you get all wet, Kathy?"

"Down there."

"Down where, Kathy. Your toes? Your ankles?"

"Higher"

"Say where you get wet, Kathy!"

"My pussy gets wet."

"What do you think about that makes your pussy so wet, Kathy?"

"I think about taking your super-big cock and licking it and sucking it and then you make me get all the way down on my hands and knees and you pull my panties off real rough and I stick my naked butt way up in the air and you slap my bare, creamy-white ass extra-good and get it all red and you stick your naughty thing in my hot cunt and fuck me there and then you take it out and shove it all up my other place and I grunt like a bad little piggy."

"That sounds very entertaining, Kathy. Thanks for listening. Stay hot! Bye."

Protocol required concluding such dialogue at the end of a particularly descriptive narrative. The necessity of editing a tape for maximum group enjoyment was considered amateurish and, importantly, one would not like to be perceived as personally becoming enticed by the call. This too suggested lack of true deviant class. Experience also dictated an intriguing and frustrating axiom. The more attractive a call, the less so its caller;

obviously a case of nature compensating, substituting brains in the absence of beauty or a talent for licentious language in lieu of lovely looks. Beware 900 lines. Still, we would always like to imagine that any given call might be the rule-proving exception and, with this hopeful thought, we recorded on, monkeying around.

The Monkees had hit #1 with "I'm a Believer" and an incredible push had been cranked-up by their record company. Everyone knew it was of artificial manufacture, but the music was well-produced and handily-crafted. The television show ripped-off "Hard Day's Night," even as the group was musically attempting to clone the entire Beatles catalogue. But it seemed to work. Within limits. The Beatles had stopped touring, and had been busily at work in their studios for quite some time on a "new project." So sprang The Monkees, offering no improvement on the original, but at least providing temporary replacement presence.

There was much more of significance coming down the line in new releases. Even as an insipid ballad by daughter Nancy and daddy Frank Sinatra (entitled, in a rare burst of unplanned truth in advertising, "Somethin' Stupid") climbed the charts, and the best-selling album in England was the movie track to "The Sound of Music," in early Spring of '67 something was happening. Stirring. Stretching. Shaping.

In March, the dream-like quality of "Ruby Tuesday" by the Rolling Stones spoke of ethereal, undefined, unstructured freedom in a passionate paean to a timeless tramp. Who could hang a name on her? "Penny Lane," by The Beatles, was another March release. Gone were simple lyrics expressing how she loved you or the benefits of twisting and shouting or seeking a hand to hold. There was a quiet rushing in this music, the lyrics taking flight over a sweet, safe, candy-land, sugar-coated metronomic pulse. What they sang was taking priority over how they sang it.

"A Whiter Shade of Pale" by Procol Harum wasn't really Rock 'n Roll. Or was it? The sounds were soft, but the visual imagery seemed dangerously decadent. Cartwheels off the floor? Spinning rooms? Magic ceilings? I had always been comforted by the notion that an Irishman was never really drunk as long as he could hold on to a single blade of grass and not fall off the earth. Procol Harum seemed to be singing about something entirely past that. It must be a Rock 'n Roll song.

Mt. Holly was about to head into a full new season. The owner had restructured a new nightly rental contract on terms more favorable to the venue and Bob Dell was more than willing to renegotiate. There was plenty to go around. Not just money either.

CHAPTER EIGHT

DEVIL WEED

Bob started spending a bit of time in Ann Arbor with several booking agents, preparing the lineup for his opening weeks. He had also hung-around a few of the Ann Arbor band-houses, which had started springing up as musicians pooled their resources and initiated communal housekeeping. Actually, house "destroying" was closer to the truth than "keeping," unless the band happened to be blessed with young ladies who would do anything to be associated with the group. Responsibilities would include washing, waxing, ironing, cleaning and dusting duties, along with important carnal responsibilities. Competition was particularly sharp in this last, highly-valued area of sexual expertise. All the better bands had "groupie" servants and, in fact, the caliber of "house staffing" was often indicative of professional popularity. The greater the hits, the bigger the tits.

It was near the end of March that I finished my air-shift and met Bob on a Friday night at Contos. "Somebody To Love" by a new San Francisco group named Jefferson Airplane was blasting on my car radio dialed to WTAC as I pulled into the parking lot. Since Saturday was a day-off for both of us, it seemed appropriate to get really hammered. This had become more routine than rare. After closing at 2:30 A.M., we decided to stop by Walli's Supper Club on South Center Road for a bite of breakfast and a final opportunity to see and be seen. You just

3337-CAVA

never knew who might be asked to participate in a PULSE Ratings interview. It was solely for this reason, we had often counseled our respective spouses, that it was imperative we remain connected with the listening public. We joined the general population in fun and frolic purely for promotional and research purposes. We chaperoned each other.

Rather than taking separate cars, we decided to head for the restaurant in Bob's new '67 Riviera. The vehicle had come equipped with an actual "stereo radio" which brought in two separate channels on the dumb Flint FM station, WGMZ. They only played bullshit "Beautiful Music," which no one we knew ever listened to anyway. The radio had come with the vehicle. It was a curiosity, not a concern. Everybody knew Rock 'n Roll was only for AM stations. We had just left the bar when Bob reached into his glove compartment and pulled out a white letter-size envelope. Handing it to me, he whispered in hushed, conspiratorial tones.

"Here. Open this. Don't spill any."

Don't spill any? Obviously, the envelope's contents couldn't possibly be liquid in nature. Spill any? It made no sense. Spill any? It was best to ask before taking further action. It might be uranium particles from the way he was acting. Were the contents glowing? What was he doing with uranium?

"What's in the envelope, Bob?"

"Marijuana!"

"Marijuana? No Shit? Holy Shit! Marijuana?"

We all had certainly "heard" about marijuana. It was understood that a few people and some musicians were even smoking it. Hearing and having were daringly different.

At Cathedral, we had been shown an instructive film called "The Price of Poison." It primarily was concerned about "the evils of alcohol," but had also included a few minutes dedicated to instructing all on the deadly dangers of a drug called "marijuana." There were several segments which seemed very strange at the time. People were taking deep drags off an oddly shaped cigarette and then laughing hysterically. Another scene showed a young couple frantically rolling-up their car windows to "not let any smoke get away" before lighting-up. Years later, I realized that "The Price of Poison" contained footage from a 1930's melodrama, later re-issued as a unintended comedy cult-classic called "Reefer Madness." Nevertheless, it was in Catholic school that I had first even heard the word "marijuana."

And there we were.

Two intoxicated Holy Roman Catholic husbands in our late-twenties from Syracuse were weaving about the dark, sin-filled streets of Flint. We were listening to "The Singing Strings" offering wimpish performance of "The Theme From a Summer Place" in stereo on a car radio. Wicked hours of weekend wandering had now led us to openly discussing and possessing MARIJUANA. Destiny could not be denied. We had gone wild. How incredibly "hip." There was no doubt in my mind. We were doing everything right. Except. What about the envelope?

"Bob, maybe we should pull-over or something."

"What for?"

"Well, if this is fuckin' marijuana in the envelope and you don't want me to spill any or anything, maybe we should stop the car. What am I supposed to do with it, anyway?"

This was an excellent question and one which Bob had not seriously considered. He had focused upon dramatically introducing his surprising revelation, rather than contemplating any subsequent logistics which might be required. Heavy imbibing had already taken its toll on our otherwise flawless capabilities to reason with lightning rapidity. It was mutually determined, after several minutes of excited discussion, that we must find a way to light up the marijuana and smoke it.

Bob had obtained a small amount of the evil herb a few days prior when he had visited a group called, interestingly enough, "The Rationals." They lived right near the main campus at the University of Michigan. Not wanting to fiddle around with it at home under the ever-vigilant eyes, ears and nose of wife Joannie had given Bob pause. He had decided, in a burst of impromptu inspiration only moments before, that a weekend night made a perfect time to fire-up the secret stash in the company of a comrade. We were initiating a spontaneous act.

It was decided that our homes were off-limits for the experiment. Who knew? We might go nuts. Not crazy nuts, just sort of screwed-up nuts. And only for a while. Bob testified that he had tried some with The Rationals. He admitted that it was just a little and it "relaxed" him, but that was about all. However, Bob reported the group said they did it "all the time." It was reasonable to conclude that the stuff wasn't permanently injurious. It could even prove mighty fine. We turned away from the restaurant, which we were quickly approaching, and headed for WTAC. Bob had master keys. The General Manager's office, once the cave of the Mighty Murphy, would be perfect. Charlie lived there now. Super vibes. It was also on the far side of the building, safely removed from the operational studios which represented the only occupied area at station in that early hour of the morning.

Safely within the walls of the WTAC's organizational heart, we approached the task with the precision of neurosurgeons. Since we had no pipe or "papers," the first order of business was carefully emptying-out the tobacco filling from several filter-tipped Marlboros, painfully practicing until we finally had a perfectly empty, untorn, unripped, would-be container. We then slowly and methodically attempted to pour the contents of the envelope into the ex-Marlboro. After a dozen or so false starts, we succeeded in getting most of the marijuana into a good two-thirds of the empty paper tube, which we then sealed on both ends with what would soon become a practiced roll. Were we ready to Rock?

With Bob's only cautionary instruction being that you were "supposed to hold the smoke in as long as possible," he bravely placed the newly formed, honest-to-Jesus joint between his teeth.

Striking a match on Charlie's desk with Murphy-like flourish, he fired-up and sucked-down deep. He INHALED. And held his breath. He extended the doobie in my direction.

I inhaled. And held my breath.

He inhaled. And held his breath.

I inhaled.

He inhaled.

So far, nothing.

I inhaled.

He inhaled.

Not going crazy, that's for sure.

I.

He.

He. He.

He. He. He.

He. He. He. He. Ha. Ha. Ha. Ho. Ho. Ho.

I felt a rush of unbelievable lightness and levity. I felt really gooooood. Really relaaaaaaxed. Really haaaaaaaaappppppy. So this was being stoned! I could see whyyyyyyyyyyyyyyyyyyyy they came up with that woooooord.

Bob used some scissors from a drawer in Charlie's/ Thaddeus's desk as a "clip," although we didn't then know what the word for such a thing was, and we finished off the joint. Neither of us had spoken a word since the smoking had commenced.

"Oh, Wow!"

"Good Shit!"

"Jesus Christ!"

"Oh, Fuck!"

"Cool!"

"Really cool!"

"Fuck!"

"Shit!"

"Shit!"

"Fuck!"

After fifteen minutes of similarly inspired dialogue, we started finding our bearings. We made certain that no evidence of our office-borrowing was left behind and got back in Bob's car which, after thoughtful review, we remembered was right outside the building. We decided that we were quite hungry and should resume our trip to Walli's. It was three miles away. After what seemed like several weeks on the road, we arrived. By then it was four in the morning, but a large crowd of diners remained. Everybody went out to breakfast at Walli's when the bars in Flint closed their doors and many "got lucky" on the way or after. "Would you like to go to breakfast?" was much more convivial, cultured, and refined than "Fuck me?" Both expressions were often synonymous.

"Fucking" was the last thing on our minds. We were trying to remember what city we were in. Several times Bob asked me if we were on "Salina Street" and once I stated that I thought we were. He wasn't kidding. I wasn't either. "Salina Street" runs through the heart of downtown Syracuse.

"Jesus, what are all those lights up there?"

"Stars."

By the time we got to Walli's, after more serious discussion, we were certain that we were in Flint and at Walli's. We kept this in mind for most of the time we were there.

"I'd like, let's see. How about three cheeseburgers and double-fries and apple-pie with ice-cream on top and a chocolate-shake and some mashed-potatoes on the side with gravy and a dill-pickle."

"I'd like the same thing, except I'd like some French-fried onion rings, too."

"Yeah, also onion rings with mine. Please."

Of course, everything was terribly amusing. Funny. Hysterically so.

When Bob had concluded his order with the polite word "please," I just had to say something as soon as the waitress left.

"Pleeeeeese. Sheeeeeeee's a sleeeeeeeaze"

Bob picked right up on it.

"A sleeeeeeeeeeeaze in the breeeeeeze."

"Up in the treeeeeeeeees. Hangin' from her kneeeeees!"

"Maybe She'll freeeeeeeeeze and catch fleeeeeeeeeas!!"

"Or drop your keeeeeeeeeys and eat peeeeeeeeeeas!!"

So that's how The Beatles came up with all that shit.

A century later, Bob dropped me back off at my car in the Contos parking lot and several decades after that I pulled into the apartment complex in Flushing. My sleeping wife and two daughters were resting comfortably in the arms of Morpheus, oblivious to their husband's/father's delightful dance with the devil weed.

It's interesting recalling the first time I got stoned with equal clarity to memories of the first time I got laid, except the former had far fewer subsequent complications and certainly involved significantly less personal commitment, particularly during the time of occurrence.

3337-CAVA

CHAPTER NINE

SUMMER OF LOVE

As summer '67 neared, Mt. Holly picked up where it had ended the previous year. The crowds were still growing. Many of the Michigan groups that had gained exposure there were developing their own followings from the Holly engagements, and were reaching headliner status, especially Seger, Nugent, and Dick Wagner from Saginaw. Release of the much-heralded new Beatles effort was scheduled for June 1.

On Monday of Memorial Day Weekend, I waited for two hours at the Greyhound Bus Terminal for a package to arrive routed directly to Flint from Capitol Records in New York. The bus pulled in at 6:45. Minutes later, I was back in our WTAC studios with an advance copy of "Sergeant Pepper's Lonely Heart's Club Band." It was all I played that night for five solid hours. Phones exploded and the Detroit stations screamed. We were among a handful of stations "breaking" the album a bit ahead of schedule. Political connections pay off in the radio business as much as they do in any other walk of life, probably even more dependably.

What clichés of the time can be used? I was "blown-away"? I was "knocked-out"? I was "turned-loose"?

Man!

Afterwards, I brought home a tape of the album which had been recorded off-the-air. I listened until dawn broke. You could hear it over, and over, and over again, and still pick up things you'd missed the first few dozen times around. Each side was seamlessly presented. "Sergeant Pepper" was, in the final analysis, a continuous stream of words, thoughts, ideas, images, dreams and schemes; all impeccably produced and musically magnificent. It was a flawless masterpiece. We knew this at once, without the slightest question or most remote reservation. And it was the Beatles.

A great topic for retrospective review in the latest hours of a good evening's "go" is the issue of whether or not anyone except the Beatles could have pulled off "Sergeant Pepper." To begin with, it was their unique popularity and astounding initial success with resynthesized American rock, rhythm and blues which provided the financial and psychological wherewithal to initiate and complete the project.

Only the Beatles were the Beatles. Only the Beatles could command such an unparalleled amount of concurrent artistic respect, admiration and cooperation. They were regarded with awe to a degree previously unknown in the new era of global communication. Even Elvis needed writers. Of even more importance was the undeniable fact that they were true innovators and originators and had now elevated Rock 'n Roll music to an incredibly advanced level. Hints of their new direction had come from tastes and touches in prior pieces, but "Sergeant Pepper's Lonely Heart's Club Band" was the complete, integral, unyielding, uncompromising whole. It is also certain that time, and circumstances, had much to do with it.

"Sergeant Pepper" threw away rules, broke down barriers, shattered preconceptions and permanently changed the face of contemporary music. It had come to Flint as a brown paper package in the bottom of a Greyhound bus.

Later in June, the Monterey Pop Festival in California created more new musical history. It was a three day event featuring performances by Simon and Garfunkle, Eric Burdon, Otis Redding, the Byrds and Big Brother and the Holding Company. Big Brother included a little sister named Janis Joplin.

Also appearing were Buffalo Springfield, Jefferson Airplane and others. The Airplane was currently #1 on WTAC with "White Rabbit." 10,000 were crowded each night into an amphitheater built to accommodate far fewer, while 20,000 more, unable to gain ticketed entry, remained outside listening to the music as best they could. At least they were there. Being there was becoming a cultural imperative, wherever "there" might be.

Ken Kesey and his Merry Pranksters were there at the Fillmore Auditorium in San Francisco where a young hustler named Bill Graham had visited the Pranksters' "Electric Kool-Aid Acid Test" experiment. This had been staged as a one-time, spur-of-the-moment "happening" at the facility. Knowing promise when he saw it, Bill had taken out a lease on the hall, and had turned the place into a regular Rock 'n Roll Emporium. He peddled Big Brother and Janis, The Doors, Moby Grape, Jefferson Airplane and The Grateful Dead. "Acid Rock" became a generic description of the Fillmore bands. Los Angeles record execs rushed up to 'Frisco. They had checkbooks in hand, stashes in briefcase and contracts at the ready. The surfer boys were catchin' the wave.

"They say Janis likes Southern Comfort."

"Murray, pull over at that liquor store!"

"Morrison's a drunk."

"Howie, make that a dozen cases of Cognac!"

"Garcia does LSD."

"Maxie, where's that goddamn, long-haired bastard we hired for the mailroom? We need somebody up there talkin' for us who can relate!"

In early August, a black Seattle-born guitar player who had moved to England, returned home. He emerged from obscurity into national prominence with his Monterey appearance, and "Purple Haze" was released as a single. Jimi Hendrix was a "Top Ten" request within hours on WTAC. Bob Dell was personally overwhelmed with happiness, deliriously ecstatic at the thought of a "Psychedelic Coon." He played "Purple Haze" every fifteen minutes the afternoon of its debut, refraining from enthusiastically using the phrase over his microphone only through admirable self-restraint. He meant nothing racist with his off-air remark, offering it more as a congratulatory exclamation than anything demeaning. When the album "Are You Experienced" was released, Bob approved most of the cuts for immediate exposure.

Bob had also appeared at several college fraternity parties with a black novelty group out of Detroit. These gentlemen dyed themselves blue from head to toe before taking the stage. They performed professionally as "The Screamin' Purple Niggers." They were booked on campuses everywhere in the Midwest for absolutely top dollar. Around Dallas, Country/Rock connoisseurs would check out "Kinky Freeman and The Texas Jewboys." It was a different time. In certain circles, there was curious, yet invulnerable pride in self-disparaged identity.

With typically strained comprehension, major promoters put Jimi Hendrix on tour to open for "The Monkees." As "Purple Haze" started ringing up cash registers from coast-to-coast, Jimi was tossed off the bill. An official complaint had been registered by National Headquarters of the Daughters of the American Revolution that Mr. Hendrix was "too erotic for young people." Who wanted to piss-off Betsy Ross? Mickey Dolenz had been "Circus Boy." He was safe.

Atwood Stadium is an old high-school athletic facility in Flint. In August, "Herman's Hermits" were scheduled to headline a major show. Among the opening acts were several young British musicians who had banded together in 1965, and had been introduced to U.S. airwaves over WTAC later that year with their first Decca single. It was called, "I Can't Explain." It is well known and acknowledged in Rock 'n Roll history books that WTAC was the first radio station in America to ever play "The WHO."

By cosmic convergence, August 23, 1967, was also Keith Moon's twenty-first birthday. At least according to his testimony at the time. Subsequent investigation would later indicate that honoring an exact score of years would have been more precise, yet, conferring "underage status" in many states, "20" might have presented certain geographic inconveniences. It matters not. Keith and the group brought a birthday cake to our WTAC studios in celebration of the momentous event and in appreciation of our earlier efforts on their behalf. We thought it was pretty wild. It was his birthday and we got the cake. "Far out!"

We interviewed the group and pushed the show. Ticket sales had been slow. Nobody knew who the WHO were. This was their first major tour of The States with little attention being yet paid by the trades or in "teeny-bop" magazines which now flourished seemingly everywhere. The promoter had been counting on "Herman's Hermits" for drawing power, but they were on a bit of a fade. "Mrs. Brown, You Have a Lovely Daughter" only sounded good under the influence of bubble-gum. I arranged to get the night off in honor of Keith's birthday. We had been promised an extraordinary treat. The promise was understated.

Under cloudy skies, and with only several thousand in attendance, the sponsors didn't break-even. The "Blues Magoos" were introduced and did a nice thirty-minute set, closing with their biggest hit, "You Ain't Seen Nothin' Yet." How prophetic. After 20 minutes of equipment changes, the WHO took charge and exploded.

Take no prisoners. Balls to the walls. It can't get any louder. Yes, it can. He's setting fire to his guitar. Shit. He's breaking everything up. There go the amps. He's kicking-in the bass-drum. What? Everything's blowing-up! Feedback's screaming!! They left the stage completely destroyed!!! The show's over!!!! ROCK 'N ROLL!!!!! The crowd reacted with proportionate appreciation. Hope I die before I get old.

Backstage, every member of "Herman's Hermits" was ashen-faced. They had to go on after that and sing twinky little tunes about some fat king with eight wives? Fuuuuuuuck.

We left with the WHO after they playfully trashed what was left of their make-shift "dressing rooms," still being pumped. The piece de resistance had been Keith making a field goal with some random wastebasket from a good fifty feet away straight over one of the stadium goal posts. This had been executed at the spur of the moment with miraculous precision. Backyard soccer had finally paid off for this lad and his mates were justifiably proud. More than half the crowd had deserted the stadium, exhausted from the WHO's remarkable presentation, and in no mood to bring themselves down. Herman's Hermits bravely started-off their set with "There's a Kind of Hush." They had that right. No matter. Within weeks, the Hermits were scheduled to play the Shah of Iran's Coronation in Teheran. Fuck Flint.

For us, it was on to Keith's Birthday Party at the Holiday Inn on Bristol Road. It was right by the airport. There was a gigantic cake and, sure enough, out jumped a half-naked girl with frosting-coated breasts. Yummie. All the heavy record guys from Detroit were on the scene. Word was out. Decca Records had rented the largest available conference room for heavy-duty celebration and it opened right onto a large poolside party-deck. Perfect. Bottles of expensive champagne lined the festively decorated table. Outstanding. The bar was wide-open and we could have as much of anything else we wanted.

"Make that a triple-Chivas, please."

There was an enormous buffet table groaning under every delicacy in the world.

"Can shrimp sail?"

"Whoa, that one did!"

"These little "poodle-pecker" hot dogs? Squeeze just right and they'll sail right down the front of that lady's dress over there!"

"I'd like another double-triple, Four-Eyes."

"I wear glasses too."

"But, I look like Buddy Holly."

"You look like Harry Truman."

The wheels were up. We were soaring with the WHO.

Food was also flying. Whoops. Someone just hit somebody else in the mouth with a whiskey bottle. Accidentally. He was aiming a friendly toss over a third party's head.

"Who gave Keith the car keys?"

"He's pretending he's going to drive it in the pool."

"Ha-ha"

"Watch, he'll stop at the last minute!"

"No!!"

"He's in the deep end, too!"

"Oh, there he is."

"Good swimmer!"

"He's O.K.!"

"But, he drowned the Cadillac!!"

"Anybody know CPR? Cadillac Pool Rescue?"

"What cops???"

Leaving havoc in our wake, Bob and I were joined by several band people and Peter Townshend in a drive to Contos. Since most of the Contos crowd didn't know the WHO from whomever, we were left alone to have a few more beverages before dropping Peter and associates back at the Inn. By that time, things had calmed down.

Peter Townshend struck me as being exceptionally intelligent and an accomplished conversationalist. He was particularly struck by the way everyone in Flint seemed to say "fuck" or variations such as "fucked," "fucking" and "fucker" with every other word . He observed that it was much more lively and descriptive than "bloody," which he defined as kind of an English equivalent rendered pale by comparison. He thought all the "fucking" gave the town a "quaint quality."

Keith later reported that he had experienced possibly the very finest Birthday Party in the history of all birthday parties. He looked forward to his next with thirsty anticipation. Decca Records was also rumored to have purchased an extremely damp Cadillac from a very irate owner. It was said over $20,000 had been expended to set things straight. Unbelievably, the party had outdone the performance. We were impressed. In 1999, VH-1 would recall the episode globally on "Rock 'n Roll Record Breakers."

As The WHO departed Michigan, The Doors entered the charts with "Light My Fire." WTAC also added "Break-On Through" as a "Hitbound Extra." We were regaled with stories of the Doors' wild singer, Jim Morrison, "eating every girl in sight" and being so screwed-up he couldn't finish most live performances without passing-out in front of one and all. Crowds loved it. This was interpreted as testimony to his incredible artistic credibility. Very dark.

Scott McKenzie saluted the end of summer with "San Francisco," where all those hippies wore flowers in their hair. Dr. Timothy Leary of Harvard had experimented with D-lysergic acid diethylamide and urged all to "Turn-On, Tune-In and Drop-Out." The streets of Haight-Asbury had become crowded with thousands of run-aways and seekers of truth and love. They wore beads and tie-dyes. They smoked dope. They did speed. They dropped acid. They worshipped at the altar of Rock 'n Roll. There was standard ritual in the absence of formal liturgy.

Chuck Berry also played Flint in early fall at the I.M.A. Auditorium. It was great hearing his music again. He was highly regarded by the Beach Boys, who also appeared at the I.M.A., and stopped by WTAC for interviews. After Berry's performance, Bob and I took him to another Flint nightclub, "The Stardust Lounge" on South Saginaw Street. He joined Johnny Gibson's band from Toledo in a few of his classics. I got to carry Chuck's guitar-case. Chuck Berry was a soft spoken gentleman, but had prison-hardened eyes from time served, and bitter experiences with the white establishment in the late 'Fifties. He had been convicted of violating the "Mann Act," which prohibited transporting a member of the opposite sex across state lines for "immoral purposes." It was bullshit. There could be no doubt he ultimately had been jailed for his success in establishing a fundamental foundation for "that music." Certain suspicions and cynicisms remained. Chuck Berry had been screwed more than once, within the industry and without. It showed on the showman. Most stars carry scars.

CHAPTER TEN

UNDERGROUND

It was in October of '67 that Bob Dell and I discussed the idea of taking the last two hours of my nightly program and featuring only "heavy" rock music, rather than continue the basic "Top Forty" mix, which was currently WTAC's normal fare throughout my entire night-time shift. Although this was unheard of in contemporary radio programming, it seemed an ideal solution for a number of reasons.

First, we had certainly seen a remarkable surge in pure rock-oriented music over the Summer season, and it showed no signs of dissipation. If anything, it was still on the upswing.

Secondly, it was becoming difficult to mix Jimi Hendrix with Barbra Streisand and Moody Blues with Johnny Cash or Nancy Sinatra with Bob Seger and maintain any sort of real programming flow and balance for younger listeners. They were starting to hate some of our regularly featured artists, whether they were selling a ton of records or not. Tastes were beginning to sharply polarize. I was getting that feedback with every other phone call off the WTAC "Hitline" every single night.

Thirdly, the Mt. Holly factor could not be ignored. Here was WTAC bringing the essence of "new music" to their doorsteps, but we weren't consistent in offering Mt. Holly attendees the product they loved over our airwaves.

Lastly, it just made all the sense in the world. After all, what did we have to lose? It would be promoted and presented as a

3337-CAVA

premium program. So what if we were the first to make the move? Who wanted to wait around for the "other guys" to jump? Why not really Rock 'n Roll?

The "WTAC Underground" made its debut the following Monday night. During the two hour block, I dropped all regular WTAC jingles and formatics and featured nothing but the best of the best from true "rock" releases. What qualified as "rock" was loosely defined. A general guide often proved to be what was definitely not rock more than what was. There could be no debate that the Beatles, the Stones, the Doors, Big Brother and the Holding Company, the Grateful Dead, Jimi Hendrix and anyone who appeared at Mt. Holly were to be included. Similarly, Frank and Nancy, the Cowsills, the Monkees, the Association, Bobby Gentry throwing her baby off that bridge and Englebert Humperdink asking for release were out. Most material off Electra was in. Motown was normally out.

There were many eccentric and arbitrary exceptions to any "general rule." I sensed it was artistically appropriate to feature an "old" rock classic such as Little Richard's "Long, Tall Sally," then segue right into the Beatles' version. One might play "Bo Diddley" by Bo Diddley, followed with "Bo Diddley" by Buddy Holly. Then you could take Buddy's "Not Fade Away" and slam right into the Stones' rendition. There was a relatively obscure California group called The Leaves who had first done "Hey Joe." This made a wonderful prelude to the Jimi Hendrix cut. As many of the new albums coming in every week included remakes, the original recordings, almost without exception, blended beautifully. They provided a perfect sense of continuity. I had personal charge of the "WTAC Underground" library, which grew larger by the day. It consisted of over 100 albums by the end of 1968. I had a storage rack assigned for exclusive "Underground" use which expanded to three large filing cabinets.

"In A Gadda Da Vida" by Iron Butterfly, which had become Atlantic Records' largest seller in history to that point in time, was regularly featured after its release. It was one of the "statement" and/or "attitude" cuts, and its length defined the "Underground" as anything but "Top Forty" in nature. Similarly, "Days of Future Past" by the Moody Blues was continually exposed with "Nights in White Satin" leading all requests. "Wheels of Fire" by Cream was played a side at a time. The first "long version" of "Suzie Q" by Creedence Clearwater Revival became an "Underground" standard long before the edited single was issued. If music was "happening" or we felt it was likely to "happen," it made its first appearance over WTAC on the "Underground."

I adjusted my announcing presentation substantially. The normal "Top Forty" style called for very highly-paced delivery and an often artificial "smiling sound," later referred to in the industry as the "yuk" approach. It was an aural "happy face." Most Program Directors insisted on this quality. They felt disc-jockeys should reflect "warmth," "friendliness" and "companionship." An accomplished practitioner sounded like Bozo on benzedrine. I certainly did. A completely different persona was evolved for the "WTAC Underground." I pulled my vocal pitch "down" rather than "up." Not a hint of "commercial hype" was left in any information conveyed. My delivery slowed to an almost hesitant semi-crawl. I was as cooooooooool as the rock was hot. The whole idea was to act as juxtaposition to the music, and to convey the feeling of being sturdy, but definitely stoned. I strived to sound "with it", but not "wasted."

Being the dedicated artiste I was, and with our WTAC parking lot only seconds away, I personally made the ultimate sacrifice by getting genuinely ripped most nights just before the "Underground." Then, with 10 and 15 minute cuts providing moments for more hits of "Fresh Air," I inevitably stayed stoned for the duration.

Let's hear it for Quicksilver Messenger Service. Most of us had no trouble at all buying an ounce or two from band connections. It was the thing to do. Premium grade smoke ran $20-

25 dollars an ounce. Jamaican Green and Columbian Gold were common-place. The legendary "Panama Red" lived up to everything heard about it. Subsequent investigation revealed the very first joint Bob and I smoked was "Panama Red." The alcoholic equivalent would be initiating your drinking experience with several tumblers of Baccardi 151, consumed in rapid succession. This relates, of course, to the magnitude of effect rather than the nature of the intoxication— the quality and manner being vastly different between booze and bud. To this day, contrary to the postulations of many self-defined "drug experts," the "buzz" was no better or worse than that available in our present times, just infinitely less expensive. "Saying No" has merely multiplied mark-up.

CHAPTER ELEVEN

DUSTIN TIME

As '68 unfolded, the Beatles took us all along on their "Magical Mystery Tour." Our hair was getting longer, our sideburns were dropping and, in my own case, a mustache took form. Buddy Holly gave way to Emilio Zapata. I thought that mine looked even better than Paul McCartney's, which he had introduced on the cover of "Sergeant Pepper." This new image looked great on our WTAC "Music Guide" which pushed the "Underground." The Lemon Pipers banged away in February on their "Green Tambourine." They were booked far ahead for a Mt. Holly appearance in the spring.

Everyone thought that Dustin Hoffman had really caught it when "The Graduate" was released in March. We agreed that the most important thing in life wasn't "plastics." We also bought the notion that successful, prosperous American middle-class parents were well-intended, but trapped in major misconceptions about life and love. We all floated at the bottom of the pool with Dustin, would also mercy-fuck "Mrs. Robinson" if given a chance, and were ecstatic when our hero stormed the wedding ceremony and ran off with Mrs. Robinson's daughter. She represented youth, freedom and a much better jump than her Mom. He had blocked the door of the church with a crucifix. What a happy ending.

Simon and Garfunkle, whose music provided an exceptional sound-track to the film, jumped from just "folking-around" to having major rock-star status. They went right into the WTAC "Underground" with no complaints. We all wanted to go to "Scarborough Fair." It sounded like it might be a place such as "Penny Lane" or "Strawberry Fields" without Beatles.

Jimi Hendrix was booked into Flint's I.M.A. Auditorium for a Sunday afternoon performance in late March. Mike Quatro, a Detroit musician-turned-booking agent, was the promoter. Mike's sister, Suzie, later gained a certain measure of Rock 'n Roll fame herself as Leather Tuscadero on "Happy Days." I was asked to help promote the concert and introduce Jimi on stage.

The opening group was an outfit called "The Frut" from Detroit. They offered an exceptional half-hour arrangement of their signature anthem, "Blow Me." Backstage, Jimi seemed quite convivial in an abstract sort of way (except he thought he was in Erie, Pennsylvania, and was desperately in heavy need of fresh cocaine). This made us more than mildly apprehensive. "Coke" was something we related to on the same level as D-Con Rat-Poison. Still, it was Jimi Hendrix and he was "experienced." Sources contacted sources, who contacted other sources. Several grams were available in less than 20 minutes.

Jimi cruised on stage as I was completing his introduction. He hugged me around the neck and gave me a great big kiss on the forehead. I'm sure he was reacting much less to my announcement than the fact I had engineered the cocaine acquisition. Right on cue, his guitar screamed the first few notes of "Purple Haze" and off we went. After 45 minutes, he was right in the middle of "Manic Depression" when he broke two guitar strings and went nuts. He was maniacally depressed. Furious with frustration, he threw down his instrument and stormed off the stage. The crowd couldn't have been more pleased. It was seen as a really "cool" conclusion to the performance.

Five days later, Dr. Martin Luther King, Jr. was shot to death in Memphis. The following week, Daniel Berrigan was convicted in Federal Court of destroying Selective Service files. After two more months, Robert F. Kennedy became front-runner for the Democratic presidential nomination by winning the California Primary. Then he was assassinated.

The Summer of '68 brought Led Zeppelin to the "Underground." I played everything off their first album, especially "Whole Lotta Love." I even took the trouble of dubbing it onto tape so I could jack things up to maximum decibel level on the trailing vocal at the end where Robert Plant talks about being a "back door man." Hey. Most stations were fading out of it before then to avoid accusations of bad taste. WTAC had to go in exactly the opposite direction. It was a matter of leadership.

We also played Steppenwolf's "Pusher Man." A station in the South had been warned by the Federal Communications Commission that the "Goddamns" in the song might be construed as "blasphemous." This was prohibited under statutory communications law. We felt that any such concerns were greatly outweighed by the message against drug abuse, providing a fine excuse. The WTAC "Underground" had to stay at the very edge. Much of the more popular material being exposed was finding its way onto the regular WTAC playlist as time went on.

The Beatles released "Hey Jude" in August. I took two copies and, after much practice, succeeded in splicing together the long chorus at the end so it just kept on repeating. Capitol Records in Detroit called and said they were catching flack from their local stations. Listeners were demanding to hear the "45 minute version" of "Hey Jude" that was being played by WTAC in Flint. As autumn leaves started to fall, the Beatles, who had borrowed older rock material in their earliest days, were themselves successfully copied by the spacey Joe Cocker. He got by with a little help from his friends all the way to #1. Who needs plastic? We had spastic.

Bob Dell had decided to try "extension marketing" and expand his Mt. Holly activities into the Saginaw area with a satellite venue. He leased an old warehouse which became "Mt.

Holly North." Its success was limited due to direct competition launched by others, particularly at "Daniel's Den" in Saginaw and at the "Foxy Lady" near Bay City. Additionally, "Holly North" would often wind up competing with "Holly South" on a given night, dividing up the crowds. After the '68 season, continuing the endeavor seemed foolish. "Mt. Holly North" was abandoned. Bob was starting to face other competitive challenges as well, some from his fellow employees at WTAC.

Although I was committed to the nightly airshift Mondays through Fridays, weekends were open for my own promotional activities. As host of the "WTAC Underground," I had become quite familiar with area bands, club managers and hall owners. Other WTAC disc-jockeys also started adding live, self-promoted band concerts to their normal schedule of high school "hops" and "dances." These were still the source of considerable activity and extra income. Since WTAC's coverage area offered a wide geographic expanse, we would rarely run into one another. There was room for all. Usually. Everyone had pretty much carved out his own "turf." The "WTAC D-J Datebook" summarizing such activities was starting to run two minutes long.

It was common knowledge that Bob was accumulating significant personal wealth from Mt. Holly and other sources. His WTAC pay-check represented a small percentage of his annual income. It was also understood that WTAC provided Bob with both a power base and an economic fulcrum that he honestly, fully and openly exploited. There was whispered speculation regarding "conflicts of interest," "serving two masters" and "divided loyalties." Human nature being unchanged through the centuries, much of the negativity was driven by basic jealousy and was nurtured by deep resentment.

Although unique in its Flint ratings leadership, WTAC was no different than most other radio stations across the country in one significant way: Although "on-air" people were the individuals most highly identified with any given facility by the general public, true power resided in Sales. As with any other business, those who directly brought in the money were ultimately regarded as priority players by upper management. Programming built the "product" that obtained "listenership," but Sales turned it all into cold, hard cash. That alone was bottom line. The average radio salesperson earned a combination of base wages and commissions easily exceeding the income earned by all but a handful of air personalities. Promotions to the position of General Manager were almost exclusively restricted to candidates from the Sales Department.

The General Sales Manager was normally second-in-line to the General Manager at a station and, in many instances, an eventual successor. While faithfully following Bob's instructions in Programming, I remained ever mindful of other organizational obligations dictated by precedent and common sense. This included offering continuing assistance to the silent radio stars behind the scenes who did nothing but ring the cash register.

"Need a guy to dress up in a sailor suit and broadcast from the top of the concession stand at the South Dort Drive-In for the opening of 'McHale's Navy'? "No problem!" After the promotion I partied with Tim Conway for a while, then my car ran out of gas and I was forced to hitchhike home garbed as a gob and got my groin grabbed.

"You want someone to introduce Bill Cosby at Whiting Auditorium next Sunday for Coca-Cola? What time do you want me there?" This was during the 10 minute period that "Nehru Suits" were in. Although Cosby had a bad case of the flu, and normally didn't need an "introducer," he was most gracious and kept me on stage for a full five minutes with incisive comments on my stunning attire.

"The client still wants a WTAC jock to host the local Miss Teenage America competition, even with long-hair and a mustache? Where do I get my tux?" A 16 year-old finalist from Birch Run High School, Nancy Dymond, would later make history in senior radio management.

I was also more than willing to spend part of my boring, unproductive, pain-in-the-ass "News and Production" shift to write copy ideas, draft promotions, speak with clients and assist sales people in any way I could. I wasn't getting a nickel extra for the effort, but it passed the time. Charlie had expressed deep appreciation for the extent of my cooperation. Bob indicated his growing discomfort.

"You know, you sometimes make me look like an asshole."

"You know better, man! But what am I supposed to do, tell these guys to eat shit? You get to do that around here, not me!" Bob and I still put in plenty of bar time.

(Ring-Ring)

"Hello."

"Hey, Peter C.! How the fuck did I get into that goddamn fight last night?"

"Well, some big mother-fucker thought I was hittin' on his lady. He came over to our table and called me a 'goddamn prick.' You stood up and knocked him on his ass. You were cool!"

"Wait. Wait. Wait. He called you a 'goddamn prick' and I stood up and knocked him on his ass? Jesus Christ!"

"He also called you a "Jew Bastard."

"A what?"

"A 'Jew Bastard.' He said I was a 'goddamn prick' first."

"Ohhhhhhh. I feel better."

"You can feel better, Bob. He definitely called you a 'Jew Bastard."

"Great. I'll see ya later."

One of the interesting speculations floating around town following the establishment of Bob's Mt. Holly money machine, was that he was Jewish. Bob was only offended by the inherent implication that Italians weren't capable of cranking out the sort of cash he was making without machine guns. With our common Catholic background, I told Bob that Jesus had been Jewish, but that most of the Popes were Italian. Who came out better in the long run? Those collection plates weren't heading for Tel Aviv. I don't think I ever mentioned Saint Augustine was a "Philosophical Coon." Bob would have run right out and picked up his "Confessions."

CHAPTER TWELVE

WILD WEDNESDAY WIN

In April of '69, WTAC assumed sponsorship of an outdoor event to be called "Wild Wednesday" at a place named "Sherwood Forest." Sherwood Forest was located in Richfield Township, just east of Flint and north of Davison. A farmer named Don Sherwood had purchased several pieces of property adjacent to his own homestead. Over several years, Don had chopped down trees, leveled off fields, excavated a small "lake," put in a baseball diamond, and brought in a number of miniature rides and games. Sherwood Forest was a self-assembled Amusement Park. Don was a big man. Had he jumped decades ahead and fought in the Gulf War, he might easily have been mistaken for General Schwartzkopf. Sliding in time, they could have been twins.

The station's idea was to sell sponsorships to car dealers, clothing retailers, food concessionaires, motorcycle shops, auto accessory outlets, jewelry stores and whoever else wanted to participate. All would display wares or sell goods at "Wild Wednesday" with the Amusement Park open for free rides. WTAC would heavily promote the event, and Don Sherwood would make all the money he could off crowds attracted to his own fastfood areas, swimming facilities and games of chance. Don was still seeking to put Sherwood Forest on the map. Three weeks of heavy WTAC advertising for "Wild Wednesday" was sure to offer long-term benefit. The missing key ingredient was a rock band line-up for the fenced-in patio area located between the lake and the unfinished new hall.

I was approached about throwing some groups together for "Wild Wednesday," and hosting the program. A fellow WTAC announcer named Johnny Parker and I entered into a partnership agreement wherein we would combine our efforts, and equally share in all the proceeds. John hailed from Tennessee and came on strong. If he liked you, you were "Ace." If not, you were "Jim," which was invariably pronounced like "Chimp." Johnny had a bite even worse than his bark. He could be one mean little son-of-a-bitch. Nothing stirred him up so much as draining a bottle of Jack Daniels and listening to The Band play "The Night They Drove Old Dixie Down." He would openly weep near the end of the song and slam his fist against the nearest wall or door. Working on "Wild Wednesday," we lined-up six local groups with The Rationals and Bob Seger headlining.

When the big day came on June 21, over 10,000 people turned out at Sherwood Forest for the rides, games, prizes, fun and excitement. WTAC sponsors who had chosen to take part in the event were more than pleased with their investment. Despite threatening clouds, 4000 rockers paid $2 to attend the 8 'til Midnight Concert on the Sherwood Patio. It came off flawlessly. After expenses and the "split," John and I each pocketed a grand. There was sudden and unexpected internal warfare at WTAC. Managers for both the The Rationals and Bob Seger quietly reported that Bob Dell had threatened to drop them from his Mt. Holly line-up if they played "Wild Wednesday." He had spurned participation in the project, after which, I then offered the partnership to John. Both camps had rejected Bob's intimidation, being aware that construction of a new Sherwood hall was nearing completion, and that WTAC was officially backing the event. We promised them this would not be forgotten. My relationship with Bob cooled considerably.

3337-CAVA

As the summer of '69 moved along, John and I started promoting regular concerts at the Center Building in Lapeer, the Owosso Armory, the Saginaw Auditorium, The "Big Wheel" Roller Rink in Bay City, and the County Fairgrounds in Midland, Michigan. The musical counterculture represented by all the Rock 'n Roll we played and presented drew its greatest emotional influence from events unfolding far beyond the powerful WTAC signal. In Southeast Asia, the Tet Offensive in early 1968 had proven costly to Communist forces with a high loss of life, but had been a major factor in turning American opinion ever more firmly against the war. Rallies were being staged almost weekly at Wilson Park in the heart of downtown Flint against the conflict with the support and encouragement of WTAC. Each new week in Vietnam was costing a thousand American lives. At the end of March, President Lyndon Johnson had restricted bombing to pave the way for peace negotiations and also announced that he would not be a candidate for re-election. Johnny Parker and his family joined the Cavanaughs on July 20 to watch Neil Armstrong step on the Moon. Daughters, Laurie and Colleen, seemed unimpressed. It was just more television.

In August, the three-day Woodstock Music and Art Fair was held in rural upstate New York. 500,000 came. No one had anticipated the enormous turnout. The gates came down. Some clothes came off. There was staring, daring, caring and sharing. The music reigned. The skies rained. It got muddy.

"Watch out for the brown acid, man."

Bob Dell was still pissed from "Wild Wednesday" and a subsequent pronounced decline in Mt. Holly attendance. The crowds hadn't vanished— they just weren't what they used to be. Competition was picking up everywhere. The Grande Ballroom and East Town Theater in Detroit were bringing in Superstars, including the WHO, Blind Faith, Creedence Clearwater and the Doors. Mt. Holly could squeeze in up to 2000 indoors at the most. Many groups that Bob had promoted in the past had now become too big for the very venue that had launched them. Exclusivity and loyalty are often passing things. Woodstock and another, less celebrated, outdoor rock concert in Atlanta provided Bob with a new spark of inspiration.

CHAPTER THIRTEEN

WORKING ON THE RAILROAD

Terry Knapp was born in Lapeer, Michigan. Charlie Speights' wife Nancy remembered the Knapp family since Terry's father used to be their milkman. The milkman's son Knapp became a radio Knight. Terry Knight had been hired as a disc-jockey at WTAC by Thaddeus Murphy and later went to Detroit, where he worked at WJBK and CKLW. Terry was an extraordinary air talent and master bullshitter. He returned briefly to Flint in late 1964 as an air personality at WTRX. While back in Flint, Terry rented the IMA Auditorium, and bought commercials on his station for a special promotion. The copy was quite clever.

"The Sounds of Chuck Berry; the Sounds of Stevie Wonder; the Sounds of the Beach Boys; the Sounds of the Dave Clark Five and the Sounds of Gene Pitney!! All for just *$3* on SUNDAY from 2 'til 6 at the IMA. BE THERE OR BE SQUARE !!!"

Two thousand showed up and forked-over their three bucks. Terry plugged in his turntables, and played records featuring all the artists and "Sounds" mentioned in his advertisements. Several attendees were quite disgruntled in the absence of real, live performers, and Terry cheerfully refunded their admission in full. Most remained. Crowds always keep crowds. Terry walked away with several thousand dollars for all his time and trouble. Although outraged at his amazing scam, we secretly had to admit he had certainly pulled off a good one.

The time was at hand for Terry to leave the broadcasting business. He wanted to be not just a radio hero, but a Rock 'n Roll Star. Joining forces with Flint musicians Mark Farner and Donnie Brewer, Terry changed the name of Donnie's band "The Jazz Masters." It became "The Pack." "Terry Knight and the Pack" started playing throughout the Midwest with Terry out front on vocals and "The Pack" in back. In 1966, Terry Knight and the Pack were signed to Lucky Eleven Records and had a minor national hit with "I (Who Have Nothing)." It was their only big single. Two albums that followed flopped, so they were dropped. The group broke up and Terry headed for the Big Apple.

He tried stints as a folk-singer and stand-up comedian. He went to work for Ed McMahon and picked-up a few minor television roles— even including an appearance on "The Dating Game." He wrote a movie soundtrack. He was just about everywhere, doing almost everything. Nothing in particular was coming down all the way right.

But wait. If Terry wasn't making it big as a "Star," what about nailing the big time as a "Star-Maker"? He returned to Flint, and called Donnie and Mark. They needed a bass player. Mel Schacher, who used to play with Question Mark and the Mysterians, was out of work. The group's popularity had collapsed after not quite two years. Mel was available.

As anyone who has ever waited a lifetime for a train to pass through one of Flint's many crossings knows, Grand Trunk Railroad ruled the rails in the Auto City. Terry pictured the trio pounding out basic rock and blues with minimal frills. They'd just chug right along and huff and puff like a big old Rock 'n Roll locomotive steam engine and— hey. That's it. Grand Trunk Railroad! No. Hang on. Wait a second. Let's think. Trunk.

Trunk-Skunk-Hunk-Bunk-Sunk-Punk-Dunk-Junk-Funk. Funk. FUNK!!

"GRAND FUNK RAILROAD!!!!!"

Terry rehearsed the band hours upon end. He told everyone who would listen that "Grand Funk Railroad" would be bigger than the Beatles. Sure, Terry. Do you mean the "Sounds" of the Beatles, or the actual BEATLES-Beatles? Mark and Donnie and Mel were well regarded in the Flint musical community, but Beatles?

Terry went to town. He called everyone he knew in the entertainment trades. And in radio. And in television. And in movies, newspapers, magazines, advertising agencies, public relations firms and every other media-connected organization he could think of. Terry sold Grand Funk Railroad like pushing pussy on a troop train.

"They're incredible, unbelievable, amazing, wonderful, gigantic, stupendous, spectacular, superlative, outstanding, unbeatable, killer and the greatest." And he was only talking about the Grand Funk road crew.

Somehow, some way, Terry was successful in booking the completely unknown group at a major musical marathon called the Atlanta Pops Festival. He then focused his attention on making contact with every major rock station in the South. He lined up interviews for the group. He arranged for limousines to sweep Mark, Donnie and Mel from station to station and town to town. He leveled his considerable talents at media manipulation toward every reporter, music critic and record executive who might come within a hundred miles of the Festival. Well, what do you know? The hype was so heavy that the world was waiting and Grand Funk Railroad came through in Atlanta. They weren't fancy. They weren't flashy. They weren't flamboyant. But they DELIVERED. They were really LOUD.

They did so well in their original time slot, they were asked to return to close the show. They tuned-up and turned-up even LOUDER. News of the concert spread like Madonna, and Grand Funk Railroad was on the front page of newspapers across America, and featured in key television clips of the Festival.

Worst to first. Lame to fame. Back of the rack to tops at the Pops. Terry had pretended, and it all came true.

We were floored in Flint and Bob Dell had a plan. Bob Dell and Terry Knight had known each other well, while working together at WTAC, then had drifted somewhat apart after Terry went to Detroit. They were outright competitors for a brief time, when Terry had temporarily returned to Flint and WTRX. When "Terry and the Pack" came into existence, their friendship resumed and Bob had used the group several times at Mt. Holly and elsewhere. Terri kept Bob posted on the formation of "Grand Funk Railroad", before and after the fact. While Bob certainly was as stunned with the group's massively heralded launch as the rest of us, he definitely had an inside lead. He immediately made his move.

The idea was to create a smaller scale version of Woodstock or Atlanta on the slopes of Mt. Holly, and headline "Grand Funk Railroad" in their premiere Michigan appearance. He would beat the capacity problem the indoor lodge presented by taking it all outdoors. The hills behind the lodge had a natural contour, which centered at exactly the right spot. Perfect. You could probably squeeze 30,000-40,000 souls on the Mt. Holly hills. Ha. At $5 a head, that would be the very heaviest of "hits" ever. Yes.

Terry Knight was excited over the prospect, and disappointed in me since I had passed on Grand Funk at a guaranteed $2,000 vs. 65 percent of gate admissions. The most I paid a group was $1,250 vs. 50 percent. It was purely an economic consideration. If word got out (which it always did) that I'd adjusted both guarantee and commission percentage for Terry, it would be impossible to maintain established norms. This would put me in a considerably riskier and less profitable series of investments.

Although I loved the music and the honor of promoting it far and wide, every concert was an exercise in basic business mechanics. I was always the last to get paid and, even with care and caution, found that nights of significant profit were necessary to fund other nights where losses might prove substantial. I surely came out way ahead over the long haul, but only by never forgetting the underlying economic realities of the game. Nine out of 10 times, one would either win or lose in structuring performance terms with a booking agent weeks or months before the actual engagement. I was always making my best educated guess. I felt that Grand Funk Railroad, at that precise moment, did not offer the draw potential to justify the amounts discussed. Admittedly, this was a few weeks before Atlanta.

The event was scheduled only two weeks in advance, and Bob arranged staggering logistics in record time. A massive sound system was booked to cover acres of land, and security planning was enormous. Heavy and expensive radio advertising was scheduled on Detroit stations, and on Lansing, Ann Arbor, Toledo, Saginaw and Grand Rapids facilities. WTAC, naturally, became the "presenting" entity. Announcements started running on an hourly basis. Numerous live references on Bob's morning program became standard. The rest of the day, "liner cards" were scheduled by the Program Director and read by all the other jocks. Since the Sherwood Forest hall was still several months away from opening and we had nothing major scheduled which might be negatively impacted by the "Grand Funk" Festival, Parker and I raced through the promos. We sat back and waited with subjective interest.

The day of the concert was hot and sunny. Bob had live "road reports" scheduled every twenty minutes over WTAC to project an image of heavy incoming traffic; the highways to Mt. Holly choked to capacity with eager throngs flocking to the slopes. The reports kicked-off four hours before performance time. The earliest "feeds" cheerfully reported "no problems." Dell was angry and suspected treachery. The next few updates sounded strange. The drift was that even if there were no traffic tie-ups then, there absolutely would be later. The rest of the "update" was a blatant recitation of all the reasons to get up off one's ass and attend the festival. It became glaringly conspicuous that the show was in trouble. Orders were given to double all "Mt. Holly" announcements on WTAC for the rest of the day.

There is always a tendency to believe that last minute volume can rescue a fading proposition. It's only natural to want to do something as the odds of success slowly slide away right before your very eyes. I'd seen it happen many times before with other concerts, promotions and, particularly, station "remotes."

"Why, sure we'll put your salesmen on the air and they can talk about all the wonderful items and prices and deals and bonus offers they want. Our listeners will love it!" Bullshit. Remotes only really work if there is enticement above and beyond the fact that there is a "live radio broadcast" going on somewhere. Vewing some live demonstration of "Mr. Microphone" is akin to watching water boil. However, if the guy on the air promises to stick his dick in scalding water if somebody comes in and buys a new Buick, then we have something else again. We have SPIN. The possibility is fair that someone listening, who was going to purchase a new vehicle anyway, might head over to the dealership and plunk some money down just to see boiled balls. Stranger things have happened. Many disc-jockeys have small endowments anyway, so we're not talking about a lot of pain. The point is that you need to have something really interesting to pull people in and broadcasting alone won't cut it. The media alone is not enough message. And the lesson learned that lovely summer day at Mt. Holly was that "Grand Funk Railroad" had become interesting, but not yet compelling to Michigan rock fans. After all, almost everyone had known Mark, Donnie and Mel for years. They'd seen them at high school dances, weddings, family reunions and out in the bars getting drunk. They were real people. "Stars" are never real people. They can't be. The magic was missing. Grand Funk Railroad played well that day before several thousand, who probably could have been squeezed inside the regular hall after all. Most of the crowd was from outside the Flint area.

After all the fuss and fury and promises of untold riches, Mt. Holly's owners were bitterly unhappy. They had taken tons of shit from township officials, law enforcement agencies and area residents who seemed the only ones convinced, along with Bob and Terry, that a multitude would assemble on the slopes. For what? To "break-even"? They barely did that. Johnny Parker and I made a note to contact them after the first of the year.

As fall arrived, work on the Sherwood Forest hall was nearly finished. A "Grand Opening Concert" was planned for the third Sunday in October. We needed a perfect headliner. There was only one group I had in mind.

CHAPTER FOURTEEN

A TESTIMONIAL

I had seen the band initially at Delta College outside the Tri-City airport near Saginaw in late January. I worked with them for the first time at the "Foxy Lady" in Bay City a few months later. The club had a capacity for 800. 1200 were packed inside. Another 500 were turned away.

The road crew had arrived hours earlier. A towering wall of Marshall speaker cabinets stood behind five microphones, four guitar amplifiers and a raised drum set. The sound system stretched across the entire length of the stage and from floor to ceiling. The equipment area was surrounded by lighting racks. Scaffolding covered with additional speakers jutted-out from the stage at almost every angle. Directly across the room were mounted three elevated "super-trooper" spotlights, each with a separate operator. There was no introduction for the first set.

The five member group simply took the stage and detonated an absolutely perfect, astoundingly balanced, 40 minute performance of the greatest early Rock 'n Roll in the history of the music form. Songs by Little Richard, Bo Diddley, Buddy Holly and Elvis Presley blasted forth with energized rebirth in staggering sequence. Their awesome salute to all which had come before was hypnotic in effect. They finished "Rock 'n Roll Music" by Chuck Berry, then took a break. Their credentials had been more than adequately presented. After 20 minutes, a tall, blond, long-haired, heavily muscled "freak" jumped upon the stage, grabbed a microphone and began to preach. J. C. Crawford doubled as road manager and "Spiritual Advisor" to the band. Jimmy Swaggert, Oral Roberts and Billy Graham, on their very best days, have never reached J. C. Crawford's level on that night of incomparable, incendiary, crowd-whipping incitement.

"Brothers and Sisters; let me see a sea of hands out there! Let me see a sea of hands! Let me hear a little Revolution out there, Brothers! A little Revolution out there!"

"Brothers and Sisters, the time has come when you must choose! You must choose, Brothers, you must choose! You must choose whether you will make a difference on this planet! You must choose whether you are going to be the problem or whether you are going to be the solution!"

"You must testify, Brothers and Sisters. You must testify! And I want to know! Are you ready to testify? Are you ready to testify?"

"I give you a Testimonial!"

"THE—M—C— FIVE!!!!!!!!!!!!!!"

The group had quietly and almost invisibly taken their places on stage behind Mr. Crawford. At "Five," they took total command. A whining, screaming, thundering, supersonic roar literally shook the walls of the cinder-block building as guitar players Fred "Sonic" Smith and Wayne Kramer hit the opening chords of "Ramblin' Rose." Lead singer Rob Tyner lunged for the microphone and wailed with abandon. All the "super-troopers" had been fired directly at Rob upon the utterance of his first shrieked syllable. The decibel level had doubled from the first set and the lighting tree had sprung to life with reds, greens, yellows and blues alternating color illumination every second drum beat. Strobe lights on either side added to visual stimulation hovering at overload.

To emphasize lyric content, Tyner reached down and shook his concealed pecker. Did he have a license for that thing? Michael Jackson "grabs his crotch." Rob Tyner went right for the cock. There is a difference. The audience was far past mere appreciation or enjoyment. It was all way too much to ever dance or bounce-around to. The crowd was paralyzed. They were captured. Taken. Frozen. Stoned. Zapped. Fried.

For their single love ballad, Rob chose a "random" female from the throng and pulled her by hand from the floor onto the stage. Fingers caressing her throat, he reached for the top of a very loose blouse and gently and slowly tugged downward until enormous bare, white breasts became plainly visible. They rose and fell, offering full spectacular view ending only a centimeter above nipple-level. Tenderly nestling his microphone into a secure resting place between the now publicly displayed pair, Rob leaned forward and whispered the song title directly into her exposed chest. As the band kicked-in and the words to "I Want You Right Now" were recited with soaring ferocity, the "volunteer" began erotically swaying back and forth in mesmerized trance. The sexual tension was finally broken only at the end of the song, when Rob politely retrieved his microphone, sincerely offered thanks for able-bodied assistance, and helped his subject off the stage. He was quite the gentleman.

The MC-5 concluded the night's performance with their quintessential anthem:

"And right now—right now—right now—right now—it's time to—

KICK OUT THE JAMS, MOTHER-FUCKER!!!!!!!!!!!!!!!!"

The song had become a hit across much of the Midwest. The words "Brothers and Sisters" had been substituted on the recording in place of "Mother-Fucker" for radio exposure. Restraint unleashed, the audience jumped up and down, undulating as one with the pulsating beat. After the group finished and left the stage, raptured applause continued unabated for ten full minutes. The MC-5 did no encores.

John Sinclair was the group's founder/creator/manager. He had moved to the Ann Arbor area years before and had attended school at the University of Michigan. When the counterculture first blossomed, and love seemed everywhere, John had grown his hair long and recited beautiful poetry in the coffee-houses and parks. He was a peaceful man who worked for an end to the Vietnam struggle and all future wars. He spoke of freedom and tolerance. Of brotherhood and understanding. Of tender thoughts and soft, sweet dreams. He was arrested by the police for smoking marijuana. They threw him in jail, then beat the living shit out of him. Fuck that.

Establishing a commune of like-minded souls on Hill Street, John founded the "White Panther Party." This was patterned after the revolutionary "Black Panther Party," except you could join without actually being black. There was "solidarity" between both Panther groups. John now believed that only a true Revolution would turn things around. Fuck the government. Fuck the "pigs." Fuck the establishment. Power to the people. Right on.

Band members Rob Tyner, Wayne Kramer, Fred Smith, Michael Davis and Dennis Thompson hailed from the Detroit area and were archetypical struggling musicians. They had played individually with various bands through time, but had yet to enjoy "making it" in any significant manner. John Sinclair loved Rock 'n Roll. He pondered how wonderful it would be if the White Panthers could have a "house band." Everyone could live together, work together, eat together, sleep together and even fuck together. John eventually got to write those exact words on the MC-5's first album cover. John and the band never fucked each other. They had plenty of females; women who waited on the Revolution hand and foot. Despite protestations to the contrary, the Revolution was really coming down as a "guys" kind of deal. "Freedom" for women meant that they would be released from the tyranny and chains of the established social order and become "free" to serve their men. For the Revolution. All in all, the musicians thought it looked like a pretty fair deal. They'd have a place to sleep, food to eat, booze to drink, dope to smoke and women to ball. It sure beat the shit out of 'Nam. They assumed the name "Motor City Five," being from Detroit and all. This was soon shortened it to "MC-5." That had sort of a hip, ethereal ring to it, like "MC2," which was Einstein's formula expressing relativity theory.

Time! Space! Energy! Light! Cool!! Love it!!! MC-5!!

And what great positioning. Talk about marketing. You want **SPIN?**

These guys weren't just a bunch of long-haired dudes playing loud music. No goddamned way. They were fucking Revolutionaries. They just might jump off that son-of-a-bitchin' stage and blow somebody's brains out right in the middle of set. Who could ever be sure they wouldn't? Bad? You want really bad? You want really, truly, capital "B" Bad, Revolutionary Rock 'n Roll Guerrillas ready to kick ass and kill? You want a **FUCKING TESTIMONIAL** to ultimate **REVOLUTIONARY EVIL?** A group parents could **REALLY HATE?**

The MC-5 totally got into it. They practiced long and hard, month after month. John Sinclair was a brilliant thinker and thoroughly in touch with raw emotions. John knew music, and production, and the art of dramatic staging. The MC-5 weren't just a band. They were theater. The band never knew exactly what the "Revolution" was, or how it might involve them, or what it might become. Who cared? They were the Revolution. They were the focal point. They were the show. That's really all that mattered. They were the best live Rock 'n Roll band I'd ever seen, bar none. I wanted them for Sherwood Forest.

John Sinclair had earned substantial notoriety from his encounters with the law and his widely publicized comments on how fucked the country was and especially how fucked the "pig/jerk-off/asshole/prick-cops" were in their "blue Nazi uniforms" with their "limp-dick attitudes" and "cock-sucking mentalities." John was quite the talker. Even though the popular press was restricted to publishing highly edited versions of his pronouncements, the essential message suggested was abundantly clear. John Sinclair was a cop-hater.

The authorities kept track of such things. The Davison City and Township Police Departments were especially sensitive to the enraged ramblings of this native son. They secretly swore that John Sinclair or his band would never publicly surface in their area of jurisdiction without severe sanction. Sherwood Forest was one slender mile north of Davison, Michigan. I was aware of John Sinclair's ties with Davison. So what? It was a free country. Arrangements were completed for the MC-5 to headline the Grand Opening of Sherwood Forest in Davison on Sunday, October 19, 1969.

CHAPTER FIFTEEN

FUCKING OBSCENITY

WTRX, still competing with WTAC for contemporary audience, had begun a series of Sunday night dances at the Davison Knights of Columbus Hall, quite near "The Forest." They increased the strength of their band line-up for the 19th with several Detroit groups of marginal consequence and heavily boosted their advertising schedule. Big deal.

We produced a killer "End of the World" announcement heralding our MC-5 opening. Posters and flyers were printed and circulated at every record store, bar, shopping mall and theater complex in a 50 mile-wide area. "End of the World" production involved using 10 or 12 music cuts within 60 seconds' worth of copy. We also combined a "Voice of God" delivery with heavy sound processing and elaborate editing, making an event sound like the "End of the World" was at hand. Anything so offered dare not be missed. One key ingredient was to use material from the group being promoted to drive the emotion and intensity of the spoken word. We also dropped in a brief sample of J. C. Crawford's harangue. It worked perfectly. It was showtime.

The event had been scheduled to run from 6 until 10 p.m. with doors opening at 5:30. The MC-5 were guaranteed $1,000 vs. 50 percent of admissions. Don Sherwood would receive 50 percent of net profits, after all expenses were deducted, and would also contribute the same percentage in the event of a loss. Parker and I would evenly divide or pay the rest. Tickets were priced at

3337-CAVA

$3. Expenses totaled $1,550. "Break-even" was 517 tickets sold. Anything past that was profit. It was the essence of Capitalism. The MC-5 did not play without pay. John and I met Don at the park shortly after 3 P.M. A few cars were already pulling into the lot. At 4 P.M., a line was forming in front of the building, and we decided to open the doors. Over 1000 had filled the new hall as we started playing records. When we introduced the opening band, the capacity was becoming strained at 1,500. At 7 P.M., we closed the doors with 2,000 bodies crammed wall-to-wall, and 300-400 more turned-away during the next hour.

Exactly at 8 P.M. — "Brothers and Sisters, I want to see a sea of hands out there! I want to see a sea of hands!"

Road Manager Crawford was in a particularly buoyant mood. We had been together in the box office only minutes before. I had counted out $3,000 in cash for the group, which represented three times their original guarantee. Power to the People. After 30 minutes or so, I heaved a deep sign of triumphant relief. I reflected. How could the Grand Opening have gone any better? A turn-away crowd, an excellent show, profits for all and happiness everywhere. But hold on, I was forgetting one last little thing. In my younger years, I willingly confess, it was often not enough that I, myself, merely win. With the "want it all" impatience, and competitive lust of unseasoned youth, it was also emotionally required that others must lose. What was happening at that K. of C. Hall?

The MC-5 had 30 minutes left to play. The crowd, although wildly euphoric over each new song the band introduced, was extremely well-behaved. Everything was under control. Plenty of time for reconnaissance. I jumped in my car and sped up along the long Sherwood Forest driveway leading out to Richfield Road. Taking a right on Richfield, hanging a left on M-15, grabbing another right on Davison Road, and there I was, smack-dab in front of the Knights of Columbus. I turned into the circular driveway. Less than a dozen vehicles were in the lot. All riiiiiiiiiiight. The win was absolute.

I headed immediately back toward Sherwood. Not five minutes had passed. As I pulled back onto the property and headed past the jammed main parking area, I saw the hall lights flash-on inside the lodge. Hmmm? The MC-5 weren't schedule to complete their performance for another fifteen minutes. People starting streaming outside. Huh? What? Directly adjacent to the lodge were at least 20 police cars parked at five-foot intervals. City of Davison. Davison Township. Richfield Township. Mundy Township. Lapeer Township. Uniformed officers milled about, waving flashlights and directing exiting concert-goers toward their cars.

Ralph Rogers was the Chief of Police of the City of Davison. He was a former U.S. Marine with a quarter-inch crewcut, a pit-bull demeanor and a general attitude wired tighter than a mouse's ass stretched across a barrel. He ran his force the way he used to run his grunt squad in Korea. Tight. Right. Tough. Rough. Steady. Ready.

Ralph had learned that John Sinclair's band, a fucking-faggot-hippy-long-haired-bunch of left-wing pukes, was coming to Sherwood Forest, right next to Davison, "City of Flags." These were the kind of people who snuck around in the dark of night obliterating the letter "L" from the illustrious Davison City Motto on all the plaques the local American Legion Chapter had proudly posted all over town. Sinclair was a useless, un-American, Commie, Prick-Bastard, Piece-of-Shit. Military training and instinctive loathing clearly called for something. But, what? You couldn't just shoot the sons-of-bitches crossing the city line. Goddamn it.

Sleepless nights of analysis, phone calls to other area police departments requesting extra manpower, discussions with the County Prosecutor's Office reviewing options under the law and careful scrutiny of the MC5 "Kick out The Jams" album (which Ralph purchased for $6.59 with clenched teeth at K-Mart) finally brought forth an excellent plan. Even as I was only seconds away from the Sherwood Forest entrance drive, the trigger was pulled.

"And right now. Right now. Right now. Right NOW—It's time to—

KICK OUT THE JAMS, MOTHER FUCKER!!!!!"

"Obscenity! Obscenity! Obscenity! They said, "Mother Fucker!" Got that on tape? Did you get the Mother Fucker? Alright!"

"Go! Go! Go! Go! Go! Go! Go!"

Fifty helmeted, riot-geared township police officers rushed through the front door at Sherwood Forest and worked their way slowly toward the stage. The crowd parted like the Red Sea. What was this? Part of the show? Heavy! The band finally saw the cops heading in their direction. As one, they collectively flashed a single, simple, solidified and unified vision. Not "Up the Revolution"; not "Fuck the Pigs"; not "Power to the Proletariat." The united thought was something much more personally powerful.

"WE'RE HOLDING!!!!"

"Holding," to the uninitiated (and in this context), means "having illegal, controlled substances on our immediate persons." The MC-5 were temporarily not interested in taking on the establishment, fighting for human rights, or upholding the sacred revolutionary codes by which they lived and for which they played. Their entire life philosophy and sole purpose on the planet instantaneously transformed into but a single ambition:

"Go! Go! Go! Go! Go! Go! Go!"

As with all great battle plans, the execution of the police maneuver had encountered a number of surprises. Although the crowd of "kids" was enormous, they were all actually quite docile. Everyone seemed more curious than concerned as the officers stormed the hall, although "waded tentatively into" would be more honestly descriptive. While many of the men had seen military action, and had visited places and enjoyed experiences they'd certainly never shared with their sisters, wives or mothers, none of them had ever been on Mars before.

They were surrounded by 2000 deliriously entertained, screaming, shouting, dancing MC-5 enthusiasts. Brilliant lights were flashing every color of the rainbow. That unearthly, piercing, pounding, rolling, strange excuse for music was shaking the ceiling, walls and floor with thundering pulsation. The cops were not only in an unknown universe, but one louder than a carrier deck at full launch. Strategy was to arrest the band for "obscenity," but it took at least five minutes to get through the crowd to the stage. They had thought of sending a few of the troops in through the back door, but had decided every man was needed in the main entry formation should there be problems with "control" or "riot."

The MC-5 finished "Kick Out the Jams" with 55 seconds to spare. They thanked everyone for coming and were out-the-door and in their van, hurriedly heading for Ann Arbor. The whole bunch were gone in almost less time than you could say "Mother Fucker." They shot by me in a blur as I entered the backstage area.

"Cops! Bye!"

I hit the stage the same split second as Chief Rogers. Only very few times in my life have I abandoned all thoughts of reason and deliciously surrendered to the full, pure, powerful passion of furious Irish rage. Rogers' eyes darted sharply about in anxious anticipation.

"Where'd they go?"

"Who the fuck are you?"

"Who the fuck are you?"

"I'm the fuckin' promoter and you're on private fuckin' property!"

"This place is fuckin' closed and you're under fuckin' arrest!"

"For fuckin' what?"

"For fucking obscenity!"

Applause for the group was just beginning to fade. Johnny Parker had joined me on stage with that look on his face that said, in no uncertain terms, they were drivin' ol' Dixie down. He joined the discussion.

"Hey, Jim! Fuck you!"

"This place is fuckin' shut down now and you're both under fuckin' arrest!"

John and I replied in exact phrasing and perfect unison, "Fuck you!"

Nothing mattered, save honor. John headed for the record booth to hit the music. I took the microphone and walked to the front of the stage.

"Ladies and Gentlemen, the MC-5!!"

There was a resumption of raucous applause.

"Ladies and Gentlemen, we have some visitors tonight. Let's hear it for the cops!"

Since the MC-5 were truly theatrical, who could tell? Maybe this was part of the show. The crowd cheered wildly for the police.

"Ladies and Gentlemen! We've got the new Bob Seger album and we're gonna play it all the way through!"

The affirmative roar drowned out Ralph's yelling for reinforcements on stage. Opening strains of "Lucifer" filled the room.

I emphatically motioned for Chief Rogers to join me in the backstage area. Several friends had whispered interesting information. I'd figured the only move. There was no turning back. The face of the Chief was scarlet red. His head was spinning. His heart was heaving. He was actually breathless with unmitigated anger. He could not contain or conceal his fierce frustration. The fuckin' Commies had flown the coop.

He couldn't call a car for interception. All of his cars and his buddies' cars were all already at Sherwood. He couldn't call the State Police or the Sheriff. He'd look like a moron, and they were a whole separate bunch of pricks. They'd laugh their asses off. But, he still had these fuckin' radio boys. That fuckin' dildo with the glasses, who admitted he was the goddamn promoter. That's at least one fish in the net; no, two, counting that fuckin' little bastard who called him a chimp.

"You're both under arrest!"

"How many, Chief?"

"You're under arrest!"

"How many cars and vans, Chief? How many?"

Rogers shifted his steely gaze back and forth between us. Were these guys druggies? Were they high? On that acid crap? What the fuck were they saying? Cars? Vans? They were ignoring an arrest. Two arrests!

"At least a dozen, Chief. At least a dozen. Probably more. You're in deep, deep shit!"

Something had strangely shifted. He was in deep shit? They were the ones in the deep shit. Weren't they? Fuck, those Commies got away. Shit! What the fuck are these guys talkin' about?

"What the fuck are you assholes talkin' about?"

"Nice move, Chief. No search warrants. No permission. No witnesses. What were you guys doing? Stealin' shit? Get any tapes? Any radios? Any stereos?"

I assumed my best Dan Berrigan mode and addressed the Chief with measured patience, as though explaining the Gospel of St. Luke to a six year-old child. My voice was evenly modulated without a trace of rancor.

"Chief Rogers, I'm afraid there were witnesses. A number of complaints have already been brought to my attention regarding uniformed police officers breaking into cars and vans tonight in the Sherwood Forest parking lot. The vehicles were unoccupied. I'm sure you are intimately familiar with specific procedures required by law concerning such entry. In the absence of signed search warrants or honest reasonable cause, there is growing speculation that thievery was involved or attempted."

The Chief glared at me with lingering contempt, but I had his undivided attention.

337-CAVA

"There are also questions concerning your entry into a private facility without permission, and potentially endangering the safety and security of a lawful public assembly." Rogers blinked. There was no other change in posture or presence. But he blinked.

"It's my own suspicion that your officers were searching vehicles for illegal contraband, and erroneously felt that they were lawfully doing so. I would also wish to apologize for any untoward language expressed by myself or my partner, Mr. John Parker, who is standing to my left. No disrespect was intended. We were stunned and confused by your sudden appearance and responded on an emotional level highly untypical of our normal demeanor when communicating with members of the law enforcement community. If you feel our conduct requires our arrest, we will offer absolutely no resistance at the conclusion of tonight's presentation"

"Where'd those fuckin' hippies go?"

"Chief Rogers, the MC-5 and their entourage left immediately, fearing an undesired encounter could create a full-scale riot."

His voice was much more subdued. Confidence was cracking. "I want this place shut-down."

"Chief Rogers, this place will be shut-down in exactly 10 minutes time. We have announced a 10 o'clock closing on WTAC. We must honor our promise or there could be severe problems with the Federal Communications Commission regarding false, misleading advertising. That could bring in The Bureau."

This was really starting to stretch it. Parker was pissing his pants. The Chief whirled about and left the room. We could see him speaking with his officers near the front of the hall. We bid the gathering farewell at 10 P.M. sharp, plugged the next week's attractions, then turned the house lights up.

Chief Rogers and his helmeted forces blended into the departing crowd until the building had finally emptied for all except employees and cleaning crew.

Don Sherwood was understandably upset. His new hall had debuted with overflowing attendance. He had earned more in one night than in an average two weeks of full operation. At the same time, Ralph Rogers was really mad. The last thing Don or any businessman needed was problems with a pissed-off Police Chief— especially a former Marine agonizing over a failed mission. I agreed that things had to be set straight, and the Chief made comfortable. I would review all options and conjure up a plan. There had to be a way.

Stewart Newblatt had been elected a Circuit Court Judge several years prior, and had resigned from the bench in frustration. He was an honest man with a superlative mind. Stewart felt that rigid requirements of sentencing had restricted him from rendering fair judgment in several situations which had arisen involving certain circumstances not adequately contemplated by, nor written into, the law. He was a man of principle and passion. Decades later, he would resign early from the Federal bench over similar discomforts relating to mandatory sentencing of drug offenders. Stewart was a good friend of Charlie Speights. I explained to Charlie all of the prior evening's events, in great detail, the following day. There was a lot I didn't have to tell him. It was all in the Flint Journal and on both major Flint television stations.

The official Ralph Rogers version was that he had been alerted to the appearance of the MC-5 at Sherwood Forest, and had assembled a force of uniformed officers to be ready, should necessity require professional intervention. As it turned out, the officers had been successful in maintaining the peace. When the group used a "blatant obscenity" during their show, Ralph and his men had approached the stage to demand the performance be stopped. The group abandoned said performance, and left the hall immediately. There were no arrests. Chief Rogers promised that all future "rock concerts" at Sherwood Forest would be heavily policed, and that there would be arrests for any violations of the law, including the use of obscenity. Don Sherwood was quoted as saying he would certainly abide by any decisions made by the Chief and wanted to "get along." My own quotes related to "misunderstandings" and "missed communications," and the like. No one had spoken to the press about illegal entry, searches or threats. Yet. These matters warranted and awaited private discussion. Charlie Speights arranged a meeting with Stewart Newblatt. Stewart was outraged.

There was no question that Chief Rogers had theoretically violated any number of rules and regulations in evidently condoning a search of "suspected" vehicles for drugs or drug paraphernalia. The searches had turned up a few roaches and a clip or two. Nothing more.

Newblatt was very clear and wise with his summary of deliberation. While Rogers had acted imprudently and might successfully be called to account, he could probably justify his actions enough to get off with a slight slap on the wrist. He would be waiting in the bushes from that point forward and had every legal right to do so. "Rock Concerts" were not Sunday School Picnics. We all knew the nature of the counterculture. It would only be a matter of time before opportunities presented themselves for Chief Rogers to gain glory. An accommodation was desirable.

After leaving attorney Newblatt's office, Charlie and I stopped for a few beverages at the Shorthorn on South Dort and thoroughly explored options. During Baseball's off-season, the Shorthorn regularly featured an aspiring organist who was much more widely known as a thirty game winner for the Detroit Tigers. Denny McClain was a fine entertainer off the field as well, substituting melodic booms for fast-ball zooms. It was at the Shorthorn in Flint that Denny McClain was said to have formed certain associations which subsequently led him to periodic difficulties with the law in matters of gambling and more serious rambling. Charlie and I were not among such associations, although we would often chat with him about baseball over booze. As Denny finished "Take Me Out to The Ballgame," a Shorthorn favorite, Charlie and I concluded that Chief Rogers had to be approached at the soonest possible time with a conciliatory gesture.

I returned home and drank a six-pack of Colt 45. There are times when the most important aspect of acute analysis is continually re-examining the obvious. Rock crowds almost always appeared wildly loose, but this was not their true nature or essential characteristic. Rock enthusiasts were at a concert to be entertained, by the performers and each other. In a large sense, they were performing off-stage as much as those elevated above the masses. The musicians were surrogates. In words and music, they expressed thoughts and emotions unspoken and unexplored in their absence. It had always been so, but Rock 'n Roll magnified the intensity of participatory experience as ever more powerful amplifying systems expanded stimulation in geometric progression.

Rock 'n Roll audiences wanted to have a good time. Any other consideration was completely secondary. Having a good time included being at peace with themselves and each other. There was a delectable dichotomy in safety within chaos. In many ways, the wilder things appeared, the more security was insured. This was decades before "moshing" offered the same point. When the fun's right, who wants a fight? Rock crowds were the easiest controlled, most cooperative assemblies on earth when given proper respect and entertainment. What was first and foremost in the mind of the good Chief? Only one, single, basic thing. To not be perceived as an asshole. Who does? Everything else was a detail.

Taking pen in hand, I composed a brief statement to the Chief, then called Western Union and dictated the message word by word. I asked that it be immediately phone-delivered to the Davison Police Department and hand-delivered to Chief Rogers the following day. This would maximize exposure within the Department and emphasize the formal importance I placed upon the communication. The telegram thanked Chief Rogers for his efforts at the MC-5 Concert and expressed how well he had handled crowd-control and traffic-routing. In fact, he was asked to take official charge of security at all forthcoming concerts. Naturally, he would be reimbursed for his efforts, as would all off-duty officers assigned by him to be present. Not a penny of City or Township taxpayer funds would be required. Although specifically rejecting any attempts at defining "obscenity," we certainly recognized a concept of "community sensitivity" which the Chief had so reasonably outlined. All future groups contracted for performance at Sherwood Forest would be asked to avoid specific limited language as a condition of appearance. I asked to meet with the Chief at his earliest convenience for further discussion.

Don Sherwood contacted me early the next afternoon. Chief Rogers had called him to express surprise and pleasure in receiving the telegram. He had shared its contents with the Mayor, a number of City Council members and the local Davison newspaper. The Chief said that I could phone him at any time. I did so at once. The concordat established was the essence of simplicity. Ralph would be in charge of security and arrange for up to a dozen other officers to be present at Sherwood Forest at every future rock concert scheduled. Ralph would also receive advance copies of every Sherwood Forest performance contract, which would specify that the word "Fuck" or any form of "Fuck" could not be used during performance. Any "Fuck" uttered would result in forfeiture of payment to the artist.

The Chief agreed that the sole purpose of the security presence was to assure peaceful assembly and guard against "Fucks." Within this understanding, it was emphasized that the police were being paid by the promoters to protect the crowd within the walls of Sherwood Forest in every way possible. This was fundamental to our relationship. This also meant policing the police.

The "No-Saying-Fuck" clause was added to all bookings and thoroughly discussed beforehand with agents, managers and musicians. It bowed to sensitivities without importantly sacrificing content. It was a relatively small thing compared to the opportunities for all presented by the venue, yet it seemed a major score for Chief Rogers. In return for not hearing a clear "Fuck" from the stage (although muffled variations or phonetic substitutes were perfectly acceptable), the Sherwood Forest audiences existed within an environment approaching unlimited liberty.

Each concert saw most of the same crowd peacefully intermingle with most of the same police. Repeated and uneventful proximity erases fear, creates familiarity and breeds content. It was an amazingly rational arrangement. Meanwhile, the MC-5 episode and corresponding media coverage had put Sherwood Forest in the public eye. That following Sunday, Bob Seger drew 1,600. The next Friday was Halloween Night.

CHAPTER SIXTEEN

PENNY AND KACHINA

We decided to promote a relatively unknown group from Phoenix, Arizona, who had moved to Michigan, and were working out of Detroit. They sounded pretty spooky to me, and had already established a significant "word of mouth" reputation after only a few appearances. The lead singer claimed to be a witch who was burned at the stake and had come back from the dead. He was the real-life son of a preacher-man. The singer's name was Alice. He played in a long-haired, rock 'n roll band.

The radio advertising for Alice Cooper was a joy to write and produce. Alice's entire set was even more theatrically designed than that of the MC5, with dozens of props, special effects and curious twists. Instead of the "Revolution," Alice Cooper was the "Reincarnation." In place of "politics," we had "horror." Where "fuck" had been daringly screamed in defiance of established standards, there was a doll's head decapitated by a monster of non-specific gender. All in all, "Alice Cooper" was an upgrade in degrade. Engorged entertainment. Timing is everything. "Halloween Night with Alice Cooper" drew another capacity crowd.

The Alice Cooper contingent arrived early in the afternoon for their evening performance. The stage was completely prepared, the sound system installed and tested, and the entire show rehearsed from start to finish. Manager Shep Gordon ran an exceedingly tight ship. Nothing was left to accidental chance. Every note was practiced, every move choreographed to the inch, every beat bolstered and balanced.

Backstage prior to performance, Chief Rogers wasn't at all sure what to make of Alice Cooper. It wasn't only the extreme application of facial cosmetics and the ancient hooded-robe with skeletal sequins which brought pause. It wasn't even the 12 foot snake sleepily coiled around his neck. It was the fact that dozens of young women were loudly and longingly chanting Alice's name outside the door, begging for entry that they might be entered. One of the oldest thoughts known to man flashed into consciousness:

"All that wants this?"

Alice put him instantly at ease.

"Hey, Chief! Wanna fuckin' beer?"

"Can't."

"Save you a cold one for after the show!"

"Thanks!?!"

"Wanna fuckin' beer?" That creature talkin' like a Marine?

Word sped around the rank and file security deployment that the Chief said "Alice" was a "nice kid." There was speculation that what the Chief had really said was that somebody ought to "ice the kid." It was double-checked. There was confirmation. No, it was "nice," not "ice." The "Alice Cooper Show" combined Vaudeville, Rock 'n Roll Assault and Ultra-Shock Theater. Could you tell who he really was? Did it matter?

A dozen plastic pumpkins, which I had donated from home (for which my two oldest daughters have never forgiven me), were kicked out into the crowd. This instigated a moment or two of fish-feeding frenzy, similar to a home-run ball at every baseball park in the land, the significance of such souvenirs being similar. Premium items. A doll was held high into the air and then placed upon a flower-decked altar for careful beheading by hatchet, "blood" squirting several feet into the air with the initial blow. Ewwwwww. Looked real. Really real. At the conclusion of the performance, Alice was spun slowly around. He was primitively perched, wearing loin-cloth and jungle rags, inside a revolving metal cage covered with purple leaves and green vines. He pounded the floor with primordial rhythm as the band played an eerie, haunting, soul-chilling rendition of "Sun Arise," an aboriginal "dream within a dream" chant brought to brief adaptation and popularity by Australian Rolf Harris in the early '60s. Suddenly, as the beat swelled to ponderous proportion, it ceased.

From the public address system came an unworldly hissing and humming, then buzzing and rumbling. Louder and bolder and wilder it came. Closer. Nearer. Approaching with fearless advance. Alice jumped from the cage and threw himself upon the stage. On his back, he began to rise forward and upward. Clenched fists came into view. With grimaced glare and dark intent, he was tightly clutching both a struggling, squawking, live chicken and the blood-soaked hatchet. A piercing scream filled the air with tormented terror and taut intent. The thundering, pumping, audio oscillations were becoming almost unbearable. Sitting upright, his face distorted by madness and malice, Alice lifted his hatchet to strike. It appeared to fall in full, evil arc. A blinding explosion of fire and light was completely unexpected. Hidden behind scenery, members of the Cooper crew instantly emptied four large pillow cases onto the blades of a giant blaster fan, spewing twenty pounds of feathers toward the crowd in an airborne avian avalanche. The howling of a hundred tornadoes filled the room, the wind from the fan adding realism and effect. The stage went dark. The silence absolute. The crowd went ballistic.

"Alice! Alice! Alice! Alice! Alice! Alice! Alice! Alice! Alice! Alice! Alice!"

The spell had to remain unbroken. No return to the stage.

Back in the dressing rooms, Penny the Chicken was gently retired to her cage. Kachina the Boa Constrictor was separately confined. Penny had been with the group for several weeks and certainly was faring better with Alice than she would have with the Colonel.

As happy Halloween rockers poured out of the building and with his evening's responsibilities concluded, Chief Ralph Rogers joined Alice for that cold beer. They talked about the Lions and The Tigers. Alice told Ralph he hoped they'd see each other at the next gig. Ralph allowed that was quite possible. He later confided in me that he'd never seen so many women go "apeshit" over a performer. You could never tell how much charisma might rub-off suckin' down a few suds.

With Sherwood Forest in full bloom, things at WTAC were becoming progressively more strained between Bob Dell and entrepreneur/disc-jockeys Cavanaugh and Parker. Mt. Holly was closed during the skiing season, even as Sherwood Forest was pulling fabulous attendance on a weekly basis. John and I were also cornering the "high-school dance" market and adding live groups to our appearances. We were starting to book a large number of bands at Sherwood Forest and throughout the entire area. With volume came increased clout. Special Thanksgiving and Christmas Season concerts sold-out within minutes after opening the doors.

Protests against United States policies in Vietnam were reaching new heights. The Nixon administration, far from ending the conflict, seemed to be extending it even further. Outlaw opportunists made their move.

3337-CAVA

CHAPTER SEVENTEEN

UP-CLOSE COMMIES

On college campuses across the nation, the toughest of the self-proclaimed "revolutionary groups" was known as "The Weathermen." They had branched off from the Students for a Democratic Society, and were preaching outright street violence. They had no tolerance for anything or anyone not supportive of total Communist victory in Southeast Asia and proportionate American defeat. Their heroes were Marx and Lenin. Che and Fidel. Mao and Ho.

Larry White was black. He owned and operated the "Giant Ballroom" on North Saginaw Street in the heart of Flint's "ethnic" district. He had become a friend of mine. The "Weathermen" had chosen Flint as rallying site for their "National War Council." They called Larry and asked about renting out the "Giant" for a 4-day run, concluding with the arrival of 1970 on New Year's Eve. They said that Larry was a member of the oppressed minority. He was a "brother" in the conflict for the minds and souls of man. He was a secret soldier in the ranks.

Larry contacted me, and asked what I thought. I suggested that he rent the "Giant" out for $20,000. He said that he couldn't believe "white boys were that dumb." I suggested that this group probably was and were also more well-funded than he might think. He called back in twenty minutes, laughing hysterically. Not only had the "Weathermen" agreed to the price after a few minutes of bitching, they had also promised a check for the full amount in advance. There was quite a national hullabaloo about the "Weathermen." Their name was lifted from Bob Dylan's line in "Subterranean Homesick Blues" about how one doesn't require a weatherman to know wind direction. Bob had been right. You don't. Evidently such irony was completely lost upon the S.D.S. dissidents who became the "Weathermen." The Weathermen seemed just like the White Panthers, except they didn't have a great rock group and really claimed to mean business. They were mean business. They got lots of press, mainly by saying they hated the press. They felt representatives of American media were "running dogs of the ruling capitalist elite." They pissed on radio, television and newspaper reporters, left and right. The more that they urinated, the more they were circulated. It was automatic that the "Press" be excluded from the National War Council Meetings at the Giant Ballroom in Flint. What more could ensure maximum coverage?

The "Weathermen" arrived in Flint by foot, rail, van, bus, plane and car. Approximately 1000 of "them" gathered at the Giant Ballroom on Sunday, December 28, ready for a four-day blow-out. It was so incredibly "hip" in such an ice-cool, "revolutionary" sort of way. The walls inside the Giant were papered with giant photos of Communist heroes from yesteryear through the present. Almost everyone attending wore torn jeans and jackets with dirty sneakers and raggedy hats. This was the class-equalizing uniform d'jour. There were scroungy blankets, boiling pots of communal soup, and hundreds of pieces of hand-out literature for all. Everyone would be staying right there at the Giant for the whole duration. You could sleep where you weep about all the bad things done by your country. One might eat where you'd greet your new leaders of tomorrow. An American flag had been torn in half and hung as a split canopy across much of the ceiling. You might even screw under Red, White and Blue should camaraderie romantically escalate to critical mass.

A movie screen covered most of one wall, where inspirational films of strife and struggle would be shown. A monstrous sound system had been set in place for the dozens and dozens of speeches, which would fill the hall with shouts and threats and raging invectives promising true democracy. The Giant was surrounded by police cordons and news crews from all major networks and regional stations including Detroit. Up-Close Commies. This was RED hot.

Admission was limited to only those with pre-issued "Weathermen Identification Badges" and was solemnly checked by scowling, menacing security forces guarding the lone entrance, as though it led through the gates of Workers' Paradise Itself. No reporters, eh? No newspaper, TV or radio folks, umm?

Larry White had us covered like sticky lives on cotton candy.

There were very few black participants in the "War Council." A majority of the handful of minority members present were associates of Larry White. They were working various assignments for Larry; primarily keeping an eye on anything which might be begged, borrowed or stolen from the premises by the cadre of white boys in charge. Naturally, these brothers weren't particularly interested in remaining within the walls of the Giant for the entire confabulation. Hanging around for more than three or four hours at a stretch was quite enough. True liberation was taking leave as soon as completed responsibilities allowed. Larry had been given a number of identification badges for his support people. Ta-da.

It was New Year's Eve; the culmination of the Flint Weatherman War Council Meetings. It was a night where everything would come together in one final blow-out celebration with all major leaders offering summary accounting of the four-day conference. Other top name revolutionaries who had been unable to attend the entire affair were flying into town to lend their presence and support. This was the big pay-off.

John Parker and I wore our rattiest rags and hadn't shaved for several days. Under burly, over-sized winter coats, we both packed a cassette recorder. Each of us had a microphone, which was concealed in our sleeves, and instantly available with the flick of a wrist. We shuffled and ambled past the outer security perimeter and approached four "Weather Police" blocking passage to the ballroom. We presented our Larry White I.D. badges. The guards were confused.

"You dudes are white!"

"We work for Larry and, if you weren't informed, that's his last name!"

Misplaced humor is never funny. They demanded we allow ourselves to be searched.

"No problem, but don't fuck with our recorders!"

"What recorders?"

"We've had the recorders under our coats perfectly calibrated. We're working for Larry White. He owns the building. You're on his sidewalk. Even though a lease has been extended, Mr. White maintains certain clear proprietary rights. We're here to obtain interviews for "The Free Black Institute" with which Mr. White is proudly associated. I'm sure it's all been cleared. Go check!"

One of the Weather-Cops headed into the hall. We hadn't expected a goddamned search. Larry would pick right up on the extemporaneously devised ploy, and probably insert a twist or two himself. Twenty G's were in the bank. Several new Weathermen returned with the original security sentry to review our credentials and allegations. It was getting shakier. One of the new interrogators was Mark Rudd.

"Mr. Rudd. Mr.White has enjoyed affiliation with the Free Black Institute since its inception. Our mission is similar to yours, but our identification as journalists for the movement is normally restricted to the black community. You will note that we are not black. This permits infiltration into many otherwise prohibited circles and prohibits the white establishment from singling us out as agents for change. Mr. White has approved and authorized our presence here tonight. We demand entry!"

Larry White was summoned. I repeated my narrative. Larry launched into the lingo:

"They get-in or you get-out! My people want to know what you honkies are up to! Everybody's on my ass! Twenty grand ain't shit to me, but if I kick your white, mother-fuckin', jive-ass butts outta here right now, Jack, you ain't stoppin' by Refund City on the way!"

Whoops. All the revolutionaries needed were accusations of blatant racism. Penetration was allowed. Parker and I frolicked about for several hours, guided by an official "Weatherman Information Officer." We interviewed a dozen or so heavies. It became quickly clear that the true would-be revolutionaries comprised less than 10 percent of total attendance. The rest of the mob, evenly divided between male and female, were there for the experience. There were numerous professorial types taking notes and absorbing the energies, obviously planning impressive future scholarly dissertations. They were certain of publication. It seemed like we were not attending a serious political gathering. It appeared to be more of a "Dress Like a Revolutionary New Year's Eve Bash." Held in a gym. No one had seriously bathed since arriving in Flint. It was part of the mystique. So was scurrilous, sinister swaggering. We mentioned to one of our interview subjects that we maintained our cover as Free Black Institute reporters by working as disc-jockeys at a local radio station.

"Which fucking station is that?"

"WTAC"

"That'll be the first radio station we burn down!"

"Mmmmm."

We ran through a half-dozen or so cassettes, filling both sides with interviews, speeches and general crowd conversation. Even when we weren't officially taping, the recorders hummed along. We thanked our hosts for their congenial hospitality and sped back to the station. Within an hour, we had edited highlights from our cassettes and included them in reports which we fed by phone to the NBC, CBS, ABC and Mutual Radio Networks. It was absolutely exclusive coverage. News is always fun when you're first. And profitable. John and I later split several hundred dollars received in rights fees. We called it as we saw it.

John, Larry and I were against American war strategy and felt that society certainly had a number of problems which required remedy. At the same time, all three of us had friends who had joined the fighting in Southeast Asia. Many would not return. The "Weathermen" were an ugly joke, yet core constituents regarded themselves with deadly intensity. If things ever went their way, shotguns indeed would sing the song. The Weathermen were not only dangerously subversive pretenders, but an embarrassment to the Rock 'n Roll counterculture and representative of the exact antithesis of freedom. They'd gone way over the edge. They represented no one other than themselves, and had signed up with Chairman Mao. Bought and paid for. War's whores.

It was all in how you looked at it and all in how you studied it. The 'Sixties were over. It was the start of a brand new decade. Welcome 1970. Happy New Year.

CHAPTER EIGHTEEN

DEAD AND ALIVE

New Year's Night saw a return to Sherwood Forest by Alice Cooper, who added a special "Baby New Year" segment to the act in honor of the occasion. Chief Ralph Rogers told Alice later over a few beers that "you could almost see balls" under the "Baby New Year" costume. He asked Alice to possibly be a little more careful the next time he donned a diaper. Although not specifically included under the "No Saying Fuck" guideline, there was a gentleman's understanding that the rock stars refrain from any public display of genitalia.

The issue had been broached in a discussion over Ted Nugent's "Polar Bear Suit." Ted made a number of clothing changes during each performance, and his last outfit had been what I called the "Polar Bear Suit." The Polar Bear Suit was more or less a wide breechcloth made of white animal fur which more than adequately covered the Nugent nuggets, not counting approximately one second. This tiny exception helped explained why the first five or six rows of fans crowding the stage when Ted played were primarily female. Ted was unusually strong, and extraordinarily athletic. He could jump a Volkswagen from a standing position. With a two-step start, he could also leap four or five feet into the air while playing guitar and land directly on top of his amplifier speakers. After a few moments, he would jump back down to the stage. It was during such descents that a momentary updraft would lift both flaps on his Polar Bear Suit. For the barest instant, Nugent offered dramatic testimony that he was not being sponsored by Fruit-Of-The-Loom. Ted was extremely casual about the entire thing, and one had to be exactly in front to appreciate the full effect. The police were never precisely in the right spot, but from where they were, it looked like something might be visible at a proper angle. Several of them had discussed it with Ralph, and he had mentioned it to me. It had become a non-issue due to lack of evidence, but it was something else to keep in mind. No flashin' cocks, balls, asses, cunts or tits. Well, maybe tits. But no nips.

January '70 also brought Mitch Ryder and his new group "Detroit" to Sherwood Forest. They played all the old stuff like "Devil with the Blue Dress On," and some new material including "Rock 'n Roll," a hit single bringing Mitch back to fame and fortune. Mitch had recorded a special version of the song for us and where he sang the part about a "home town station," he inserted WTAC's call-letters. He did this for several dozen other facilities, as well, and it didn't hurt national airplay a bit. All promotion is good promotion.

John and I were due back at the Giant Ballroom again on January 17 for a co-promotion with Larry White. Black promoters paid premium prices for all artists, white or black. White promoters had an edge, especially those booking a high volume of acts. Parker and I contracted "The Parliaments and Funkadelic" featuring the inimitable George Clinton. We extended to Larry the same split percentages we used in working with Don Sherwood.

Saturday nights started late and extended far into Sunday morning for many members of Flint's black community. The Giant Ballroom had gained regional prominence as being the most important black after hours club north of Detroit. The Parliament and Funkadelic were booked as an "After Hours WTAC Cabaret Showcase Performance" with a $10 admission price. "Cabaret" in Flint also meant you could bring your own adult beverages. Free mixers and ice cubes would be provided at table settings for up to six. Larry felt comfortable that we could safely expect at least 500-600 in attendance and, with any luck, could comfortably seat 1000. Fate intervened.

A week before our scheduled promotion, another Cabaret being held at the Giant drew 500 offering only local groups as a draw. At 2:30 A.M., a young lady and her date were accosted by an irate gentleman, who spoke harshly to both. He was allegedly the young lady's husband, justifiably upset over the circumstances in which he found himself. He was quite belligerent and irrefutably drunk. When asked to take his leave, he refused and was forcibly ejected, literally kicking and screaming. His car was parked outside. Inside the glove compartment was a fully loaded .38 caliber pistol. Very, very drunk and very, very mad can lead to very, very mean and very, very bad. It was fast. Six shots were fired in blind fury at the Giant Ballroom entrance. No specific targets were selected. It was an undifferentiated gesture of unbridled hostility.

One shot sailed 50-feet through the entrance door and across the ballroom floor, grazing the right thigh of a woman sipping her cocktail. She was later treated for superficial wounds and released. Four other shots sailed above and between party-goers with no real harm done. A sixth shot blasted through a box office window, and took off much of the attendant's head. Police arrived almost instantly and arrested the assailant. The crowd was thoroughly freaked. Who wouldn't be? And I expected them back the following week? I called Larry White and asked his opinion. Larry agreed we were looking at the genuine possibility of an astronomical self-inflicted fucking. Larry was in a far more serious situation. John and I were focused on just one promotion. Our friend Larry owned the scene of the crime.

Parliament and Funkadelic had cut us a fair deal by offering a valuable Saturday night in the midst of a very busy schedule. Larry White could now use the extra bounce a big name act would bring to the club in a very important, although unintended way. Who's afraid of a few stray bullets? What the hell.

Rock 'n Roll! A day before the show, John was rushed to the hospital after doubling over with stomach pains. Ulcers. Nothing too serious. He'd be released Monday. He felt bad about having to miss the event. He needn't have.

The morning of the 17th, it started snowing early. It continued snowing all day. It was snowing at Midnight when I pulled into the nearly empty parking lot at the Giant Ballroom. It was still coming down at 1 o'clock when the Parliament and Funkadelic equipment truck arrived for set-up. They'd left Detroit four-and-a-half hours earlier. Flint was only 50 miles to the north. It was snowing harder 10 minutes later, when a Cadillac Limousine careened down the driveway and slid to a stop. Out jumped George Clinton and his group. They were troopers.

"Don't blame this snow shit on us Africans, Peter C.!"

15 inches had fallen in less than 18 hours. Most roads were only marginally passable. The temperature was -5 degrees with a heavy northerly breeze dropping the wind-chill index to -30 degrees. A total of 118 tickets were sold that night at the Giant Ballroom.

I sat alone in the box office, shivering as an icy wind whistled through a three-inch bullet hole just above my head. Larry was busy policing the crowd. According to Mr. White, although sparse, the turn-out included "the baddest niggers in town." Who-the-fuck-else would come out on a night like this? Everyone seemed to be armed. I was the only white boy present, but had grown up with blacks on the wrong side of the tracks in Syracuse. I was much more unnerved by the dark stains still covering much of the box office walls and floor, than I was by dark faces in the night. Parliament and Funkadelic played a full two-hour set. I sat down with Larry as we killed the better part of a fifth of scotch. The show was superb. We'd lost about a grand each. All the baddest niggers left at 5 A.M., having been highly entertained.

1970 was still young, and there were other promotional avenues to be explored. In early February, I convinced the General Sales Manager of Channel Five and the Regional Advertising Director for Pepsi-Cola to fund a television pilot. The idea was a half-hour weekly program to be called "Five Alive," which John Parker and I would host. We had a set built. We rented a bus to transport 50 Grand Blanc High seniors to the Channel Five WNEM-TV studios in Saginaw for the taping. The main ingredient of Five Alive would be appearances by all of our prominent Michigan bands. For the pilot program, we used Bob Seger, Dick Wagner and the Frost, The Rationals, Ted Nugent and Frijid Pink.

We had a "sports segment" featuring Dan West. Dan was a long-haired freak who started coming to WTAC when I had first kicked-off the Underground show. He liked to sit on the floor in the studio with his head inches away from the rumbling monitor speakers. His older brother, Dave, was in the audio manufacturing business and had designed all of Grand Funk Railroad's equipment. They used nothing but West amplifiers, speaker cabinets and sound systems. So did a lot of other Michigan bands, including Bob Seger and Dick Wagner. Dan was to be our Five Alive Sports Director. When he was 14, he had vigorously campaigned for Barry Goldwater. Subsequently, he became convinced that Bob Dylan had been brought to earth on a flying saucer to change his life.

Dan West had a piece of paper from Selective Service which officially described him as a "manic depressive with paranoid delusions and schizophrenic tendencies." Dan attributed such designation to a dozen hits of acid and a handful of speed ingested before and during his Army physical. He was an excellent drummer. Dave West felt his brother's basic problems could be traced to the absence of a real job in his life or any serious interest in seeking same. A brief passionate liaison on the lawn next to our Sherwood Forest lake after one concert had given Dan both temporary pleasure and a more lasting case of the crabs. He selected a few dozen, placed them in a glass jar, and mailed them to his paramour. "I believe these were left behind.," said the note. You just had to love Dan. He agreed to appear on our TV show wearing nothing more than swimming trunks and a coach's whistle around his neck. He was incredibly skinny. He would read area High School basketball scores and make predictions on future competition based on astrological charts and tarot cards.

The taping was completed February 5. We were ecstatic. Everything clicked just right. It was awesome. It was a state-of-the-art "Bandstand," but completely localized, and utterly contemporary. We waited for a decision by Pepsi-Cola. Detroit loved it. It went to New York. We were looking for a 13 week commitment and possible syndication into Lansing, Grand Rapids and Detroit itself. We were ready.

Word came back. New York hated it! What? They hated it! Why? Because disc-jockeys and all the musicians weren't wearing proper attire. **"WEREN'T WEARING PROPER ATTIRE!"** I saw notes from the agency boardroom meeting in big, bold marker print. **"NOT ONE PERFORMER WORE A TIE!"** One last phrase summarized the notations: **"PROTECT PEPSI IMAGE!"**

Channel Five attempted to sell the concept to Coca-Cola, but we had liberally laced the pilot with Pepsi references, which didn't help. Coke also thought the program was way too "hippy" in nature. After a month of effort, Channel Five backed off. We were so busily engaged in our concerts and dances and regular radio work, we just didn't have the time to pursue the project and enlighten ancient 40 year-old mindsets along the way. I still have portions of the program preserved on film. It was ahead of the mass culture curve, but only by seconds and centimeters. I learned an important lesson. Other than in retrospect, a cutting edge is invisible except to those involved. I'd always thought that most things were obvious to all.

Johnny Parker and I had successfully cornered a large share of the Michigan Rock 'n Roll scene and had become, by far, the most highly visible and continually active promoters in the Flint and Tri-City area. There was one target that remained.

3337-CAVA

CHAPTER NINETEEN

SPIRO WHO?

The second week of February, after completing work on our hippy TV show, John and I met with the owners of Mt. Holly. Bob Dell had mistakingly assumed that Mt. Holly was a permanent lock.

Our basic proposition was that Sherwood Forest had become established as the hottest rock entertainment venue in the area during the Winter months as the slopes of Mt. Holly were covered with skiers. We had big plans for the Spring and Summer. We would be scheduling sporadic one-time concerts and four major all-day outdoor events to be called "Wild Wednesdays" from June through September. Rather than compete with Mt. Holly, we preferred to become associated. We could therein coordinate scheduling, booking, advertising and overall strategy. We would contribute our time and effort on Mt. Holly's behalf and everyone would benefit from the combined leverage of joining forces. Otherwise, necessity would require that we counter every Mt. Holly presentation with one of our own, splitting attendance between us. We would also request a two month exclusivity option be included with any future bands contracted to play Sherwood Forest. This would sharply curtail entertainment availability elsewhere in Southeast Michigan. We would offer everything that Bob Dell had in the past, and put the agreement in writing. We would also seal the bargain with $10,000 upon signing as a guarantee against future net profits. The Mt. Holly owners thanked us for our proposal and said they needed time for review and proper consideration. They also felt, in all fairness, that they should speak with Bob before making such a significant change. This was not unexpected and fully appreciated.

Two weeks before we made our call on Mt. Holly, the station had received a copy of a letter written to Vice-President Spiro T. Agnew by a gentleman named Frank Patrick. Although in his late fifties and not part of the "g-g-g-generation" sung of by The WHO, Mr. Patrick was an astute businessman and had entered the rock concert promotion business himself. He ran "Daniel's Den" in Saginaw, and bought advertising time on WTAC. The rambling, bitter diatribe sent to Spiro complained of favoritism, conflict of interest, and unfair competition. Patrick's main issue was that the disc-jockeys of WTAC were getting free publicity on the airwaves for all of their endeavors, while he had to pay for his. He specifically cited Bob Dell's Grand Funk Railroad campaign the preceding summer, an appearance by Neil Diamond that Bob had presented in early January at Flint's Whiting Auditorium, and all Sherwood Forest activities of Peter Cavanaugh and Johnny Parker. In unusual concurrence, John and I agreed with Bob that Patrick was a "whiny little bastard." General Manager Charlie Speights thought the letter to Agnew was particularly unsophisticated, and tossed it in the trash.

WTAC had always encouraged its air personalities to become involved in outside activities. The dances and concerts contributed greatly to WTAC promotional visibility at no cost to the station. Extra outside income to staff members so involved made requests for raises from that group almost nonexistent. The radio stars were happy being paid like engineers, providing they could double or triple their personal cash flow with lucrative activity on the side. Everybody won. The station operated in complete conformity with established FCC Rules and Regulations in this regard. All of the activities were totally legit with the Commission. Fuck Frank Patrick. Spiro WHO? There was unanimity in the ranks on this one.

It soon became clear that Spiro had a bit of time between counting paper bags of secret cash delivered to the Office of the Vice President. He read some mail. Official correspondence from the Federal Communications Commission hit Charlie's desk three days later. They had sent a "Letter of Inquiry." It would not be an overstatement to suggest it was a "Summons from the Inquisition." The Commission covered the highlights from Patrick's complaint, and then requested that specific information and/or materials be submitted to them within thirty days. Their shopping list included:

(1) Copies of all WTAC Programming Logs for the preceding twelve months.
(2) A complete list of all activities mentioning WTAC air personalities that were broadcast over WTAC in the prior year.
(3) A further list indicating the nature of each activity mentioned, the number of times broadcast, the amount charged to the disc-jockey in every instance, details of any financial arrangement between the disc-jockey and other entities, total compensation to the disc-jockey and method of payment utilized.
(4) A complete list of all activities not involving WTAC employees which related to live-music promotion for the prior 12 months, complete with invoices indicating rates charged and schedules run.
(5) Recordings of all "live-music" announcements carried over WTAC for the last full year, whether or not employee-related. In the absence of such recordings, written copy of all scripts used could be substituted.

The shit had not only hit the fan; it was whaleshit into turbo-props. We hadn't been found guilty of anything, yet we had to spend literally hundreds of hours putting together dozens of exhibits and thousands of bits of information. In terms of incentive, the more we assembled, the more we might be constructing an ultimate hammer of just retribution with which the Commission could pound our collective nuts. If we left anything out, it would even be worse. Would they share this stuff with the IRS? Did I log all those plugs for Alice Cooper at Sherwood when I might have been secretively taped? How long does it take to establish residency in Quito, Ecuador?

The President of Fuqua Communications at the time was a big, balding, heavy-set man from the world of television named Jackson Beaudry. Even on a good day, he thought of radio as a simple pimple on the illustrious ass of broadcasting. He would painfully visit Flint once a year from Communications Division Headquarters in Augusta, Georgia. Fuqua Communications owned big television properties in Columbus, Georgia; Chattanooga, Tennessee and Evansville, Indiana. Television revenue accounted for more than 90 percent of Communications' profit line. The other 10 percent came from WTAC radio in Flint, and WROZ radio in Evansville, Indiana. At least WROZ was a Country station, and didn't play music that made you want to throw your receiver into the nearest manure pile. WTAC's programming exactly fulfilled that dubious distinction for the head of our division. The disc-jockeys had long-hair, and even the General Manager was starting to look a little shaggy below the ears. He was also under suspicion of playing trumpet. Then, too, the whole operation was up North. In the best of times, even though operating at a 50 percent profit margin, WTAC was bothersome and annoying. Now this.

Any FCC investigation theoretically put the license of a station in jeopardy. An FCC license was really the only significant asset of a radio property. Highest level executive presence was mandatory in such a tense situation. It was the middle of winter. Mr. Beaudry hated "Yankee Winters" with the snow and ice and sleet and hail and terrifying roads. He arrived at the station in the foulest of moods.

"Do you all realize this horseshit is going to cost twenty grand just in lawyers?"

Actually, he was wrong. It was more like $35,000.

For two solid days, there was constant repetition of a continuous theme.

"Goddamn Disc-jockeys." "Goddamn Disc-jockey dances." "Goddamn F.C.C."

I suspect Jackson would have just as soon fired everyone and blown-up the station for insurance value, but there were complications. Fuqua attorneys had reviewed our vast assemblage of data, and were perplexed. According to FCC law, everything seemed in order. The exhaustive retrieval of factual data had uncovered no "smoking guns" or improper behavior. It was true that WTAC disc-jockeys might obtain certain benefits from their employment unavailable to others, but they were employees and entitled to receive non-cash compensation at the discretion of the company. Everything had been logged. This was a critical requirement and one with which WTAC had completely complied over the course of the entire year reviewed. The only viable position recommended by Fuqua attorneys was that the corporation and WTAC had done nothing wrong. If the "D-J Datebook" or the employee discounts were abolished, this could be interpreted as an admission of guilt.

Jackson pissed and snorted, feeling thwarted, but hopped on a plane at Detroit Metro and headed back to his warm, sunny South. It would take the Commission a full year to decide that, while WTAC had abided by all governing Federal rules and regulations, there was a vague, anti-competitive quality to the practices questioned which should be addressed. A $2000 fine was levied along with a vague admonition to remember the spirit of the 1934 Radio Communications Act in matters of future policy. It was not even a slap, but a tap on the wrist. None of our lawyers knew what the hell the decision meant in terms of direction and had been unofficially told that the Commission was loath to pursue the matter any further. The fine was paid, and nothing changed.

Yet earlier, as Mr. Beaudry's plane crossed the Mason-Dixon Line and he heaved a massive and heart-felt sigh of relief, another potentially more injurious and far-reaching problem had arisen. WTAC had suddenly started to encounter strong radio competition, and not from other Flint stations.

CHAPTER TWENTY

RUTHLESS EFFICIENCY

CKLW in Detroit had moved to a tighter, highly controlled and very well programmed Top Forty approach consulted by a Californian named Bill Drake. He was shortly to be acclaimed the best in the business. The Drake Format essentially cleaned-up many elements which had wandered into Top Forty. Drake had streamlined everything with razor-sharp precision. Playlists were reduced from 50 or 60 cuts to 30, with the Top Ten played every hour and a half. Radio identification jingles were cut from twenty or thirty seconds to two or three. With a few rare exceptions, disc-jockey talk was limited to reading standard slogans in an exact, pre-determined manner. Clutter was completely eliminated. Commercial load (the number of announcements per hour) was slashed in half, and advertising rates were doubled in compensation. Newscasts were presented with extreme editing and maximum hyperbole. It was back to the basics, with ruthless efficiency, and brilliant execution.

With 50,000 watts,"The Big Eight/CKLW" had an enormous signal. It was #1 in Detroit, Lansing, Toledo, Cleveland and, with the release of the Fall '70 PULSE survey, in Flint. That it was happening in other markets was of no consolation to Charlie Speights. Ultimately, a radio station sells its listening audience to the advertising community. When that audience is reduced by half, which is what had happened at WTAC, decrease in revenue can become proportionate.

Anticipating a hit from CKLW, Bob Dell had made some adjustments of his own at WTAC, pirating a number of concepts from the Drake school of programming. They had come too late to reverse a powerful trend. Suddenly, there was a dreaded bad ratings book with which to deal. Then, Mt. Holly owners met with Bob and asked him to counter our offer. He was infuriated. He detonated. He told the owners of his primary source of personal income they could go fuck themselves. He told Charlie Speights that unless Johnny Parker and I were instantly fired, union or no, he could go fuck himself. Bob had been entertaining a major offer from Westinghouse for their 50,000 watt Fort Wayne dreadnought, WOWO. Within 24 hours, John Parker and I signed a contract with Mt. Holly for the 1970 season; Bob Dell resigned from the station; I was appointed Program Director; and Parker demanded a change in shift to prime-time afternoons, and a pay raise.

Bob eventually moved to New Orleans, where he and wife Joannie would make millions running an annual "Fishing and Outdoors Show" for many years in the Superdome. He'd gotten the idea back in Syracuse.

While John and I were equal partners in the dances and concerts, I regarded my new position as Program Director as a serious threshold and a personal challenge. Reluctantly, and with great reservation, he agreed to honor certain new definitions. There was no other way. It was a time of critical commitment.

The revenue from concert promotions had been more-than-a-bit handy with a wife, two daughters and a third child expected in September. I loved the music and challenge of the game, but had come to realize that limitations in the pursuit were increasing every day. Rock 'n Roll was becoming big business. Prices for major groups were starting to escalate. Competition was increasing. Interest in promoting Rock 'n Roll had evolved as an ancillary aspect of my radio career, and was only secondarily driven by monetary considerations. The degree of expansion I envisioned necessary to maintain credibility and capability as a truly major promoter would require entering Detroit and other large markets with significant financial funding beyond my personal wherewithal. It would require investors and partners. And I would need to leave radio.

I had given the matter much thought and prolonged consideration. There could never be a new choice. This had been determined many years before when I first listened to "Let's Pretend" as a 2-year-old on Lancaster Avenue in Syracuse and had come to know an old floor-model Zenith receiver as my invisible window to the world. Could I bring WTAC back to the top? It was now my personal charge. I spent the next week almost exclusively devoted to completely revamping the station.

I contracted for a new jingle series that was even tighter than packages commissioned by the Drake organization, and included phasing and spacing technology just being introduced to radio. The sung call-letters were surrounded by electronic sounds which would be blended and merged with other programming elements for continuity. The WTAC list of current music was cut to 30 records. Several new categories of music were introduced, including "recurrents" (monster hits which had dropped off the sales charts), "powers" (developing mega-hits) and five types of "oldies" (rated by style, popularity, tempo and artist). News quantity was sharply curtailed, and quality increased by editing, heavy production, and use of "actuality" inserts. Non-music features were totally eliminated. Music was added to all commercial production, without exception. Disc-jockey talk was eliminated unless executed over the fade or intro of a record.

Only creative contesting was allowed. Just a handful of audience members ever enter radio station contests. The goal became "interesting to listen to" more than "winning anything." Positioning was a priority. Every aspect of the programming product offered excitement and entertainment. Imagery was imperative. Everything counted. My work schedule had shifted rather dramatically. I replaced Bob on the weekday morning show, and would spend the rest of each day involved in the programming area. WTAC began to take shape in a unified fashion, all elements moving in the same direction. With one or two school appearances, along with Sherwood Forest and Mt. Holly efforts, I was typically working well over 100 hours a week and enjoying every instant. It never seemed like work at all.

CHAPTER TWENTY-ONE

BE YOUR DOG

On April 11, Apollo Thirteen lifted-off from Cape Kennedy, providing an exciting saga which Ron Howard cinematically reproduced to great advantage two decades later. On April 12, "The Stooges" came to Sherwood Forest.

James Osterberg was rumored to have been valedictorian of his Senior Class in Ann Arbor. He eventually moved in with John Sinclair and the White Panthers at their commune on Hill Street, and helped form a band called "The Stooges." Sinclair used The Stooges as an opening act for his MC5. Mr. Osterberg became Iggy Stooge. In 1995, he would help open the Cleveland Rock 'n Roll Hall of Fame performing as Iggy Pop. Other Stooges of the time were Ron Asheton on guitar, his brother Scott Asheton on drums, and Dave Alexander on bass. Although none of The Stooges could really play music that well at the beginning, that was no concern. They were attempting something far beyond music. The Stooges were intended to be a Rock 'n Roll/Guerrilla/Comedy/Theater of the Absurd sort of phenomenon, and three chords were about as musical as things originally got.

Iggy was extraordinary. Manic comedy became dangerous weirdness transforming into frightening chaos, changing to raw depravity, shifting to laughable lewdness, transcending into utter madness and concluding with the most disturbing kind of electrified shock-rock imaginable. Iggy was a sight to behold, although not one to share with any female relative, living or dead. The Stooges were a natural complement to the MC5. They were a graphic, hallucinogenic, mind-wrenching, outrageously-overblown depiction of a decadent problem for which the MC5 would provide a solution. And absolution. It was all quite artistic if you took the time to think about it, which very few did.

Iggy had several tricks that had become hallmarks of his remarkably creative performance. Iggy would smash a glass bottle over his head, then carve his chest with the shards until interesting and uniquely decorative patterns emerged. Iggy often stood at the very edge of an eight-foot high stage, then toppled-over, diving head-first to the floor below. Iggy might conceal several tablespoons of peanut butter in his shorts and, at the height of performance, plunge his hand down the back of his pants and retrieve a covered finger which he would slowly lick with delight. Of course, no one in the audience knew precisely what the substance was and automatically assumed the worst or best. That was the whole idea.

The Stooges had enjoyed marginal success with their first single release, "Now I Wanna Be Your Dog." They found even greater popularity with "1969," which had been issued a short time later. I had seen the group perform at Delta College with the MC-5 and, as I introduced them, Iggy had goosed me. It was nothing sexual, just pretextual. Iggy was quite well-behaved off-stage, and we had entered into an engaging conversation. He was equal parts of bafflingly brilliant, and truly fucked-up. He had been busted a few nights before in Romeo, Michigan, for exposing himself, which he honestly didn't remember doing. "Bummer," summarized Iggy.

With our anti-obscenity requirements at Sherwood Forest and with Ralph Rogers' continuing cooperation as we honored community sensitivities, The Stooges were the last band I would ever consider booking. I might as well unveil, "Butt-Fuck-Bob and His Masturbating Monkeys."

But, it's a world of change in which we live. Electra Records, having signed The Stooges as well as MC5, was into a little heavy image adjusting. You just couldn't get on American Bandstand pretending to stick your finger up your ass or using your head as a floor-ram. Dick Clark was not into suggesting psychotic self-mutilation was a pleasant pastime either. The word was out that The Stooges had radically cleaned-up their act. Electra Records was begging me for a Sherwood Forest date. Our reputation had spread. An appearance there could do the group a world of good in converting disbelievers who were hesitant accepting news of Iggy's conversion as other than wishful thinking. John Sinclair called me and confirmed the transformation. The Stooges' Personal Manager was on the phone every day. Diversified Management Agency in Detroit, with whom I worked continually, positively guaranteed The Stooges were now sparkling, shining, shimmeringly clean.

Well, O.K?

I drafted a contract rider which, in addition to the No-Saying-Fuck clause, went on to forbid anything remotely resembling anything I had ever seen The Stooges do which might be interpreted as offensive and plenty of things I never had seen them do, but that they might think of. I discussed the booking with Chief Rogers, and he threw in a number of things I hadn't considered. The Stooges were not to leave the stage during performance. No crude language, actions, conduct, behavior or facsimile of same would be permitted. Any breach of conditions would result in double forfeiture of payment. And arrest. I wrote the rider in a way I thought would not be signed unless the group was absolutely sincere in their pledges of altered attitude. Unlike most union contracts, each member of the band had to agree to the rider provisions and stipulations by signature. The contract was returned to me, signed by all. There were no changes or alterations.

The Sherwood Forest parking lot was already full early on the day of the show. 1500 were admitted by 6:30. It was wall-to-wall once again. Their equipment had gotten there, and had been set-up on stage, but The Stooges had yet to arrive. They were still missing at 7:30, when the opening act finished performance. It was 7:45 and we were stalling with records. Where were they? Representatives from Electra, Diversified Management and Creem Magazine wanted to know the same thing.

It was 7:55. The Stooges were supposed to start at 8:00 sharp.

It was 8:05. I asked Parker to find out what the deal was.

It was 8:10. John had returned ashen white and righteously rattled. His voice was barely above a whisper.

"They're downstairs. I think they're shooting."

"WHAT?"

"I think it might be heroin. I don't know. They're probably shooting something. This biker-dude told me to get the fuck out of the dressing room."

The first thing I reflected was that I had left "No Shooting Heroin" out of the contract. Wait. This was crazy. Jesus Christ. There was sudden turmoil behind me. I whirled about and saw The Stooges approaching. They looked pretty bleary-eyed and unfocused, but when hadn't they? Maybe John had been wrong about this "shooting heroin" business. Possibly several members were diabetic and were just taking a little insulin before a long, hot, 90-minute set. Perhaps they were volunteering in a scientific experiment conducted by the Medical College at the University of Michigan, wherein blood samples were being taken before and after each concert to determine the effects of high-decibel music exposure on plasmatic development. Maybe Daisy Duck has a diamond dick. Too late for further speculation.

The group appeared ready for introduction. Well, they hadn't publicly violated any contractual provisions yet. We had a full house clamoring for their appearance. Only Parker had witnessed theoretical peculiarities in the dressing-room. Might as well jump.

It was customary to begin each introduction with a quick billboard of future bookings at Sherwood. Everyone was paying attention. Advantage had to be quickly taken. There was an unwritten 20-second window in which to squeeze all extraneous information before getting on with the actual introduction. Anything past 20 seconds would make the crowd restless and prompt cries of "Let's Go!" or "Kiss My Ass!" from antsy clientele. John Parker was doing the honors this night. At about the ten second mark, he was abruptly and rudely interrupted by Iggy

"Fuck this guy. Kick it in!"

The band immediately exploded into "Down in The Streets" from The Stooges' "Funhouse" album and the audience went crazy. Parker wanted to kill the show right there and then. After all, Iggy had said the magic word and he had cut John off, which was a supreme professional insult. But, the "fuck" had gone unnoticed by the police, who were way at the back of the hall. Pulling the plug was certain to provoke a small riot. I reminded John that we had taken in an excellent gate and had plenty of time to get even later. Meanwhile, I suggested that skeptical patience seemed the wisest course. He went along.

Miraculously, the next 55 minutes went wonderfully well. No fucks. No cutting chests. No peanut-butter from the butt. If the group had been shooting heroin, you sure couldn't tell. The energy was extraordinary. Maybe they'd been shooting cocaine. Maybe they'd just been sticking needles in themselves, administering self-acupuncture to unleash karmic power flow. I thought we might just pull it off. The Stooges always liked to finish things up with their love song. It was time for their last number which, by tradition, was an extended version of "Now I Wanna Be Your Dog." Iggy was pretending that he was going to do one of his head-first falls off the stage. Heh-heh. Shit. The fucker did it!

Iggy was now standing shirtless in the middle of the first few rows of floor-seated enthusiasts. He was holding a microphone in his mouth and sucking upon it heavily. He was barefoot. He started dancing and twirling and spinning around. Several roadies starting feeding foot after foot of microphone cable in his wake. He stopped, suddenly attracted by the heaving chest of a strikingly well-endowed female fan directly before him. He extended one bare foot forward and started vigorously massaging her breasts with his toes. Maintaining the overall theme of his closing selection with instinctive artistic grace, Iggy nevertheless chose to depart from normal lyric content and repeatedly starting screaming an incredible intonation.

"Dogs lick assholes and chew big titties!"

THAT'S IT!!!

The police were already wading through the crowd in Iggy's general direction. The quickest way to kill the music was to unplug the band. Parker moved like a flash. Everything on the stage was rendered silent in under five seconds flat. Except Iggy. He was on the floor and his microphone operated separately off a sound system that was wired behind and under the stage. It was out of immediate reach. Iggy wasn't. He was now a good 30 feet in front of the stage and, in all of his swirling and twirling, had wrapped the microphone cord six or seven times around his neck. The attached cable ran straight through the crowd to a sound-mix amplifier set beneath the edge of the stage. Iggy noticed that the music had disappeared. His band had stopped playing. He was alone on the P.A. system.

"What the fuck's wrong? Where's the music? What's happenin'? Where the fuck is the

ARRRRRRRRRRRGGGGGGGGRRRHHHHHHHHH!"

John Parker had been cut-off by Iggy. He had gone along with letting things continue against his better judgment, and had been the picture of perfect patience. When Cavanaugh ordered the band silenced, he had experienced a feeling of total release, almost orgasmic in quality. Iggy had managed to evade the consequences of his first actions. Not now, *JIM*!!

Parker quickly bent over the front of the stage, firmly grasped the microphone cord twined around the neck of the unsuspecting Mr. Stooge and pulled with the strength of a thousand Tennessee Volunteers. Iggy was almost garroted, then spun into several almost perfect pirouettes. He was then slammed to the floor and dragged through the crowd toward the ferocious John Parker, who was reeling him in, hand-over-hand, fist-over-fist. Chairs were flying. People were shouting. Mayhem reigned. I took a still active stage microphone and ran a play-by-play:

"Ladies and Gentleman! Only here at Sherwood Forest! You'll never see the likes of this again anywhere on the planet. Stand back! Step Aside! It's a life and death struggle before your very eyes. Iggy will die for Rock 'n Rollllllllll!!

It was a completely appropriate end to the performance. As Parker reached down and yanked a very groggy and confused Iggy onto the stage, I concluded:

"Ladies and Gentlemen, "The Stooges!!!"

Wild applause thundered for a full five minutes as several police pulled Parker off Iggy and escorted everyone backstage. The hall lights went on, and cheering continued as the crowd peacefully departed.

Creem Magazine offered an extensive feature story on the concert in their next issue and Dave Marsh described my concluding narrative as "sounding just like Chris Schenkle on ABC Wide World of Sports." It became quite the story in Michigan music circles. The most amazing aspect was that almost all in attendance had been convinced it was carefully and entertainingly staged.

Electra Records had an important investment in both The Stooges and MC5, and they were not amused. Iggy, for the purpose planned, had completely blown the gig. Trust and confidence in the band disappeared. Consequences for The Stooges and John Sinclair were serious. Electra executives had already been pluperfectly pissed when Sinclair had taken out a full-page ad in the Ann Arbor Argus which included only two words above the Electra logo: "Fuck Hudsons!" Hudsons was a major Detroit area department store that had refused to stock the original MC5 album due to Sinclair's extensive use of "fuck" in his published liner-notes. The album package had been re-issued without Sinclair's comments. Hudsons saw the Argus and pulled all of Electra's products from their stores. Now this? Electra stopped all further promotional efforts on behalf of both The Stooges and the MC5. It marked the beginning of the end for both bands.

Iggy was arrested backstage and charged with obscenity. He was quickly released on his own recognizance. The following day, the Genesee County Prosecutors Office told Chief Rogers they had no interest in pursuing the matter, and that such charges would never hold up in Court. Per agreement, the group was not compensated. Many months later, the Musicians Union demanded that payment be rendered. I refused. Picketing and blacklisting were threatened, then delivered. I paid.

John Parker was glad he had gotten a piece of Iggy, and went home a happy man. He would not leave the next "Wild Wednesday" as filled with content.

CHAPTER TWENTY-TWO

A WILDER WEDNESDAY

The regular Sunday night concerts at Sherwood Forest were suspended by the end of April as we moved into a regular weekly Saturday night schedule at Mt. Holly. The first six weeks included performances by Ted Nugent and the Amboy Dukes, SRC, Bob Seger, Brownsville Station, Frijid Pink, The Ides of March and the Electric Prunes. Attendance was decent, but we were starting to regularly recycle a number of major Michigan artists in relatively limited time frames.

"Wild Wednesday" was scheduled for June 24 at Sherwood Forest. Although WTAC would be participating as it had the prior year, with client booths and exhibits, 90 percent of the focus was on our first live rock spectacular. We were pulling out all the stops. We would run 12 groups in 12 hours, from Noon 'til Midnight, with Twin Concert Stages and no recorded music. Admission would be $5. When one group finished, the next would immediately begin. It would be continuous, non-stop, live Rock 'n Roll without pause or intermission. The introductory endeavor would feature Bob Seger, Ted Nugent, the MC5, The Rationals, Brownsville Station, Alice Cooper, Frijid Pink, Teegarden and Vanwinkle and three opening acts, including a group from Pontiac which John Parker had started managing called "Dream Delight."

Don Sherwood mowed acres of adjacent fields for parking. Security was to include all of Ralph's regulars and an extra two dozen off-duty Sheriff's Deputies, many on horseback. Additionally, my own "Roadies Squad" now numbered close to 50. These were divided into five teams with various tasks assigned each unit. The Roadies Squad had added volunteers as it went along and had become more organized. We had Captains and Lieutenants and all wore "Sherwood Forest Rock 'n Roll" T-Shirts. The roadies helped with equipment, assisted on security duty, guarded dressing room areas, and were generally available for anything or everything that might require manpower and/or ingenuous resolution. A number of old Flint biker friends became "Concert Associates." The Concert Associates acted as unofficial and discreet enforcers of prevailing promoter policies. They were exceedingly effective, and absolutely trustworthy. Word of their presence alone discouraged all manner of bad behavior, except in the most rare instance.

The morning of June 24 was warm and sunny, with a favorable weather forecast for the remainder of the day and evening. We had advertised "Wild Wednesday" in Detroit and throughout the rest of Michigan. We met at Sherwood Forest shortly after dawn and prepared to open the gates at 10. As the first group started playing, 3000 had been admitted to the park. The crowd doubled and doubled again during the next four hours. By late afternoon, a crowd of 20,000 was assembled between the Sherwood Forest Lodge/Hall, and our adjacent lake area. Everything had been going along without a hitch. Except that appearance by "Dream Delight."

Although John and I had worked out the playing schedule weeks before and his group had been set to appear third in sequence, "Dream Delight," felt a later hour was desirable and had so informed John. John had agreed, but never told me.

When 12 groups are being coordinated in close fashion, rigid time discipline is a must. All band members and managers had received copies of performance times along with their contracts. There would be no changes. We had balanced the lineup with draw value, performance quality, style sequence and a certain amount of Rock 'n Roll politics in mind. Dream Delight was not available as scheduled. I crossed them off the list and had the second and fourth bands fill the gap. When they appeared later and informed me that Johnny Parker said they could go on "after Seger," I suggested that they just sit back and enjoy the rest of the show. They found Parker and brought him to the stage. John had been drinking. John demanded that the group be scheduled. I took John aside and told him what an asshole he was and that he was getting fucked-up. We had an absolute understanding that neither of us would drink a drop or take a puff of anything stronger than tobacco until any show had been concluded, the people sent home, and the money counted and deposited. As dark fell, John was getting exceedingly drunk and very belligerent with a wide variety of people. Several managers insisted he be removed from the backstage area. He started a fight, and was quickly subdued. He reeled toward me and shouted that he was going out to his car and would return shortly to "set things fuckin' straight, Jim." John kept a handy, dandy .45 under his front-seat. This was decidedly not a matter for the police. My Concert Associates were on hand for just such delicate moments.

John was firmly guided by four Associates to a basement area in the lodge, where he was given a full bottle of Jack Daniels and locked in a broom closet for the duration of the program. The Associates reported that he had pounded on the door, then started singing and laughing for approximately 30 minutes. Loud snoring was then heard. At least one Associate remained on guard duty for the rest of the evening.

At 1:15 A.M., I awakened Parker to release him. He had slept peacefully, but was suddenly experiencing a violent hangover and sweeping waves of nausea. He remembered nothing from the previous day except showing up for the concert. I presented him with a full accounting. He was sincerely penitent and meant it. He promised it would never happen again. I told him that was fine with me and I would count on that. I told him that I believed everybody should get "one," and he'd just gotten his. We concluded our business and headed home. The day had been a complete success.

(left)
Great-Grandfather Peter Cavanaugh and Grandfather John Cavanaugh.
Fulton, New York. (1861)

(below)
Donald J. Cavanaugh (far right) and World Heavy-weight Boxing Champion Jack Dempsey.
Syracuse, New York. (1935)

Dr. Vincent Cavanaugh.
Syracuse, New York. (1927)

Cavanaugh at WNDR Control Board.
Syracuse, New York. (1957)

WTAC Staff Photo.
Flint, Michigan. (1963)

Peter C. Cavanaugh and Bob Dell Meet the Beatles.
Olympia Stadium. Detroit, Michigan. (1964)

Northland Drive-In Marquee.
Flint, Michigan, (1964)

WTAC General Manager
Charlie Speights.
Flint, Michigan. (1966)

Keith Moon's "21st" at the Holiday Inn.
Flint, Michigan. (1967)

Wild Wednesday '70 Admission Ticket. (1970)

Wild Wednesday '70

MICHIGAN MONSTER

$5.00
ADMIT ONE PERSON
TO FESTIVAL AREA

No 126

IMPORTANT: You MUST Retain This Ticket For Admission

Peter C. Cavanaugh and John Parker.
Davison, Michigan. (1970)

Peter C. at Sherwood Forest. Davison, Michigan. (1970)

Wild Wednesday Crowd. Sherwood Forest.
Davison, Michigan. (1970)

Bob Seger. Sherwood Forest.
Davison, Michigan. (1970)

Backstage with Ted Nugent.
1:30 AM. Sherwood Forest.
Davison, Michigan. (1970)

Sherwood Forest Lodge. Davison, Michigan.
Christmas Night. (1970)

WTAC Air Staff.
Flint, Michigan. (1976)

Detroit Free Press

Volume 148, Number 77 ON GUARD FOR 148 YEARS Friday, July 20, 1979

Friday, July 20, 1979	
THEATER	2
CLASSICS	5
MUSIC	6-7
FEATURE PAGE	13

YET ANOTHER INCREDIBLE WTAC FIRST!!

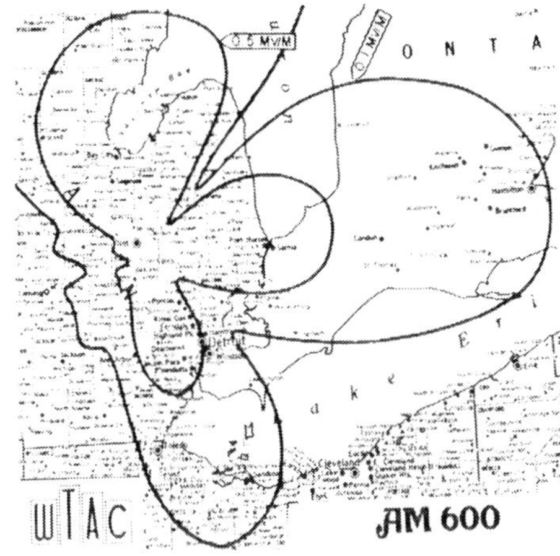

on top of it

Flint radio takes a slice of the Detroit market pie

★ FOR THE FIRST TIME, a Flint radio station has made inroads into the Detroit market, according to the most recent Arbitron ratings book.

The station is WTAC, known up there as "Big 6 Radio." The station got impressive numbers, especially with teens (12-17). In the mornings (6-10) the station had more teen listeners than WNIC or WMJC. At night (7-midnight) it out-drew CKLW and WDRQ with teens.

Woody Allen

If the station can sustain that gain for more ratings periods WTAC could stand to gain by attracting more advertisers into the station and going head-to-head with its Detroit competitors.

The trouble is WTAC did not subscribe to the Detroit Arbitron book and therefore cannot legally use those figures in advertising sales pitches. Instead, it must wait another mouth for the release of the Flint book it subscribes to.

The question is, how long will it take for WTAC to get caught up in talent raids, on-the-air Arbitron announcements and all the rest that ratings mania brings.

WTAC Promotional Piece.
Detroit, Michigan. (1979)

WWCK Air Staff.
Flint, Michigan. (1982)

JOURNAL TEMPO D1
THE FLINT JOURNAL · SUNDAY, APRIL 24, 1983

"He was the one who really made rock 'n' roll in the area. He started it all."

"He was one of the promoters we really enjoyed working with — he was just very good. We always got paid."

"When you needed to be uplifted, you'd go to see Peter... this business isn't full of people who are associated with the music for the music's sake, but for the glamour. And when they find out there's no glamour, they take it out on everybody else."

"Cavanaugh is still a rock 'n' roller. He is still a partier and a rock 'n' roller and Led Zeppelin is his love. Many a night we have sat down after closing up the bars and been blared out by Led Zeppelin."

... comments on Peter C. Cavanaugh

Goodbye, Peter C.

Though climbing the corporate ladder, his heart still beats to rock 'n' roll

By DAVE GUILFORD
Journal staff writer

Perhaps it all started the day Mrs. Cavanaugh's boy, Peter C., burned down a neighbor's garage.

Young Cavanaugh — who left the world of Flint radio last week after nearly 20 years as the godfather of local rock 'n' rollers — was not yet a rock fan.

But, as he recalls, he had achieved a certain prominence as head of a gang of fourth graders in a "tough Irish neighborhood" of Syracuse, N.Y.

On the day of the fire, Cavanaugh and gang had seen a Tarzan movie that featured a flaming-arrow attack. Shortly afterwards, the group was hard at work in Cavanaugh's yard with sticks, strings and lighter fluid.

THE RESULT, in Cavanaugh's words, was "a tremendous flaming-arrow apparatus."

A single shot to the roof of a neighbor's garage proved that the weapon worked. In fact, results were more flamboyant than Cavanaugh expected, with dire results for the garage and a new Dodge parked inside.

When the smoke cleared, Cavanaugh said, he was faced with a choice between "reform school or Catholic school." He chose the latter, entering a parochial school where, he said, he quickly became a model student.

"One thing a street education teaches you is to analyze power very quickly," said the former vice president/general manager of Flint radio stations WWCK-FM and WWMN-AM. "It took me two days to realize that the nuns were in charge and if you did anything wrong, they'd hit you, so I got along very well with them."

But he still hung out with his friends in the neighborhood "and had the experience of living in two worlds," he said.

THAT TRAIT continues today. Cavanaugh is outwardly a businessman, neatly coiffured and dressed in a dark suit.

He can reel off his civic activities — United Way, the Cystic Fibrosis Foundation, Easter Seals, Goodwill Industries, Boy Scouts, and many others. Earlier this year, he was chosen the business person of the year by the Sales and Marketing Executives of Flint.

And last week, Cavanaugh was promoted to chief operating officer and executive vice president of Rentle Broadcasting of Toledo, Ohio. There, he will oversee six stations — including WWCK and its AM sister, WWMN — in Michigan and Ohio.

Yet underneath Cavanaugh's neatly buttoned vest beats the heart of a rocker.

His local radio career started when, freshly graduated from LeMoyne College in Syracuse, he took a disk-jockey job at WTAC-AM. At the forefront of local rock radio during the turbulent 1960s and 1970s, he rose to become president of WTAC before switching to WWCK in 1980.

"HE WAS the one who really made rock 'n' roll in the area," said Michael Stone, promotions and marketing manager in Detroit for the Warner-Elektra-Atlantic Distribution Corp., a major record wholesaler. "He started it off."

Cavanaugh's friends and peers say the thudding chainsaw rock WWCK plays is not a mere commodity to him. He is kin to every 15-year-old who jerks the volume up when a cut by the rock band AC/DC is played, they say.

"If and when he dies of old age, at 118, they will play 'Stairway to Heaven' (a Led Zeppelin song) at his funeral," said "Pete the Cat" Flanders, who was a D.J. with Cavanaugh at WTAC-AM in the early 1970s. "It'll be in his will.

"Cavanaugh is still a rock 'n' roller. He is still a partier and a rock 'n' roller and Led Zeppelin is his love.

"Many a night we have sat down after closing up the bars and been blared out by Led Zeppelin."

JIM MELTZER, vice president/general manager of a competing rock station, WTRX-AM, recalled that last year, Cavanaugh dragged him to a concert by Kiss, the quartet famous for its demonic costumes.

"He's very comfortable in that scene, whereas I'm totally burned out on concerts," Meltzer said. "So I'm bored to death, surrounded by 13-year-olds thinking, 'The amplifier just blew up — that's an interesting effect,' and I look over and Pete's bouncing up and down and saying, 'Hey, that's great.'"

Cavanaugh makes no bones about his musical tastes. "I don't like the slow stuff. I like it real loud and hammering till 2 or 3 in the morning. That's how I relax."

He said his affection for rock goes back to his youth, when he hung around a Top 40 station in Syracuse, listening to early rock artists like Buddy Holly, Little Richard and Chuck Berry.

And, of course, Elvis Presley.

"WHEN I first heard Elvis Presley — and this is going to sound very, very melodramatic — but it changed my life," he said.

Cavanaugh has stayed with rock through its changes.

In 1964, he said, he and a fellow WTAC D.J., Bob Dell, had some buttons made reading "official police pass." Wearing them, they talked their way backstage at the old Olympia Stadium in Detroit and interviewed the Beatles on their first American tour.

When "underground" rock emerged in 1966, Cavanaugh devoted two hours of his nightly WTAC show to playing album cuts, songs by new groups and the like, anticipating the FM rock format.

In the Vietnam War era, Cavanaugh was active in promoting concerts at Mount Holly and at Sherwood Forest, in Richfield Township.

THESE EARLY "rock festival"-style concerts aroused the ire of local authorities, and were closed by legal and political pressure in 1974. But while they ran, Cavanaugh was not shy about slugging it out with detractors.

In a 1974 story in The Journal, for example, he called opponents of the Sherwood Forest concerts "a handful of small-minded, bigoted officials exerting enormous pressure on township officials to bury the children of our society under a mountain of their own prejudices."

Those concerts provided paying gigs for a number of then-struggling Michigan rockers, like Bob Seger and Ted Nugent. Julie Sherr, promotions and publicity director for the Birmingham-area firm that manages the now-successful Seger, said Cavanaugh was "very supportive of Bob."

"He was one of the promoters we really enjoyed working with — he was just very good," Sherr said. "There was never any problem with shows Peter booked. We always got paid. The shows always came off on time."

Sherr, who promoted records in those days, said Cavanaugh had a reputation for breaking national hits.

"HE WAS great out at TAC," she said. "He would always listen when you brought in a record and he'd tell you what he thought. If it was good, he'd say it was good, and if it wasn't, he'd say it wasn't."

Stone also recalled Cavanaugh as having a sure ear.

"You'd play him a good rock 'n' roll record and he'd say, 'That was great,' and he'd put it right on the air," Stone said. "He was the excitement in the business.

"When you needed to be uplifted, you'd go to see Peter. In the main, this business isn't full of people who are associated with the music for the music's sake, but for the glamour. And when they find out there's no glamour, they take it out on everybody else."

Yet it would be a mistake to peg Cavanaugh as a rock groupie who dabbles at the radio business. He said his dual life as a rock fan and radio executive is "a very natural dichotomy with me."

"JUST BY need, I suppose, I'm still the street kid, but really there's not as much conflict as it would seem. Good business is like good rock — it requires intensity, dedication and results."

The high ratings WWCK scored under Cavanaugh's reign — it's been No. 1 or No. 2 in the market for the last two years — are a measure of his skills. His peers also call him a good manager.

"He's just 100 percent professional," said WTAC vice president/general manager Ray Nelson. "He's a good egg in our business."

Meltzer also credited Cavanaugh with being "a very, very good manager. His people skills are some of the best that I've seen and he knows how to get publicity."

Yet Meltzer pointed out that Cavanaugh's career is not one of unbroken triumphs. The "new woman" musical format of WWMN has been low-rated for its entire 16 months, and WWCK's "Trip to Flint" contest reaped bad publicity when its winners publicly complained of their experiences on their trip to [illegible].

BUT MELTZER praised Cavanaugh for being adventuresome. "I always had to be careful about what Cavanaugh was going to do. He was my challenge."

Likewise, Flanders described Cavanaugh as having "the type of mind that takes things just a little farther out than anybody else.

"He's always been like that. It comes from his strict Catholic upbringing — at least, that's what he always told me."

Cavanaugh did not debunk the theory.

"I never shot another arrow at a garage," he said. "So I thank the sweet little sisters and the Jesuits."

Peter C. Cavanaugh in 1957. Top photos of Cavanaugh today by Leo Johnson

Flint Journal.
Flint, Michigan. (1983)

ABC Rock Board.
West Palm Beach, Florida. (1984)

CHAPTER TWENTY-THREE

JERRY AND ME

In early July, I was at home randomly scanning the dial on a new multi-band Panasonic radio recently acquired when, roaming through telephone frequencies and hoping to hear wild sexual exchanges, I happened to accidentally come across even more interesting communications. Instinctively and illegally, I recorded around 30 minutes worth. There were several different conversations involving the highest echelons of General Motors. The President of Buick Motor Division was speaking on his car phone with superiors in New York and Detroit. Many serious things were under discussion. The executives appeared privy to governmental information which had not yet been made available to the general public. There was talk of strained relationships with Opel in Germany, pending safety standard guidelines, and price control data. There was also an abundance of corporate intrigue evident in factual variations presented in the accounting of specifics to different individuals and assessments volunteered on the efforts of others. I was most intrigued by the fact that they didn't sound like typical milquetoast General Motors types at all. How refreshing. At the top of the pyramid, they talked like Rock 'n Rollers.

"Those fuckin' Germans are a complete pain in the ass!"

"We're sayin' we'll put the goddamn things in for cost, but there's 25 points in every one of those cocksuckers!"

"Sure Ed's secretary's got big tits. She's top-pick for the top-prick. Ha-ha-ha-ha!"

What wonderful men. They seemed quite likable. Did they know they were "on the radio"? I thought not. I should just call up the President of Buick Motor Division and slip him the word. Why not? What goes around, comes around. As partially expected, I was stopped at the lowest rung of the Buick internal communications ladder by some junior executive who needed to know specific information before I could possibly be referred upward. He was a snotty little jerk. To tell him anything seemed indiscreet. An indirect method offered a better solution.

Dan and Dave West's Dad was an artist at Buick. He'd been there for 30-some years, and was looking forward to retirement. I called Dave and asked him to stop over. Dan would have wanted to make 2000 copies of the tape and throw them off Flint bridges at every Buick passing underneath. Dave was considerably steadier and infinitely more responsible. I played several minutes of the tape, and Dave couldn't believe his ears. I told Dave I had tried to reach the primary conversationalist, but wasn't allowed through. He did believe that. I suggested that Dave simply tell his Dad that telephone car communications could be a sensitive thing and why. No specifics regarding content were to be shared. I would be glad to confirm interception only with those involved.

Holy Motors!

Dave called his Dad early the next morning and, within 20 minutes, Buick Motor Division's Director of Public Relations was on the phone to our WTAC Vice-President and General Manager, Charlie Speights. I was still on-the-air, but had briefed Charlie earlier about the curious affair. He was utterly fascinated.

As the story had rapidly raced up through the Buick command, it had become radically enhanced. Charlie was told that a WTAC employee named Peter Cavanaugh had recorded hours of secret corporate conversations and was "playing them at cocktail parties all over town." What's more, these tapes were going to be broadcast on the radio and offered for sale. No threats were made, but it was quite clear that any assistance he could offer in limiting damages would be greatly rewarded by the corporation.

"Oddly enough," reported Charlie, "the main thing the Buick boys want to do is listen to the tapes." You bet. Although I had no intention of taking the matter any further, adventure is where you find it. Charlie and I discussed an approach.

We called the Director of Public Relations on Charlie's speaker-phone.

"Hi, Jerry Rideout!"

"Jerry? This is Peter Cavanaugh!"

"Peter—ahhh—Peter Cavanaugh?"

"That's goddamn right! Did you just call my fucking boss?"

"Ahhh. Ummm. Errrr. See. I've known— known Charlie for years and he's an old— an old friend— and—"

"You called my fuckin' BOSS???"

"Now. Well. You see—"

"You get your ass out here!"

CLICK.

Within seconds, Charlie's private line rang.

Charlie told Jerry that I had gone completely berserk when informed of his call. Charlie said that while I was normally a fairly nice kind of a "cat," I had a vicious Irish temper and was given to bursts of uncontrollable rage, as is true of many performers. Charlie reported that I was running around the building screaming about having my job threatened. Charlie said I had so far shared the entire tape with no one, not even him. Now I had a call in to Ralph Nader, and was talking about making copies for all the networks here and overseas, especially in Germany. "Whatever that means," added Charlie. All because the Buick Motors Division Director of Public Relations had fucked up. Mr. Rideout was looking at a one-way ticket to No Snatch, Saskatchewan.

The Director arrived at WTAC within minutes, perspiring heavily and minus his coat-jacket, which, for a General Motors executive of the era, was like not wearing pants. He had literally run to his car and headed south on Center Road. Riding out. At the time, I looked quite anarchistic. My mustache was Fu Manchu and my hair was shoulder-length. I was wearing sneakers, ripped jeans and a T-Shirt that said: "So What?"

In spite of every effort to maintain practiced composure, Mr. Rideout couldn't help but radiate the feeling he was in the presence of an honest-to-God anarchist who was holding the keys to his career in one hand, and preparing to crush his balls with the other. This hadn't been addressed at General Motors Institute.

"Jerry, I'd like to cover a few things quickly and cleanly."

"Absolutely, Mr.Cavanaugh. Absolutely!"

"Jerry, I'm of Irish descent and like to handle things in Irish ways."

"My wife is part-Irish. She's a wonderful woman!"

I couldn't resist.

"Well, that's good, Jerry. That's very good. And you screw Irish gentlemen too?"

"Oh, no. No. No-no-no-no-no! That's not what I meant at all!"

"Jerry, when you called Charlie Speights, you were trying to screw me. Charlie happens to be just about my very best friend in the world, but you didn't know that. You thought you would call my boss and tell on me. Do you know what that's called in Ireland, Jerry?"

"In Ireland?"

"In Ireland, Jerry, that's called informing. Do you know what happens to informers in Ireland?"

"In Ireland?"

"In Ireland, Jerry, informers stop informing. At WTAC, you're in Ireland."

"In Ireland?"

337-CAVA

"And here's the Irish deal: First, the next time you have a question for a common Irish worker, you will ask him directly to his face. You will not contact his "better," for there's no such thing. Is that understood?"

"Understood."

"Secondly, there is absolutely no way you or anyone else connected with Buick, is going to listen to any recordings which may be in my possession, except the President of the Division if he should so choose, and only then to verify the extent of his vulnerability. He should watch it on his goddamned car phone. That's my only message here."

"I see."

"And lastly, Jerry. You seem like a decent guy. Tell your people I'm erasing the tape and that you talked me into it. You came right out here and behaved respectfully. You may come back to Ireland any time you wish."

"To Ireland. Yes. Yes. Then, we don't have to worry about—"

"All you need worry about, Jerry, is keeping your wife happy. Irish women are creatures of deep passion. The tape will be erased."

The Director of Buick Public Relations left WTAC in a state of joyous shock. Charlie and I fell on the floor in hysterical laughter. By the close of the day, all car phones were removed from every executive vehicle in the entire Buick fleet. I played the tape for no one else. It was not erased.

CHAPTER TWENTY-FOUR

JESUS JUMPS JOHNNY

Things at the station were picking up and I was confident that listenership was climbing. The new format sounded dead-nuts-on and the nightly WTAC Underground was giving us an important edge over CKLW in ambiance and texture. Unfortunately, new ratings would not be taken until the autumn and released in January. Continuous listenership surveying was still years away.

Two more 12 hour Wild Wednesdays were lined up for Sherwood Forest in July and August. Wednesday and Friday night concerts continued at Mt. Holly with pronounced attrition. Even with a dozen strong Michigan-based headliners and new national groups becoming available, such as "The James Gang" out of Cleveland, "REO Speedwagon" from Champagne, "Blue Cheer" from San Francisco, the "Guess Who" of Canada and Chicago's "Ides of March," we were starting to regularly compete with ourselves. Better that than with others. I was enjoying life to the fullest, but John Parker was not. There were too many hours. Too many shows. Too many late nights. It was getting to him. He desperately needed time-off. He left on a 2 week vacation the first of August. He returned to work on Monday, August 16. He stormed into my office with unaccountable intensity.

"Jesus Christ is my Lord and Savior!"

He kicked at a dozen albums with rock artist covers stacked against the wall.

"I am through with Satan's disciples!"

Was he joking? On drugs? Stoned? Fried? Drunk? Fevered? Crazy?

He was saved, Children. He was Saved. Big time SAVED!

John had completely snapped. He was Heaven-Bound on the Road to Glory, a path initiated by being continually and spectacularly drunk the first few days of his vacation. His wife had brought in a Preacher. John was ready. He had been shaken awake in the agonizing vise-like grip of the most massive, cosmic-class, better-off-dead, "I'm-the-most-useless-piece-of-shit-in-the-history-of-the-whole-wide-world" hang-over he had ever experienced. It was a giant, black, swirling whirlpool of deep, dark, depressing despair. It sucked him ever-downward, even lower than the Portals of Hell. His body ached, his head was pounding and his stomach heaved like he'd swallowed six jack-hammers set to maximum-pound.

"Oh, Jesus," moaned John. It was his lucky day. Jesus was right there. Jesus, through the Preacher Dude, told John that he was suffering from Sin. The tortured pain that tore through John's very being was called the "Wages of Sin." John would keep paying those wages until he stopped sinning. I had often suspected why men of the cloth saved their preaching for Sunday morning. I theorized that Sunday was "The Lord's Day" because Saturday was "The Devil's Night." More men have been brought to their knees by Jack Daniels, Johnny Walker and Jim Beam than all twelve apostles combined.

John Parker now joined the ranks of thirst-conquered quenchers. As soon as I became convinced that John was absolutely, irrevocably, undeniably serious, I asked him his intentions. The Preacher Man had explained that the reason John did all the bad things he did, like drinking, swearing, working at the radio station, and hanging out with "hippie-queers" at rock concerts, was because of Satan. Satan was the cause of all Evil. It was Satan who made John also do those other things that he did, so that he was worried all the time about picking up diseases, or getting caught.

Guilt is the Vaseline of Salvation.

The nice part was that all of John's troubles and woes were the fault of Satan. All those terrible sins weren't really John's responsibility after all. No. John could escape the influence of Satan and be forgiven of everything and not have that godda— that darned— hangover ever again, if he would only reject Satan and accept Jesus Christ as his Personal Lord and Savior. This meant:

(1) Leaving WTAC
(2) Joining the Church (10 percent Tithing)
(3) Abandoning Rock Concerts
(4) Bringing others to Jesus (10 percent Tithing) and
(5) Testifying against the Evils of Rock 'n Roll (100 percent Personal Income)

Praise the Lord!

Jesus was looking for someone just like John

Pastor Parker would be traveling all over Detroit and the Midwest doing the Lord's Work. He would be accepting small honorariums of two or three hundred dollars a witness to talk about his experiences as a Rock 'n Roll Disc-Jockey promoting Rock 'n Roll concerts and doing heavy-duty Rock 'n Roll SINNING until he found the Truth and the Way and the Light. Christian teenagers would hear the REAL STORY of SATAN'S SONGS! Make that $500. Obviously, he could also pick his own shift.

I voiced a certain amount of healthy cynicism about the witnessing John would be doing, and was verbally thrashed and soundly chastised. It seemed that the Preacher Man had a few unkind things to say about Catholics, too. Catholics, explained John, were not personally saved. I worshipped under, and was governed, by Papist Power. It was impossible for me to know

The Lord, let alone understand John's conversion and commitment. His eyes started to tear.

"Peter C. Cavanaugh. The Lord is calling you now! Take my hand and kneel down with me to pray!"

"John, get off the floor.

I could hear voices. Half the WTAC Sales Office was gathering outside my closed door, attracted by John's rising supplications.

"Jesus! Jesus! Jesus! My friend Peter is a Catholic Sinner!"

Enough.

I reached over John and opened my office door. That didn't break the spell. Moreover, John's passionate performance had already drawn a crowd.

"Jesus! Jesus! I am surrounded by Sinners!"

I gently asked the sales personnel, secretaries, announcers and several total strangers who were hovering in hushed disbelief to provide John and I with privacy. Compliance was immediate.

I again shut the door and quietly told John that unless I spoke honestly, I would feel guilty of abject betrayal. I suggested that we had known each other for a half-dozen years and he was certainly not being himself. I told him that it would absolutely be no problem in getting another week or two off. This seemed like an advisable idea. I expressed my opinion that he was making important decisions without full and proper consideration, and that he should spend more time in personal reflection before making anything final. He spit on my framed, autographed picture of Alice Cooper.

O.K.

He said he still wanted to be my friend, and would like to get together for some Bible Study in the not-too-distant future.

Couldn't wait.

He said he wanted no settlement on our partnership. It was "Devil Dollars."

Certainly so.

We shook hands and he left. He would become a major attraction for the next year, and even address a crowd of 10,000 gathered at Cobo Hall in Detroit with fire and fury. John was a pretty good Preacher Man himself. And John's departure made things infinitely easier for me. I resolved to avoid partnerships in the future.

On September 4th, our third little girl was born at McLaren Hospital in Flint. We named her Candace Elizabeth Cavanaugh. She instigated false labor several times, then kicked right into gear, and was screaming her little lungs out in less than 20 minutes. I should have known she would study for the bar.

CHAPTER TWENTY-FIVE

REBOUND

On September 12, a major act played Mt. Holly for the last time. Bob Seger drew a disappointing crowd of barely 500. It wasn't his fault, since it was Bob's fifth area appearance in less than three months, and he was scheduled to headline "Super Sunday" at Sherwood Forest on October 4—our final outdoor show of the year. The market had reached maximum saturation. Major expansion was scheduled for the Mt. Holly Lodge to accommodate a growing number of skiers in the winter months. Construction required early closing of the concerts in any event. It was time.

On September 18, a coroner's inquest found that Jimi Hendrix had died from inhaling vomit in London, England. It also stated that there was no evidence of drug usage. He was 27.

Al "Blind Owl" Wilson of Canned Heat was found dead in a Topanga Canyon, California garden. An empty bottle of barbiturates was at his side. He was 27.

On October 4, Janis Joplin was found dead at the Landmark Hotel in Hollywood. It was a drug overdose. She was 27.

27 is the number three to the third power.

"Super Sunday" was attended by 5000. Regular Sunday indoor concerts resumed on October 11 with Frijid Pink and Third Power.

Detroit's Frijid Pink had sold over two million copies of "House of The Rising Sun" over the course of the year, and were the first Detroit rock group to score a #1 global hit. They were heading to Australia on Quantas the following week. Third Power also hailed from Detroit. Jim Targal, Jim Craig and Drew Abbott made up the extraordinary trio, and were always just one hit away from shooting to the top. As with many frustrated groups, that elusive "super single" never materialized, although Drew was to find enormous success not too far down the road with Bob Seger's "Silver Bullet Band."

Terry Knight had spent $100,000 on a New York Times Square billboard promoting the new Grand Funk Railroad album "Closer To Home." Mark, Donnie, Mel and Terry were now Superstars.

The #1 single on WTAC was "War," by Edwin Starr. The struggle in Vietnam continued. In early December, Paul McCartney filed a writ in the London High Court against The Beatles, seeking legal dissolution of his partnership. On December 8, Jim Morrison of The Doors recorded poetry at Electra Record in Los Angeles. It was his 27th birthday. On Christmas Night, Brownsville Station from Ann Arbor drew a capacity crowd at Sherwood Forest. Their "Rock 'n Roll Holiday" was hitting the charts nationally and they were a sensational act. Cubby Coda played lead-guitar.

Christmas Night had become a new Sherwood tradition, and attendance was considerably enhanced by the closing of all bars in Michigan from Christmas Eve through Midnight on the 25. We were the only action anywhere. "Sock It To Me, Santa!" Bob Seger had recorded a tune of that very title based on a WTAC listener contest. It was kind of a spur-of-the-moment deal, and had taken on a life of its own as a hit single in Detroit, Flint, Lansing and Grand Rapids.

On New Year's Eve, Alice returned with plenty to celebrate. His recording of "Love it to Death" had become a major, unexpected smash in Canada. It had been released by Warner Brothers in the States. It had a new name and was gaining airplay everywhere. "Eighteen" was already #1 on WTAC.

On January 11th, the long anticipated Fall '70 PULSE Radio Ratings came in. WTAC had moved from a 9.3 percent to a 15.8 percent share of audience, and had reclaimed Number One status. CKLW had plunged from a 13.6 percent rating share to a 7.1 percent. Of equal significance was WTAC's performance in the Tri-City area. There we had regained major strength at the expense of several Saginaw stations, and were also rated #1. 250,000 people listened to WTAC every week. Fuqua Communications was overjoyed, and even Jackson Beaudry called to express his appreciation and congratulations. We were on the rebound.

CHAPTER TWENTY-SIX

LOCAL DJ

I received a call from a Detroit booking agent the day after the amazing ratings came out. It turned out that the legendary Chuck Berry was spending several weeks in Lansing. He was recording a new album with the Woolies. The Woolies had constructed their own recording studio in a garage annex next to their house, and were highly honored being chosen by Mr. Berry for professional collaboration and/or advantageous utilization.

After incredible success in the mid to late '50s, and a period of incarceration (brought about, as previously mentioned, much more by his skin complexion and unparalleled popularity among white youths than overt acts of felonious illegality), Mr. Berry had fallen on marginal times. He had never been the primary beneficiary of his earlier triumphs and had made only thousands as his record company made millions. As a black artist, he was not unique in this distinction, but his experience was singular in terms of magnitude. His contributions to, and influence upon, a newly emerging music form were staggering. His financial rewards had been minimized by crafty agents, crooked promoters, and slick attorneys.

As a consequence, Chuck Berry had become a lone rider on the Rock 'n Roll range. He was his own manager now, and all he carried on the road was his guitar. His contract specified amplifier requirements (Twin Fenders) and support musicians of acceptable ability. Since any rock musician claiming such distinction always knew the entire Chuck Berry catalogue, it was usually just a matter of choosing four or five good players who would spend several hours rehearsing, and then meet Mr. Berry only moments before show-time. There weren't that many chord changes. After Chuck Berry had worked with The Woolies a few times, they became great friends.

In addition to being outstanding musically, The Woolies really enjoyed playing with Chuck and they added an animated, enthusiastic quality to each performance. This was sometimes lacking with typical "pick-up" bands. Whenever Berry was booked in Michigan, Illinois, Indiana or Ohio, The Woolies were his first choice. Promoters were instructed accordingly. Chuck was also without a recording contract. When The Woolies offered him use of their humble, but adequate, facilities at extremely favorable terms, Mr. Berry was most pleased. He had set aside much of January for the project.

Chuck had also reflected upon the possibility of generating a few dollars in the immediate vicinity during his stay in Lansing. Berry and the Woolies wanted a guarantee of $1,250 against 50 percent of the gate on Sunday, January 24. I agreed instantly. Having briefly met Chuck a few years earlier, I was incredibly excited about being afforded the opportunity to actually present him myself. I had carried that guitar.

Even though the Sherwood Forest audiences represented a second generation of rockers, the turn-out was excellent. Mr. Berry's show was magnificent, and the audience was exceptionally responsive. Backstage, we had gone through a ritual prior to performance, which I came to learn was standard when dealing with Chuck. He carefully reviewed the ticket-count, and had then audited the money given him. He had gone into percentage and was thus entitled to $1,770. for the night. As usual, this amount was presented in cash, mostly in $1 and $5 bills. These were sorted and labeled into $50 and $100 packets. Mr. Berry unwrapped all the packs and carefully counted each and every dollar. It took approximately ten minutes. Satisfied that all was in order, a giant, tooth-filled grin crossed his face. With the single word: "Mellow," he signified his satisfaction. One would not wish to see Chuck Berry frown.

During one of several encores, he introduced a novelty tune. It was chanted like a nursery rhyme, although the lyrics danced about with an unmistakable ring of double-entendre. It was about a little boy and his bell. Crowd participation was requested and given. A studio version performed with The Woolies was later discarded in favor of a live recording made during an appearance the following winter at the Lanchester Polytechnic College Arts Festival in Coventry, England. The BBC resisted severe pressure to ban the song after being accused of being "a vehicle for mass child molestation" by self-styled protector of British morals, Mary Whitehouse. "My Ding-A-Ling" sold over two million copies around the world.

In March, Peter, Paul and Mary broke up. A year earlier, member Peter Yarrow had pleaded guilty to taking immoral liberties with a 14 year-old girl. I assumed she had puffed his magic dragon. I was saddened when 55 year old Frank Sinatra announced his retirement from show business to "write and teach." Although I was not a Sinatra music enthusiast, I was always an attitude fan.

Rather than attempt concerts every Sunday at Sherwood Forest, I had initiated a pattern of scheduling two or three presentations a month based on availability of proven attractions. In practical terms, unless a group had significant radio exposure, and people had heard of them, only several hundred could be attracted by even a stellar group of unknowns. I had tried packaging two or three emerging bands of excellent merit and selling the concept as supporting new music. It just didn't work. Without a hit, you couldn't draw shit. Even attendance for a Bob Seger concert would rise and fall, proportionate to recent chart success. When he played Sherwood in late March and introduced a new composition about life on the road called "Turn the Page," only 300 were present for the historic moment. Bob later said that the smaller turn-out had encouraged him to try some new material for experimental purposes.

On Easter Sunday, Badfinger packed the hall. "No Matter What" on Apple Records had gone through the roof and their connection with the Beatles didn't hurt. They were very proper Englishmen, and enjoyed a bit of Sherwood Forest horseback-riding prior to appearance. They also were fascinated that I had obtained an advanced copy of the new Rolling Stones album, "Sticky Fingers," which I played in its entirety during a break. It had debuted the prior evening on WTAC, much to the renewed chagrin of our colleagues at Detroit stations. They once again had found themselves fucked by Flint.

Creem Magazine was having financial difficulties, and Shep Gordon had promised publisher Barry Kramer an Alice Cooper date for old times' sake. Creem had been good to Alice, and Shep was not one who forgot a favor. Wednesday, May 12, saw us stage a "Creem Benefit Concert" at Sherwood Forest. Creem writer Dave Marsh was delighted over my choice for opening act. Rudy Martinez had reformed his group.

"Question Mark and The Mysterians" kicked things off with a fine 30-minute set. It was to be the first of many failed reincarnations. Too many teardrops had fallen. "Q" had ended his brief earlier career penniless and without direction. He was working at a gas station in Clio, Michigan. I gave him $200. It was his first paid gig in a year.

I decided to try a promotion at the Rollaire Skating Rink in Bay City with the MC5. John Sinclair was in prison, ostensibly for possession of two marijuana cigarettes. John Lennon would later appear at a massive "Free John" rally in Ann Arbor and write a song about Sinclair, which would precipitate an early release. Meanwhile, the MC5 were functionally rudderless without Sinclair's impressive management skills, and were taking any work that came their way. Less than 100 tickets were sold. Their new album on Atlantic had been well-produced, but lacked adequate record company support. "Sister Anne" and

"High School" were as good as anything they'd ever done. The "Revolutionaries" had ammo, but no guns. It was a shame.

On June 23, the first "Wild Wednesday" of the year was scheduled outdoors at Sherwood Forest. It was to be a notable milestone in Bob Seger's career. I had put together the usual "best of the best" Michigan line-up and was looking forward to another great summer kick-off. Bob's manager, Punch Andrews, called me a week before the concert.

"Pete, listen. I've gotta tell you something. Don't panic. Don't panic!"

I experienced a "klong," which author William Safire later coined and defined as "a sudden rush of shit to the heart." Seger was canceling? Punch was going to sell me on a substitution? The radio announcements had already run a week headlining Bob. Posters and flyers had been distributed throughout the state. There goes the whole show. Don't panic?

"I won't panic, Punch. Seger's still on the date??"

"Sure. Sort of."

"Sort of? What do you mean "sort of?" He's phoning in his appearance?"

"No. No. No. No. Bob will definitely be there."

"Punch, what's the 'sort of' thing?"

"Don't panic!"

"Punch, you're making me very fucking scared."

"Seger wants to do an acoustical set. Solo. Just him sitting on a stool with his guitar and a single microphone. It's what he wants to do."

I was absolutely silent. As all great managers do, Punch kept on talking.

"I know it sounds weird. I tried to talk him out of it. Honest-to-Christ! I tried. I really tried. I did. I tried. Pete?"

A single acoustical number strategically placed in the final half-hour of a 90-minute rock performance was one thing. It could even be elegant. And it set things up for a crashing, slamming, thundering finale.

Bob Seger playing a purely acoustical set would be like Johnny Carson opening with a joke free monologue. It would be viewing a Tarzan movie without Cheetah, Jane, or that one scene where he always stabs the same crocodile while the jungle birds go, "Aaahwooow. Aaaaahwooow. Aaahwooow." Or paying $5 to see "Deep Throat", and discovering that you're watching a 3-hour cinematic opera on the life of Enrico Caruso in Italian without sub-titles. I patiently explained all of these illustrations to Mr. Andrews.

Punch entirely agreed, but was powerless. Bob had been wanting a new direction. He was tired of the same, old shit. He wanted to expand as an artist. He wished to grow as a performer. He desired more personal contact and communication with his audience in a more meaningful, dignified way. Punch was guessing that this was a phase that Bob was going through and that it would be short-lived. But the phase would not pass before the 23rd of June. Of that, Punch was certain.

Rather than close the show, the set-times were adjusted and Bob was scheduled for a 35 minute "all acoustical/solo performance" at 7 P.M. It would still be broad daylight, and jagged projectiles from the crowd thrown at the promoter could be more easily avoided. All radio copy was changed to stress that this would be an all ACOUSTICAL appearance by Bob Seger WITHOUT his BAND. I used a "first-time-ever" approach, not knowing how understated those words would shortly become. We had great weather on the 23 and another record crowd for "Wild Wednesday '71."

As Frijid Pink finished on stage "A" at 6:55 P.M., Bob took his position on stage "B" in anticipation of my introduction. There was Bob on the promised stool with his guitar and a microphone. Nothing else. Next to naked.

I used my 20 seconds of introduction to explain what a rare and special moment it was, and how pleased we all should be to witness such a splendid event at that particular point in our respective lives. The crowd applauded correctly and Bob launched into something from his "Beautiful Morning" album about flowers, and love, and feeling, and touching. He finished his first number, and there was polite, if somewhat tentative, applause. His second selection was a 6-minute ballad about a lonely coal miner and his pet canary or something similar. The crowd was straining under the challenge. There were a few muted cries indicating restlessness, disenchantment and discomfort. Bob's third tune about quiet loss and gentle heartache broke the dam.

Exclamations of dissatisfaction and demands for "Heavy Music," "Ramblin' Gamblin' Man," "Noah," and/or anything other than "That Shit," (which was the collective critique quickly emerging) echoed through the park. Screams for "Rock 'n Roll!" and shouts of the ever-dreaded "Fuck You!" were building with every sweet, delicate note sprung forth. This wouldn't even qualify as a debacle. It was outright, unimaginable, unmitigated, unadulterated disaster. The crowd had lost even a pretense of tolerance. Impatience had given way to anger. Rage would come next.

If Necessity is the Mother of Invention, Terror is the Father of Inspiration. During the first twelve (which seemed like a trillion) minutes of "Seger/Solo," an amazing opportunity for unplanned intervention had presented itself through pure coincidence. Is random chance no more than luck? Are miracles what they seem? Is fortune destiny or draw?

As soon as "Frijid Pink" concluded, their equipment had been struck from stage"A", replaced by that of the next musicians, who would follow Bob Seger. Since their gear consisted of one (1) organ and one (1) drum-kit, normal set-up time of 25 minutes was reduced to 10.

David Teagarden and Skip VanWinkle hailed from Oklahoma and had worked out of the Detroit area for several years. I had never seen a duo of their kind. David played drums with forceful precision, while Skip VanWinkle pounded the organ and sang with equal power and talent. Skip looked, acted and spoke like Festus Hagen on "Gunsmoke." When they had first appeared at Sherwood Forest the preceding Christmas season, audience members had stormed the stage in adulation during their last of three encores. Their recording of "God, Love and Rock 'n Roll" had sold 500,000 copies across the nation. Teegarden and VanWinkle were ready to totally save the day.

In the middle of Seger's second song, I had noted that David and Skip were almost through with their preparations. I was standing next to Punch Andrews, who knew his artist was in serious trouble. The "Fuck-You" birds were just beginning to chirp. I loudly whispered to Punch that we both knew how bad it was, and how much more so it would soon become. I suggested that if Teegarden and VanWinkle would go along with it, assuming that Bob wanted to quickly bail from his game plan, a remarkable solution might be right at hand. I speculated that, although they had never played together before, there were probably dozens of songs in their mutual repertoire. Chuck Berry stuff. Bo Diddley music. Little Richard material. All Bob had to do was run over to the other stage, plug in an electric guitar, compare choices with Teegarden and VanWinkle and then, just fucking jam.

Punch quickly visited with Teegarden and VanWinkle. They were watching Seger, and were acutely aware of his predicament. It was a crazy idea. It might be a trip. No problem. Bob had finished his third piece, and was staring into the face of a potential lynch mob. The audience was devastated in disappointment. He reflected upon even the most remote options. He contemplated faking a heart-attack or stroke. Possibly no faking would be necessary. The eyes of 12,000 bitterly bummed-out fans bored into his very soul. He had heard all the shouts. He had seen the questioning looks of lost allegiance. Where he had sought artistic extension, he found collapsed credibility. He had misjudged. He had wandered. He had committed the most Mortal of all Rock 'n Roll sins. In attempting to lead his audience up, he had proportionately brought them down.

All Punch had to do was begin the first few words of hypothesis. Bob was in full stride toward stage "A," his electric guitar was waiting, and amplifiers set to maximum volume. Skip and Dave shook hands with Bob and spoke but a few seconds. The introductory guitar notes were as known to me as my calling in life. It was the very first record I had ever played on WNDR more than a dozen years before. Seger grabbed the microphone and screamed opening lyrics.

"I'm gonna write a little letter; gonna mail it to my local DJ!"

Electricity cracked through the crowd like a bullwhip. The energy rush was nothing sort of breathtaking. 12,000 involuntary and self-administered doses of raw adrenaline surged into the body collective. It was SEGER!

"It's a jumpin' little record I want my jockey to play!"

The mood-swing was incredible, as though a giant spring had been wound to the last possible degree of tolerance by 12 minutes of almost unbearable restraint, then instantly sprung-loose with full, abandoned, utterly reckless release. The acoustical beginning had become an inadvertent catapult, launching the audience into sudden unexpected heights.

"Roll over Beethoven, I gotta hear it again today!"

Teegarden and VanWinkle were exploding under Seger's guitar as though created solely for that exact moment. The musical synchronization and balance were perfect. There was no way they could be any tighter. They played and played and played. Song after song. Classic after classic. They raced through the duration of Seger's allotted time and through all of Skip and David's. I allowed the three an extra 15 minutes for encores. There was no way not to. The accidental performance was everything that Rock 'n Roll ever should be. It was true magic. Nothing else made sense.

Bob and Punch and Skip and David spent hours in post-concert discussion. Agreement was reached. A pact was formed. A new group was born. The album "Smokin' O.P.'s" was released several months later with resounding success, more than half the material having been performed impromptu that night at Sherwood Forest.

Jim Morrison of The Doors was found dead on July 3 in a Paris bathtub. He had not finished his 27 year. July 14 brought another "Wild Wednesday" headlining Edgar Winter's "White Trash." A friend picked up Edgar at the Flint Sheraton, drove him to Sherwood Forest, and then returned to the Sheraton for his hat. Edgar couldn't play without his hat. He got back to the park with 30 seconds to spare. That hat sounded great.

Parliament and Funkadelic closed another "Wild Wednesday" show August 11 in spectacular fashion. George Clinton had been thoroughly briefed about voluntary behavioral requirements while playing at Sherwood Forest. We had reviewed the constrictions again upon his arrival in early afternoon. Somehow during late-evening performance, George suffered a serious attack of major confusion. As he later apologetically explained to me:

"Hey, Man. I know we talked, but I couldn't remember whether you said to do it, or if I was supposed not to do it. I knew it was one or the other. I decided to do it. I'm right half the time!"

He did do it.

Fortunately, it was during their final number of the night that George stripped-down to nothing more than a purple, iridescent jock-strap. Admonishing the crowd to "move your ass and your mind will follow," he then started moaning loudly. His next message was quite distinct and clearly delivered. He wanted to "Suck and Fuck and Lick and Dick!!!"

In and of themselves, the words and thoughts alone were more than enough to warrant immediate police action. And it was a large black man who was standing there, two super-trooper spotlights savagely illuminating his jock-strap. It glittered and sparkled and shot-off shimmering, multi-colored, laser-like rays into the night. The combination of language and imagery immediately offered unnerving, unswerving visions of an ultimate hell to dozens of white men with badges.

Chief Ralph Rogers was frozen in shock. The rest of the Township forces, tired after nearly 12 hours of security detail, looked to Ralph for an indication of intent. Ralph looked at me. I looked at Ralph. The group was ending their last song anyway and George had already left the stage.

"Ladies and Gentlemen! George Clinton! Parliament and Funkadelic! Thank You and Good Night!"

The police report ran six pages, and was completed by Chief Rogers and four officers. Along with what George actually said, there were many creative interpretations of what he might have been thinking about saying. Most of the writers were former Marines. George was taken downtown. He was instantly released. Again, the Prosecutor's Office refused to officially charge "obscenity," but Ralph had done his best, and certainly that was all that should be expected. Payment that would have gone to the band was donated to several charities. Ralph requested that his eyes never again set sight on the group within 50 miles of Davison City Hall. George had made a lasting impression.

Two days later, a Friday the 13th brought good luck with the much-delayed release of the PULSE Spring '71 ratings book. WTAC continued its strong performance from the prior Fall and actually gained a little ground in Flint, shifting upward to a 16.4 percent share of total audience. It was the last completely dominant measurement the station would ever experience.

CHAPTER TWENTY-SEVEN

ARMSTRONG'S CURSE

WMRP was an AM/FM religious combo in Flint owned by the Methodist Radio Parish, hence the "Merp" call-letters. Simulcasting programs of a spiritual, inspirational and uplifting nature to the Flint community, its audience was negligible. We used to say that you could broadcast Anything at all on "Merp" in complete confidence.

FM radio had been perfected in 1933, but had been relegated by common consensus within the industry primarily to public radio facilities, including many college stations. The background offers excellent testimony to the many wonders of American free enterprise.

"Frequency Modulation" (FM) technology had been developed by Edwin Howard Armstrong. Armstrong was asked by David Sarnoff, Chief Executive Officer of the Radio Corporation of America (which also owned the National Broadcasting Company), to craft a system which would eliminate static from AM ("Amplitude Modulation") transmission. After years of experimentation, Mr. Armstrong's achievements with FM went far beyond Sarnoff's wildest hopes or expectations. Although somewhat limited in reach compared with AM signals, the quality of sound reproduction was vastly superior to AM. It was like night and day. RCA and NBC had made incredible investment into AM transmitters, receivers and radio stations. Sarnoff was enormously impressed by Armstrong's remarkable achievement with FM. He ordered the project shelved. Why screw yourself for the public good?

Armstrong decided to forge ahead on his own. He built thousands of FM receivers, and had plans for several dozen transmitting sources. He had the future on his side. After Armstrong had manufactured his receivers according to Federal Radio Commission guidelines, Sarnoff put on the heat in Washington, and the Commission changed their approved FM frequencies. Oops. Sorry. Armstrong's new radio receivers couldn't even pick up static. He eventually went out of business and committed suicide, nattily dressed in an overcoat, hat, scarf and gloves, plunging to death from the 13 floor of a very tall building. Hitting an overhang, he wasn't discovered until the following day. I am certain, in his final seconds before terminal impact, he uttered a lasting curse against Amplitude Modulation, and all stations so processed.

My own experiences with FM had been extremely limited, not counting watching television. Sarnoff had made sure that television sound was processed by Frequency Modulation when RCA starting building TV stations and receivers from scratch, following World War Two. He knew a good thing when he heard it.

A group of Flint investors bought "Merp." The daytime AM at 1570 would play Country, and the call-letters were changed to WCZN, "Your Country Cousin." The FM call-letters, in hopes of creating listenership confusion, due to CKLW's earlier success, became WWCK. WWCK-FM hit the air the last week of August '71. Several Detroit FM's had gone rock a bit earlier with mixed results. Listening to Bob Seger at 105.5 in high-frequency stereo made me increasingly uneasy. A lot of folks I knew were buying FM converters for their cars.

September 1 was our last "Wild Wednesday" of the season at Sherwood Forest, and Chuck Berry closed the show. He invited me on stage and I jumped around with him during the performance finale. I can't dance, but it was a close approxima-

337-CAVA

tion. He closed the show with his famous "Duck Walk." Later, we proceeded to a friend's house with several close acquaintances and partied. I just listened to his stories. Who wouldn't? I was on the air at 5 a.m. and he co-hosted the first hour. All we played were Chuck Berry hits. He made it to the Flint airport for an early morning flight.

"Every Picture Tells a Story" by Rod Stewart was the #1 album on WTAC in October. We were playing the title cut every two hours. On November 20, WTAC exclusively introduced the new Led Zeppelin "Four Symbols" album in the Midwest. "Misty Mountain Hop" was initially my favorite cut. The Friday and Saturday after Thanksgiving, I presented a double-header at The Saginaw Auditorium. Friday night was a touring production of "Jesus Christ, Superstar." It successfully sold over 4000 tickets. I had played the original album on Christmas Eve, at Midnight, on WTAC, for the last several years. On Saturday, we staged the world premiere of Alice Cooper's new "Killer" show. It had sold-out within hours of our first announcement.

Alice was now a huge act, and preparations for the Killer Tour had been months in planning. Alice's manager, Mr. Gordon, wanted to use Saginaw as a kick-off to work out any production problems before hitting major venues. I was delighted to act as promoter for the test-run. With major funding from Warner Brothers Records, the theatrics were now even beyond Broadway quality. At the end of the set, Alice was seized by eight mad monks, chained, whipped, and then hung from gallows. The crowd went wild. He came back to life and encored wearing top-hat and tails, singing "No More Mister Nice Guy." The cheering continued for ten full minutes after he left the stage. Shep was happy. Everything had worked with efficiency. The big cities were about to be blitzed.

On Saturday night, December 25, Brownsville Station and The Plain Brown Wrapper performed Christmas honors at Sherwood Forest. New Year's Eve saw Frijid Pink and The

Woolies on stage. Alice was playing Madison Square Garden. Ralph Rogers needn't worry about his balls.

The Fall '71 PULSE came out in early February '72. I was on the air when it arrived, so Charlie Speights brought it right into the studio. WTAC had dropped five full points in Flint to an 11.4 percent audience share, while upstart WWCK-FM had come out of nowhere to register a 6.1 percent. Between 7 and Midnight, WWCK actually beat WTAC 10.9 percent to 10.7 percent. Jesus Christ Superstar, they only had one tower to our four! What the fuck? Charlie was not as alarmed as I.

"Relax!" he commanded. "Maybe it's just a novelty factor!"

That's what they'd said about railroads, television and indoor plumbing.

As usual, Charlie was right. Temporarily.

WWCK-FM had vast technical superiority to WTAC, but the initial surge had been more a harbinger than permanent beachhead. The scales wouldn't be tipped forever until a few more years had passed. Yet, WWCK-FM was there and had to be factored into every formatic equation. Moreover, they were running five or six minutes of commercials per hour, to our 15 or 16.

We reduced our hourly load level to 10 minutes, and drove-up the rates. We convinced local advertising agencies that we had the history and would not regard the use of WWCK as an act of friendship. In the finest radio tradition, we used threats, promises and intimidation with clients. Music rotations were tightened even more. Select rock album-cuts were worked into overall programming with added frequency. Contesting was loaded with bigger money pay-offs. The WTAC "Underground" was extended until 5 a.m., with enhanced musical depth for all-night listeners. We controlled the local live rock market and used this leverage to the fullest. We borrowed time in staving-off the inevitable.

CHAPTER TWENTY-EIGHT

HEY-HEY!

Concerts at Sherwood Forest were becoming ever more infrequent. Band prices were starting to soar, and major booking agencies were grabbing up the bigger acts, and demanding much higher guarantees and percentages. Without exception, all of the Michigan-based attractions still worked with me on a 50/50 basis when they were available. Bob Seger was now playing regularly throughout all of the Midwest, and had developed a strong following in Florida and Texas. Ted Nugent was appearing throughout the entire country. Alice Cooper and Frijid Pink were international. I was grabbing occasional dates on new national talent by spotting them early and booking them far in advance, before the rest of the world caught on. Other than that, Rock 'n Roll had become quite corporate.

In the early '70s, almost every city had one or two promoters who would bring in major headliners and use area talent to open each show. The exposure and identification afforded the opening acts by this procedure made it possible to use the same local groups to draw 500 or 600 to area halls, amusements parks or smaller auditoriums as the baby bands developed individual followings of their own. It was a natural progression.

As Premiere, ATI, Banner, IFA and other New York/Los Angeles agencies starting signing acts and calling shots, middle rungs of the extant Rock 'n Roll ladder disappeared.

With consolidation came compression. A requirement in obtaining a major band was to use other artists represented by their agency on the same bill. Local acts were out. Unless one could ante-up with massive guarantees for staggered dates in multiple cities, a local promoter was out. Everything went big-time. As a generation aged and became legal, the only remaining venues for local or regional acts became taverns and inns. The Rock 'n Roll world became divided between stars and those playing bars. Musical Darwinism had seized the scene. Only the strongest survived. How could it ever have been otherwise? The most natural form of society is feudalistic. The most natural form of music is Rock 'n Roll. We all listen to the Master's call.

Easter Sunday of '72 brought Frijid Pink back to Sherwood Forest. Australia had been wonderful, and they even scored Quantas hostesses going and coming, so to speak. There was an issue of playing listener-friendly music. Frijid Pink saw "House of the Rising Sun" as a blues, rather than rock hit. Consequently, their set was almost all blues. The group believed that their live audiences would learn appreciation. No, people just didn't come back. We pulled around 500, filling less than half the hall. Much of the world thought Frijid Pink was Norwegian or something. They were just from Detroit and thought "frigid" had a "j."

On May 26, I promoted Big Brother and the Holding Company at the Forest. It was the original group with one notable and obvious exception. In performing without Janis Joplin, they played quite well, but attendance was marginal. The group was much better received later that evening at The Sandtrap Lounge on South Dort, our new WTAC hangout.

Then it was time for a powerful combination.

On Tuesday, June 20, Alice Cooper broke in his new "School is Out" tour at a sold-out Flint Industrial Mutual Association Auditorium. Alas, this time there was a major production problem at the end of the show. Shep Gordon, now challenged to top the hanging from the neck until dead finish to "Killer," had reached into his wizard's bag of terrifying tricks and came up again with what promised to be a real winner. At the end of the act, Alice would be loaded into the barrel of a cannon, and shot through the air over the audience to a net stretched across the very back of the auditorium. Talk about cool.

The dramatic staging was far past intense. It was transfixing. Alice slowly donned his cannon-suit with masterful suspense. The band was droning a solid, throbbing tone. He courageously marched up to the giant cannon and, waving a last, pathetic salute to the anxious throng, bravely climbed into the weapon and disappeared. The cannon was flooded with lighting. A drum-roll began. The moment of sheer climax was at hand. Everyone held their breath. There was an ear-shattering explosion of fire and light. Smoke was everywhere. Protruding from the cannon's mouth was a life-sized, sad, rag doll dressed like Alice. The mother-fucker hadn't even cleared the barrel.

The real Alice, of course, was hidden inside the cannon. It was goddamned dark in there, but he could sure hear the explosion. He counted to five. The stage lights would be struck by now with the attention of the crowd diverted by spotlights on the flying dummy. In the absence of ejection, the lighting operators kept their massive beams trained on the main set. Alice emerged. Now there were two Alice Coopers on stage. Which one was the dummy? Ummmmmmmmmmm. "Hi!"

Mercifully, the crowd enjoyed a special treat during Alice's encore. WTAC had brought Mickey Dolenz into Flint, in conjunction with a major client campaign. I had escorted Mickey backstage to meet Alice prior to the performance. Alice was thrilled to be greeting a real "Monkee." Mickey was excited meeting Mr. Cooper.

After his roadies removed the "fuckin' cannon" from the stage, out came Alice Cooper, his band and Mickey Dolenz. The encore turned-out to be a spontaneous ten minute rendition of "Hey-Hey-We're the Monkees," which Alice and musicians knew by heart. They had been fans of the TV show in their early teenage years back in Phoenix. No rehearsal was needed. As soon as the crowd recognized Mickey, it erupted in loud, rapturous celebration. Six thousand voices joined right in.

The cannon episode was completely forgotten. This was a FINALE!!!

Alice Cooper went on to perform before hundreds of thousands as he traveled across the land with "School is Out!" The cannon was also out. It stayed in Flint. So did Mickey Dolenz. He was part of our next day's "Wild Wednesday '72" at Sherwood Forest.

I always used a fairly obscure instrumental track by The WHO called "The Ox" from their very first album under all "Wild Wednesday" advertising and had done so since "Wild Wednesdays" were born. I would pick it up a few seconds into the cut at the exact instant Peter Townshend established his first guitar note and it had become the "Wild Wednesday Theme." Copy was delivered with dramatic precision, and measured intonation against the frantic background energy of the music. It was powerfully effective. 1972 was no exception.

:60

(Establish "Who" Bed)

(Double Phasing/Heavy Read)

"A Single Point in Time and Space! Outdoors! Under the Summer Sun and Stars at Sherwood Forest in Davison! Twin Concert Stages Explode with Non-Stop Rock 'n Roll For Twelve Solid Hours from Noon 'til Midnight!"

"Wild Wednesday '72!"

"Ted Nugent and the Amboy Dukes! King Biscuit Boy! Bo Diddley! Mitch Ryder and Detroit! Sunshine! April Wine! The Whiz Kids! The Mike Quatro Jam Band! Julia! Chase! Ormandy! Bob Seger with Teegarden and Vanwinkle!"

"Wild Wednesday '72!"

"Twelve Groups! Twelve Hours!"

"Wild Wednesday '72" is Tomorrow! Rain or Shine! At Sherwood Forest!"

"Take I-75 to I-69 and the Davison Exit to Richfield Road."

"Gates open at 10. Admission $5."

"Wild Wednesday '72!! A Peter C. Rock 'n Roll Presentation!"

We drew 14,000, more than half the crowd from Detroit. We introduced Mickey Dolenz on stage, but didn't repeat the "Monkees" number, since it had already been done the night before and we wanted it to remain an Alice thing. There was no violence or trouble of any kind. Marijuana smoke filled the air. There was not a drop of alcohol in the crowd, nor a single empty beer can to be found anywhere on site following its departure. 1972 marked the last "Summer of Love." 1973 was to become "The Year of the Quaalude" in Michigan.

1972 also witnessed the last year of the engineering staff at WTAC. The Federal Communications Commission in the first Nixon term had eliminated a key provision in their rules requiring a "First Phone" technician to be on-duty at a transmitter site while a directional pattern was being broadcast by an AM facility. A first-class Radio-Telephone Operator's License was issued by the government after the applicant successfully passed an FCC-administered examination. There were also "Second" and "Third" class "tickets" which also were obtained through FCC testing. Each level of classification reflected the amount of knowledge mastered. Most disc-jockeys had "Third Class" certification, which covered most of the general basics of Commission law and little else. A "Fourth Class" category, requiring only U.S. citizenship and registration with the Commission, had been eliminated.

Any AM station with more than one tower broadcasts a directional pattern, usually between sunset and sunrise. This is because AM signals travel much farther at night, bouncing off an invisible electronic field above the earth called the ionosphere. A handful of AM stations are clear channel and romp all over the place. To prevent all sorts of signals from interfering with each other, a directional pattern points an individual station in a certain direction and away from other distant signals on the same frequency. Most people think that having a lot of AM radio towers generates a stronger, more superior signal. Exactly the opposite is true. One tower is the primary antenna attempting to radiate a pure, concentric circle. All the other towers try to screw it up, so it only takes a certain shape and goes out in a limited direction or pattern. That'll be 5 cents, please.

The WTAC engineers were fucked again. For a final time. Without a mandated need for transmitter supervision by holders of a "First Phone" license during night-time hours, what was their job? Disc-jockeys could now read the meters and could operate broadcast equipment as long as a Chief Engineer regularly reviewed logs, meters and overall operations.

At WTAC, there was one Chief and four-little-full-time-engineer-Indians.

Everything was still fine until the current NABET contract expired. There were negotiations. Four engineers were retired with generous severance, including Clair Bowser, President of Local 46.

Disc-jockeys moved into the Main Studio, and operated their own controls for the first time in the history of the building. Functionally, it was more efficient. NABET had never officially recognized the position of Program Director at WTAC. In the eyes of the union, I had been "Chief Announcer." Upon my insistence, I was deemed "management" and removed from the group. Clair Bowser warned that the departure of technicians would deteriorate union bargaining strength, and that most of the announcing staff would have their day come.

Eventually, it did.

The reality about unions vs. management is simply this: Whichever side has the most shit together wins. Everything else is irrelevant.

Had the United Auto Workers come to the aid of NABET engineers in Flint, it wouldn't even have been a struggle. NABET could have forced job security for all through natural retirement. The station might have gone bankrupt in later years, but all would have gone down together. The engineers asked. The UAW couldn't be bothered. They had theirs back then. Brotherhood? The WTAC engineers weren't dues-paying employees of the auto industry. Fuck 'em. Clair Bowser also said the auto workers' day would come. It has.

CHAPTER TWENTY-NINE

RETRO RULE

Bob Seger's "Back in '72" provided an excellent summary of the entire year. Comparatively speaking, something had happened. Absolutely nothing. Nothing was new. All-of-the-sudden, there was no more all-of-the-sudden.

When I had graduated from High School in 1959, the advent of the Rock Era had already come and gone. Even Elvis had lost excitement. Five short years later, the Beatles had burst upon the scene. In another five years, we had "Woodstock." Everything big had always somehow been replaced with something bigger and better. Finer. Faster. Hotter. Heavier.

We were convinced the continual escalation of innovation and improvement would never end. To question this wasn't remotely considered. Of course there would be "another Elvis" or "another Beatles" or "another Woodstock." To suspect otherwise was inconceivable.

Less than a dozen years had separated Elvis's first recording of "Heartbreak Hotel" on obscure Sun Records and "Sergeant Pepper's Lonely Heart's Club Band" on global monolith Capitol/EMI. What a roll we were on. Most of us thought of '72 as a temporary lull. With occasional moments of passing surprise and raised expectation, the lull is now three decades old.

There has been synthesis. Recording technology has vastly improved with digital compact discs replacing analog vinyl and hundreds of dials replacing ten, but the music is essentially unchanged at every level. It can be argued that "Rap" is nothing more than George Clinton at a Square Dance. "Grunge" is cement-flavored heavy-metal. "New Country" is good old Rock 'n Roll wearing cowboy boots and a great big hat. "New Age" is elevator music with an attitude. "New Rock" is Frank Zappa without an attitude. Retrograde rules.

Lee Abrams has been one of America's foremost and most successful rock programmers through the years. One very late night in 1984 after many adult beverages had been consumed, Lee discussed with me his growing suspicion that 1972 marked the end of musical ascension. While there had been no absolute decline, we'd all been floating under a mathematical ceiling ever since. Lee theorized that all the important notes and chords had been uncovered by 1972 and there just weren't anymore. Everything could be re-worked and re-examined and rediscovered and re-lived and re-invented and re-issued and reestablished, but true expansion had stopped without warning or notice. Lee was the first to eloquently articulate the discovery of no more discovery. Only a retrospective review of a full dozen years brought the reality into focus. He was correct in his hypothesis and remains so to this day. But, "Back in '72," we saw nothing more than a blurry blip on our Rock 'n Roll radar.

"Play Misty For Me" with Clint Eastwood became a major motion picture and made every disc-jockey at WTAC more sensitive to phone conversations with listeners. The film dealt with a hit-line-honey, as we used to call them, who develops an obsessive attraction to a DJ. Our all-night jock even took down his "Shrine of the Unknown Virgin" from a prominent position on one of our studio shelves.

The Shrine was an expensively-framed wedding picture of an unknown female listener who had stripped naked and run around our WTAC parking lot in the loneliest hours of a bright, moonlit night. She had started banging on the studio window and our announcer peered out. She pranced seductively hither and fro, offering a number of enticing and exceedingly personal poses, revealing her most tender and private parts in prolonged exhibition. She then ran to her car and took-off. She left the photo behind. General recollection was that she had a "pretty face," "cute tits," a "nice butt," and very "fast wheels." She later had called and explained that, although she had left a wedding picture, she was still a virgin. She and her husband had never gotten along. Oh.

Such happenings were not that uncommon around WTAC. Erotic and psychotic could present an unhappy blend. "Play Misty" pulled the boys back a few notches. Yes, we were all boys, just like Mr. Chips' students as they said "Goodbye" at the end of the movie. The only female announcer in Flint radio was Betty Clark who did a "recipe show" on WFDF. Sometimes I would raise my voice and imitate Betty Clark on WTAC. "Peas. That's green peas. One-half can. Boiled, not broiled. Steamed, not creamed. Exhumed, then consumed." I could be a riot.

A new, powerful WTAC promotional tool had come along with our introduction of "Midnight Madness Movies," in cooperation with ABC, which owned two major theaters in Flint. Every two or three weeks, we would run a rock-oriented movie such as "Woodstock" or "The Song Remains the Same" or "The Concert for Bangladesh" and pack both theaters on Friday nights at Midnight. Then we added Saturday nights.

WTAC disc-jockeys would greet the crowd before each showing, and give away a few prizes, plug several station features, and then bring-on the film. A pre-recorded tape was played as the audience entered and left each showing, filled with great rock music and station hype. Each "Midnight Madness" weekend would provide in-person WTAC exposure to 3000 or 4000 listeners and generate $2000 to $3000 in station revenue. I assisted with the bookings and eventually expanded the menu to include such classics as "2001," "A Clockwork Orange" and "Catch-22," which were attitudinally "Rock 'n Roll," if not musically. It worked. Three Stooges Marathons and Road Runner and Bugs Bunny Cartoon Festivals also were highly favored.

Memorial Day Weekend of 1973 was particularly unique. I attended my first national radio convention and, although frequenting dozens of others in future times, it turned out to be the very best. Then again, none like it was ever held again.

When I had first entered the industry, Broadcasting Magazine was the radio trade publication of choice. On the music side, one had either Billboard and/or Cashbox. In the late '60s and early '70s, a West Coast disc-jockey and radio guru named Bob Hamilton started a new publication called the "Bob Hamilton Radio Report," later changed to "The Radio Starship Report." The "Radio Report" had made an astounding leap into the future. Its format is what "Radio and Records" became and is today, more or less.

I was an early and enthusiastic subscriber. When the publisher announced a "Radio Carnival" was going to take place over Memorial Day Weekend '73 at Estes Park, north of Denver, I signed-up in half a hurried heartbeat. Friday morning, May 25, I drove to Metro in Detroit, and boarded a non-stop flight to Denver. I was seated (by fate) next to an 18 year-old, long-haired, hippie-type who had been brought in by ABC to program their Detroit FM, WRIF. He was the youngest ABC executive in the entire chain by at least a full decade, and was rumored to be a genius. It was thus I first met Lee Abrams. We talked for most of the flight, primarily about the relationship between relativity theory, pagan religions and rock culture. There was unanimity in agreement.

When we arrived in Denver, a number of us radio radicals gathered together and waited for buses to arrive, which would swing us north to Estes Park. It was a motley assembly. Onlookers suspected another Woodstock was being clandestinely sprung somewhere near, but these flower folks were traveling up the country by jet and motor coach. As soon as our bus departed the airport, spontaneous demand was issued to stop at the first convenience store en route. Twenty cases of Coors were added to our collective luggage and immediate consumption initiated. Within 45 minutes, as the bus wound its way up mountain roads, an unsuspected physiological phenomenon presented itself with painful reality. We all learned that copious Coors consumption, combined with rapidly ascending altitude, brought bladders threateningly close to bursting-point after mere moments.

"Stop at a Bush!" we all cried at our driver in agonized unison, even though drinking Coors. Three minutes later, groaning with every bump and gear-shift, we were let off the vehicle at a small rest area overlooking a 200 foot ravine. There was one facility, and everyone properly lined-up in queue. Except Lee and me.

The mathematics were quite simple. There were 45 people who needed to relieve themselves, and at 60 seconds-per-leak (much beer had been drunk, and that was a conservative estimate) we would be there more than a half-hour. Moreover, those near the end of the line would require morphine injections to tolerate much more waiting. There was a giant rock overlooking the deep ravine, and it offered both gorgeous scenery and immediate resolution.

I climbed to the top of the rock and pissed over the ravine's edge, my flow joining yet another stream 200 feet below. I felt a pure, natural poetry was inherent in the act, and reflected that I was returning the Coors from whence it came. Lee joined me and estimated that, factoring gravity-velocity, wind-speed and air-resistance, it was taking 3.25 seconds to hit the creekbed below. We instantly created a trend. Suddenly everybody wanted to piss off the rock. Well, it was a radio group. Lee and I had finished and zipped-up before a Greyhound Sceni-Cruiser filled with senior citizens went by. We pretended we didn't know any of those people pissing off that rock.

We arrived at the Stanley Hotel in Estes Park. A short time later, Steven King would stay there and use the Stanley as inspiration for "The Shining." There were only around 200 registered for the convention. That turned out to be plenty. 90 percent of us were either from FM "Progressive" Rock facilities, or very aware "Top Forty" stations such as my own. The other 10 percent were corporate stragglers who weren't too sure what was coming off. There were two major assemblies. The first was when we initially arrived Friday afternoon, and the second was Sunday morning before we left. The rest of the time was "do it yourself." I barely slept until we returned to Denver. The way it worked was simplicity itself.

There was a large blackboard in the hotel lobby where our 25 "experts" would "register." The blackboard said who they were, and where they were. That was it. You would decide who you wanted to hang-out with, and just go there. The experts weren't tied-down, either. They might want to be in their room, or in the bar, or walking the grounds, or climbing up a tree. They would just return to the blackboard when wishing to change location, or even take time out. They would just write it down so anyone interested could keep track. The experts were categorized by areas of specialization.

The experts in Parapsychology were Dr. and Mrs. Rhine from the Rhine Institute at Duke University. You couldn't do any better. They were in their early eighties and had a hell of a time.

One of several experts in "Comedy" was a virtual unknown named Martin Mull. He was usually in the bar, calling in truckers with a CB radio hidden in his guitar.

Representing "Art," we had Shel Silverstein of Playboy, who had written "A Boy Named Sue" for Johnny Cash.

For "Music," we had Judy Collins and my buddy Alice Cooper.

Another former Monkee, Michael Nesmith, was our expert on "Mass Communication."

Shep Gordon was there for "Artist Management." We spent time together discussing Shep's plans to have Alice play the part of Bunny Hoover when Robert Altman got around to making a film of Kurt Vonnegut's "Breakfast of Champions."

Alice and I shared a deep admiration for Vonnegut. The movie was never made by Altman, and a later attempt recently failed.

The biggest names in the record industry were experts, as were top radio programmers from across the country. There was one room in the attic where "2001," and "Electra-Glide in Blue" were shown continuously for the duration of the meetings. There was snowfall Saturday night throughout the Rockies. There was also some "California Snow" available in certain suites, mostly occupied by West Coasties. There was high quality marijuana and hash in abundance everywhere which circulated freely. Even the Rhines took a polite toke or two. On Sunday morning, the Edwin Hawkins Singers serenaded with "Oh Happy Day" as the sun came up over majestic, snow-capped mountains. Everybody clapped and sang right along.

Bob Hamilton gave a speech about how we all had "Come Together," just as in the title of the famous Beatles' tune. He said it had been "sociologically transcending" and "psychologically profound." He had spent much of his time in the West Coast suites. We all bid adieu and headed back to L.A., San Francisco, Dallas, Miami, Chicago, Boston, Houston, Philadelphia, New York, Detroit and— Flint. On June 28, Eileen gave birth to another baby daughter at McLaren. Susan Elizabeth became the youngest of four sisters, which, she has always reminded me, clearly fits anyone's definition of a "dubious distinction." I promised her a trip to Paris someday in consideration of her sequential placement, although that has now been replaced with a trip to Dublin with a weekend in Paris. I'm not too sure where the Paris idea came from, but believe I was drinking cognac at the time.

Sherwood Forest concerts had continued on a monthly basis in the Spring and our first "Wild Wednesday" was scheduled for June 20 with Michigan bands and "Sugarloaf" of "Green-Eyed Lady" fame. The second "Wild Wednesday" of 1973 on July 11 offered a special treat. "Blue Oyster Cult" was headlining, and had arrived in Flint the prior evening, but REO

Speedwagon contacted me the morning of the event and explained a horrid dilemma had arisen. They were in a major bind due to a recording deadline that had not been met, and open studio time had become severely limited. I agreed to the cancellation, in return for a rescheduled date and because of an outstanding substitution offered by their booking agency. Joe Walsh had left the James Gang and had just completed his first studio album as a solo artist. He wanted to try his new band and material out without advance advertising at a location not yet selected. He had been contacted and had agreed that circumstances presented a mutual opportunity.

For many Wild Wednesday enthusiasts, the event had become more of an attraction than individual bands, as long as music quality was maintained. The sum was greater than its parts. It seemed half of those in arriving cars would ask our gate-keeper, after buying their admission tickets, "Who's playin'?" I announced that REO had been unfortunately detained, but had been rescheduled for the following Wild Wednesday. There were a few murmurs of muffled disappointment, but a great roar of approval went up with my introduction of a super surprise. Joe Walsh took the stage and premiered his "Barnstorming" album for the first time before a live audience. He closed with an extended, 15-minute version of "Rocky Mountain Way," which all present saluted with tumultuous cheering and applause. Such moments were always mystical, but darkness lurked on the horizon.

The invisible and still largely unnoticed cultural shift, which had somehow begun the prior year, had started pointing certain things sideways and downward. Methaqualone had become the rage of the day. Instead of getting "high," and attempting to view reality from a heightened, expanded perspective, many people started wanting to get "down." Who wanted to get "into" it? Getting "out" of it and "away" from it had become a popular urge. Echoes of undefined disappointment were now resounding with discomfort, and resonating with discouraged hope and tenuous trust.

The stabbings at Altamont before the Stones were safely 'coptered-out had dispelled many expectations of the peace and love so faithfully chronicled at Woodstock. Safety in numbers was no longer seen as an automatic attribute of, or guarantee from, the rock counterculture. Although viewed in many circles as a national disgrace, the Kent State shootings of college students had broken the back of the more militant anti-war movement.

Richard Nixon had celebrated his overwhelming electoral victory by raining bombs on Hanoi and Haiphong. In 12 days, beginning on the 18 of December, 36,000 tons of explosives were dropped on North Vietnam, exceeding a total of the three prior years. Fifteen B-52 bombers had been downed, and forty-four pilots captured. Nixon had ended the war with more war.

The Paris Peace Accords had been signed January 31, 1973. The agreement provided for U.S. withdrawal and the return of American prisoners-of-war. It was a "peace with honor." Who knew what that meant? Who knew who had won what? But we were out. Was it a premature evacuation? Who cared?

Where there had been heated confrontation, there was now hesitant conversation. In the absence of protest, came no test. It was time to stop thinking and start drinking. Anxious, dudes? Try quaaludes!

CHAPTER THIRTY

INVISIBLE DUCKS

The summer outdoor concert season had ended. Another local radio station approached me about doing a Country version of "Wild Wednesdays" on Labor Day. What the hell. They weren't really competitors. We agreed to a 50/50 split. The "WKMF Country Carnival" drew 4000. We had Bobby Bare, of "Detroit City" fame, and Jeannie Pruitt as major draws, and a dozen or so local country bands. Jeannie Pruitt had a #1 Country-Western hit with "Satin Sheets to Cry On." Jeannie sat in her mobile home as fans lined-up outside for autographs. "Look at 'em fuckin' squirrels," several members of her entourage reflected aloud. Well, they weren't all wrong.

The Country audience in Flint during this period was demonstrably rural in both background and predisposition. There were quite a few exceptions, but those were far in the minority. There was a pronounced lack of sophistication, and a tangible aura of subcultural angst highly evident and prevalent from the moment we opened the gates. The "WKMF Country Carnival" had been promoted as a family affair. That it was.

There were picnic tables, fold-up chairs, beer kegs and blazing grills as far as the eye could see. Little kids were running around everywhere with no obvious supervision, many falling into the lake completely unnoticed. There were near-drownings every five minutes. Frisky with whiskey, major fist-fights were breaking-out everywhere. Women were punching other women and pulling-off each other's wigs.

A number of younger couples had playfully headed back into a wooded area where, according to reliable sources, they were pulling down each other's pants and screwing their brains out in broad daylight, otherwise remaining fully-clothed and decent. Many families had brought their dogs along. These were starting to pack-up, rummaging through unguarded food baskets and over-turned trash cans with reckless abandon. My entire long-haired roadie team locked themselves in the record room and refused to come out without police protection. A giant of a man grabbed one of the country jocks and proudly announced that he was a "favorite fan." He demanded to meet Jeannie Pruitt. When it was allowed how that just wasn't in the cards, the son-of-a-bitch drew a foot-long butcher knife out of his pants. The "favorite fan" was arrested and brought downtown. He was back an hour later with three brothers. They were all hauled-in.

By the time the day ended, there had been a dozen arrests. Those detained were just the obvious ones who moved slowly and were caught. The park was a wreck. The net profit was a grand total of $200. Security costs had tripled due to a number of off-duty officers wisely called-in by Chief Rogers. Oddly enough, there were no serious injuries reported. The folks had obviously practiced this sort of thing before.

There was absolutely no disagreement from anyone that the "WKMF Country Carnival" had wrought more havoc and had engendered more flat-out trouble in 10 short hours than every "Wild Wednesday," "Super Sunday," and regular Rock 'n Roll concert ever held at the facility all put together. There was no press coverage whatsoever. The day went unknown by most and forgotten by almost all.

It was refreshing to return to the "wild" rock scene at Sherwood in the following months of autumn with Ted Nugent,

Bob Seger and other house bands running every other Sunday through the end of the year. On Thanksgiving Night, for the first time, I encountered serious head-on competition.

Edgar Winters' White Trash pulled in 900 at Sherwood Forest. It was a decent night, but only half a house. Alvin Lee and "Ten Years After" drew 5000 to the Flint I.M.A. Auditorium for Detroit promoter Bob Bageris, who had booked them in five cities with a guarantee of $20,000 per performance. He lost money on three of the shows, but made it back and a little more with the other two. That was reconfirmation of the new game. Only big action could play.

Bageris returned to the I.M.A. on December 8th with Fleetwood Mac opening for Deep Purple. He used WTAC as his exclusive advertising vehicle and I introduced both groups. If you can't beat 'em, greet 'em.

On Christmas Night back at Sherwood, REO Speedwagon defied horrendous weather conditions, including a major ice-storm, to play before another sold-out crowd. Their cover version of Chuck Berry's "Little Queenie" had already become a major Midwest hit and they were finally realizing long-awaited national recognition.

Instead of staging a concert, I decided to welcome in New Year 1974 with a party in my home on Concord Street in Flint. I had the basement area wired for serious sound, a most understanding wife and delightful daughters who knew nothing different. WTAC staff members mingled with my Sherwood Forest crew and other guests well into the following morning. A handful hung around for football games later in the day.

WTAC was still operating at a technical disadvantage to WWCK-FM, but we were countering with everything we could throw at them. Even psychological warfare was bought into play. I made it a habit of pulling into their parking lot on Lapeer Road late in the deep winter night and pounding on a studio window. When the disc-jockey on duty would look out, I'd wave and relieve myself on their lawn, penis-painting our WTAC call letters in the snow. My picture was posted in their control room on a dart-board. They knew who I was.

A challenge was suddenly presented when the ABC television network started their "In Concert" series Friday nights at 11:30. "In Concert" featured major rock acts performing for 90 minutes. That part was fine. What sucked was that rock FM stations were offered an opportunity to carry a simulcast of the program in stereo. That meant that Channel 12 in Flint would run the telecast, and fucking WWCK would get to do the simulcast. That would offer them a huge competitive advantage, in terms of image and marketing definition. One of the first "In Concert" telecasts would feature Alice Cooper. Goddamn it.

Well, now. What do we have here?

Satellite dishes at radio stations were still years in the future, and the "In Concert" television audio feed was monaural. The stereo signal could be delivered to FM partners over equalized phone lines from New York, somewhat expensive, or could be re-broadcast with network permission off a nearby ABC FM signal, providing one was available. Good old WRIF-FM, owned and operated by ABC, was right down the road from Flint in Detroit. A well-tuned quality receiver at WWCK could grab the WRIF signal, and patch it right in. Talk about saving money. It wasn't just the mechanics, but the art of utilization with which I was most gratified.

It was ridiculously easy constructing a twenty-watt audio generator which would oscillate for limited distance with a screeching roar on WRIF's exact 101.1 frequency. More difficult was rigging battery-powered operation, but only temporarily. The entire package fit handily into a Harley-Davidson saddle-bag. The Concert Associates were pleased to offer assistance. The first "In Concert" simulcast on WWCK went very well. For the first two minutes.

What the hell was wrong with them? Jesus Christ, you'd be totally into a group and then: "WAAAAAAAAAAHHHH."

It only lasted ten seconds or so. Everything would be fine again, then, look out. The noise would be back, but with rhythm, like someone was knocking on your door.

"Waah-Wawa-Wa-wa.Waach-WAAAAAAAAAAAAH."

It would leave again for 15 minutes, then come back in beat with the music. Alice Cooper might start playing "School Is Out." There it was.

"Wah-wah-wah; Wah-wah-wah-Wah-wah-wah-WAAAH."

A Concert Associate was riding up and down Lapeer Road wearing head-phones tuned to "The Riff," one hand on a switch in his saddle-bag. The WWCK FM receiver was straining to pick up every broadcast whisper from WRIF on 101.1, 50 miles distant. A flick of the wrist kicked on the "WAAAAAH" with substantially less originating power, but much closer proximity at the same frequency. Talk about coincidence. The exact scope and manner of interference had been discussed at length. There were only six "WAAAAAAAH" appearances during the initial simulcast, and none in the last ten minutes.

The WWCK folks couldn't figure out what the problem was. Maybe some kind of weird moon activity or something. Anyhow, it had disappeared at the end. Next week might be better.

Next week had nine interruptions, but the "WAAAAAAH" had become a

"THA-THA-THA-THA-THA-THA" "thumping" sound, like you'd just blown a tire. It would come and it would go. What the hell? ABC technicians couldn't figure it out. A WRIF engineer brought a brand new, highly calibrated receiver up to Flint for the third simulcast. It worked fine for fifteen minutes, and then on came the sonar.

"PUH-DI-DOW—CLANK. PUH-DI-DOW—CLANK. PUH-DI-DOW—CLANK."

Who turned on the submarine movie?

Word was out on the street all over town that you were much better-off just leaving the Channel 12 television audio up at full-blast for "In Concert" than listening to that stupid FM station with all the disruptive noises. What assholes. Word was also out that the WRIF guy and ABC had come to the conclusion that somebody might be intentionally generating signal interference. We left it alone for the next three weeks and then came back for the seventh broadcast with an attack by invisible ducks.

"QUACK-QUACK-QUACK! QUACKITY-QUACK-QUACK-QUACK!!

WWCK went to phone-line reception, but credibility had been damaged.

Intentional interference with a broadcast signal is a Federal felony, punishable by up to 5 years in jail and a $10,000 fine. Do not attempt this in your home. Unless you are a trained professional.

CHAPTER THIRTY-ONE

F.U.C.K.I.T.

Another Terry Knight group graced our Sherwood hall in late January.

Their claim to fame had been found in an incredibly successful record about remaining undetectably awake through a gruesomely prolonged, terrifyingly detailed experience of accidental and agonizing death. The cheerful little tune was called "D.O.A." Terry had appropriately named the group, "Bloodrock." They were surprisingly good musically, but all the crowd wanted to hear was their "hit." It was saved for the last number. The dirge-like sirens were particularly enjoyed.

"Bloodrock" was to return on Easter Sunday and draw another decent crowd, but they refused to play "D.O.A." They were trying to resurrect themselves from the dead professionally, and felt that the religious significance of the day might add moral endorsement to the effort. For the omission, they were soundly booed at the end of their performance. They broke-up a short time later.

The middle of March had been set aside for our annual WTAC Client Trip, wherein dozens of clients would receive a free vacation with the station to somewhere interesting, in return for purchasing more advertising than they really wanted or needed. This time the destination was Nevada. Any place good enough for Elvis was good enough for us. Viva Las Vegas. An entire plane had been leased for the journey. It had been airborne for under 5 minutes when two stewardesses came charging down the aisle, demanding to know who was "smoking marijuana?" They zoomed in on "B. C." like avenging angels of death.

"B.C." was William "Billy" Coleman. He already looked like Willie Nelson eventually would. If the long-hair, handlebar-mustache, red bandanna and purple shades didn't attract the attention of an anxious stewardess, the snakeskin cowboy-boots, orange sombrero and twelve-inch silver belt-buckle marked "F.U.C.K.I.T." might. Those things, and the fact that Billy had been passing ice-cold bottles of beer around the cabin after first opening them with his teeth, raised suspicion to convictive levels.

"F.U.C.K.I.T." was the name of B.C.'s "social club," which included many of our Concert Associates. It stood for "Fraternal Union of Casual Knights-Integrity Tomorrow." He was on the client trip as guest of John Smith, advertising manager of a local theater chain.

I had first met Mr. Coleman ten years earlier when he worked as top salesman at World-Wide Furniture Warehouse where WTAC did remote broadcasts from time to time. He had an extraordinary line of bullshit. Many were lured to the establishment by my irresistible broadcast offers of free records and hot-dogs. Billy had excelled at convincing those so enticed of their absolutely undeniable need for at least five or six rooms worth of cheap furniture. He wore expensive suits, had slicked-back hair, and used to drive two or three gorgeous women all over town in a brand new Lincoln convertible. "B.C." had been "born-again," but he had saved himself. He had become tired of the job and felt that money for purchases beyond the basic necessities of life just came down to points on a scoreboard. He could win anytime he seriously played anything, so why bother? If ever existed a "Rock 'n Roll Renaissance Renegade," it was "B.C." Billy's wallet was lovingly filled with pictures of his Triumph motorcycles. He supported himself as a projectionist, and specialized in removing a few seconds of intriguing moments from various films passing through his booth. These bits and pieces had been spliced-together into a stream-of-consciousness epic called "Tits and Creases." It was constantly being upgraded and improved upon as a continual work in progress. The current version ran approximately twenty minutes. I had included it in several WTAC "Midnight Madness" showings as a special bonus with excellent response and many requests for repetition.

Coleman lived in a old ramshackle, brown-shingled, dog-infested house almost falling into the Flint River near Flushing, Michigan. Billy referred to Flushing as "Toilet Town." He was definitely crazy Irish. We were bonded closely by genetic predisposition. Billy noticed the stewardesses and frantically beckoned them to approach quickly. He assumed a look of frustrated intensity and an attitude of patronizing impatience.

"Look, sir, we—"

"Ssshhhhhhhhhhhhhhhhhhhh!!!"

He reached in his vest and withdrew his "credentials." It was an impressive leather-folder. You could clearly make out the highly-visible "F.B.I." in bold, raised-lettering on the gold badge and an agent's picture on the card underneath. It looked very official. Prolonged inspection would have revealed small print which noted: "Fucking Bastards Incorporated." The photograph was that of an old man grinning at the camera with no teeth. Billy had found it in a magazine at his dentist's office. It was from an article on the dangers of periodontal disease. Billy flashed his identification and demanded rapt attention. It was granted.

Billy's voice was a strained whisper.

"Special Agent Coleman. Undercover."

The girls simultaneously bobbed their heads with excited appreciation.

"I've got a radio group. I've been on 'em for months. This is it."

The nodding increased.

"I need your complete cooperation. Don't stop anything these people are doin'. You're destroyin' government evidence."

Both stewardesses looked shocked and ashamed. Billy produced a small notebook and extended it.

"Here. Write down your names, addresses and phone numbers. I'll be in touch. Don't say a word to anyone about what we've discussed. This is a "Code Green" case!"

"Code green?"

"Green. How long have you known the pilot of this aircraft?"

The ladies looked at each other and one softly confided.

"We've flown with him before, but we don't really know him."

"Good. You both looked clean. Remember, not a word to anyone!"

"Yes, Sir." "Yes, Sir."

"Now, don't come near me again. Oh, and bring that guy with the glasses up there as much booze as he wants. He's one of the leaders. I need him loosened-up a little."

"Yes, Sir." "Yes, Sir."

We were ten minutes out of Flint, with three hours left to go.

Much of the "WTAC Las Vegas Adventure" is lost in a Technicolor blur, but I do recall highlights.

Upon arriving in Vegas, Coleman jumped me from behind as I passed through the terminal entrance and screamed "You're Under Arrest!" for the benefit of his stewardesses. Since I had not heard his exchange and was carrying an ounce of "Mother Nature's Finest," I was momentarily convulsed in raw terror.

Charlie Speights, again a single man, was changing female partners every twenty minutes. Everyone stopped keeping track.

John Smith, known to most as "Mr. Goodbar," lost his toupee on the giant bumper-cars at Circus Circus and made them stop the action so a thorough search could be conducted. It took 5 minutes. A crowd of spectators grew to several hundred. Word filtered though that there had been a fatality on the ride. A little kid found the hairpiece tightly wedged under a tire. It looked like a small, dead animal. Goodbar put it in his pocket and abandoned pretense of disguise for the rest of our stay.

We all went up to Mt. Charleston, just north of town, and rode horses. We then rented dirt-bikes and took them out into the desert. My wife Eileen spent 12 consecutive hours at the nickel slots.

Goodbar spent 15 hours at the dime slots.

Billy Coleman spent no time at the slots, but 10 minutes at "Blackjack" netted him $700. He retired from further gambling for the duration.

We partied. We drank. We smoked. We laughed.

No one slept.

On the last night, Charlie was missing. We split up into teams and combed the casino area. No Charlie. We checked in his room. Billy popped the lock in less time than it takes to read that he did. No Charlie. We looked in several other rooms where it was suspected he might be. Three were empty. A fourth revealed a couple enjoying mutual oral sex. Billy produced his ID and apologized for our presence. No Charlie.

Around 4:30 a.m., we abandoned our search and decided to have last call at the top of the Landmark. As we exited the elevator and approached the lounge, a wailing trumpet could be heard high above the din. It rose and fell in ecstatic release. Charlie!

He had brought his horn along to Vegas just in case. He had talked his way onto the bandstand and had been playing there for hours. He told us all later that he was sick of radio, and had always wanted to play horn in Vegas. He said that he was going to move there, and pretty damn soon. He wasn't kidding.

I introduced "The Guess Who" in April at the I.M.A. Auditorium. Burton Cummings sounded great, but Randy Bachman had left the group and was recording with a new outfit called "Bachman Turner Overdrive." They would shortly release an album called "Not Fragile." It would enjoy phenomenal success.

· A New York promoter brought The New York Dolls to the I.M.A. in June and lost a fortune. Less than 100 tickets were sold. The next day, I called the A.T.I. booking agency, and contracted with the opening band for a November 10 date at Delta College, near Saginaw. I had entered an agreement with the college to use Delta's gymnasium for a few productions in the new school year, needing a facility larger than Sherwood Forest for continued and slightly expanded enterprise. Although five months distant, I had been blown-away by what I saw. The opening group for the New York Dolls had their initial release coming out shortly. They were four nice boys dressed-up in the weirdest possible way, had unusual and highly creative stage effects and played basic, three-chord, ball-kicking, hard-core Rock 'n Roll as loud as the MC-5. If instinct demands, one must gamble. I obtained them for a guarantee of $1000 against 50 percent of the gate, including all expenses for sound and lights. I thought I would take a chance with a band called "KISS."

Our first '74 "Wild Wednesday" had been scheduled for June 24 at Sherwood Forest. With Bob Seger and Ted Nugent again heading the Michigan roster, I decided to close the show with another new band that had recently obtained enormous national radio exposure with their first album. They seemed just perfect in chemistry and content. A single release, "Rock The Nation," was in our WTAC Top Ten. Tracks called "Bad Motor Scooter" and "Rock Candy" were getting tremendous request action. The group was named after guitar player Ronnie Montrose. The lead-singer for "Montrose" was Sammy Hagar. In later years, Sammy would enjoy considerable fame as a solo artist, then find permanent membership temporarily with Van Halen.

The last "Wild Wednesday" crowd exceeded 10,000 and was a financial and artistic triumph. Everything went perfectly within the park. One mile to the west on Davison Road, an ambulance raced toward Sherwood Forest late in the day. It had been summoned by phone to a drug emergency, which was never later verified. It may well have been generated by a crank call from some anonymous irate citizen seeking to impact the day with unfavorably publicity. There had been many such calls. A soft, light rain had started falling, which went almost unnoticed on the grounds. It was enough. The ambulance slid out of control at a high rate of speed and the driver and his assistant were killed, leaving wives and children behind.

Media coverage didn't directly place blame on the concert, but the aftermath provided an emotional rallying point for those who sought to have "Wild Wednesdays" ended. Postures were assumed. I voluntarily pulled the plug. The latest controversy converged with the changing nature of the rock promotion industry. 1974 would have been our last season, regardless of community climate. Rock 'n Roll had outgrown Sherwood Forest and the "single point in time and space" had passed after five short, exciting, wonderful years.

It wasn't alone in change. On September 20, Charlie Speights announced his immediate departure for Las Vegas. He was packing all his worldly belongings in a '74 Buick Station Wagon and heading-out, taking along with him our 21 year-old, strikingly attractive station receptionist, "B.J." Furman. She would provide comfortable company.

"B.J." stood for "Barbara Jean" and she deeply resented casual joking about any other interpretation her initials might suggest. Ironically, "B.J." had lived only two blocks away from me in Syracuse when I grew up. Being a dozen years my junior, our paths had never crossed until she started working at WTAC in Flint. What a small world. She thought Charlie was just about the coolest guy she'd ever met. Charlie was equally enamored, and thought he probably wouldn't miss radio at all. He felt the whole business and, in fact, much of which seems important in life was only "snow on the water."

A horrible corporate accident accompanied Charlie's resignation. Fuqua Communications President Jackson Beaudry had died of a heart-attack a few months earlier. Fortunately, he was not felled by another FCC inquiry into "D-J Datebooks," but a sudden coronary brought on by normal broadcasting stress and strain, combined with high blood-pressure and decades of fine, deep-fried, home-cooked Southern food. He had been replaced by the Vice-President and General Manager of Channel Nine in Columbus, Mr. Joe Windsor, a tight, taciturn man with a sparse, gray crew-cut. Mr. Windsor had briefly stopped in Flint for no more than several hours in the midst of a whirlwind tour of all the broadcast properties via corporate jet and was, understandably, not that familiar with the operation. All he knew was that WTAC's Vice-President and General Manager was resigning to "play horn" in "Vegas" with "B.J." in tow. The official corporate chart indicated an immediate successor was available and one who had already secretly campaigned for the position behind Charlie's back.

Robert Nottingham Hill had been hired by Charlie as National Sales Manager. Later, "R. Nottingham," a sniveling, supercilious bore with dark, beady eyes, was made General Sales Manager just to stop his whining. He was from Chicago and had sent his resume directly to Jackson Beaudry, who had passed it on to Charlie. Charlie was impressed with the fact that Hill had worked for Empire Broadcasting, a corporation which enjoyed high reputation within the industry. He'd been released from employment following a personality conflict with a visiting engineer who, unknown to R. Nottingham, was a Corporate Vice President. Shit. They should wear uniforms or something. Hill was regarded by Charlie, most of the Sales Department and all of the Programming people as our "Station Honkie." We borrowed this black term of derision, since nothing else said it better. Hill hated long-hair, rock music and hippies. He despised "drugs," although he considered copious consumption of Canadian Mist a refreshing adult pastime. He walked out of Pine Knob Music Theater, just north of Pontiac, during a performance of "Hair" since they "desecrated the American flag." He had openly wept when Nixon left office.

Hill had been excited over the appointment of a new Fuqua President, since he hadn't made much of an impression on Jackson Beaudry, who always thought his name was "Hillingham." R. Nottingham had composed a Confidential Memo, which he sent to Mr. Windsor. This discussed at length all the things wrong with WTAC, and Charlie, and how Hill could straighten it all out. He said all the right things. The arrival of this communication coincided with Charlie's resignation. Joe Windsor thought the best thing to do was to set Charlie loose and give "Hillingham" a try. He immediately flew to Flint to effect the decision.

A staff meeting was called. Joe announced Charlie's resignation to a surprised staff and Hill's appointment to utter silence. I stood up and shook R. Nottingham Hill's hand in congratulation. Then I resigned on the spot. Five others followed suit immediately. After several weeks of negotiation, we all returned.

I had agreed to tolerate the appointment, but only if I could report directly to Joe Windsor on any matters concerning programming. Mr. Windsor had spent more time in Flint than planned, hearing negative testimony regarding his new General Manager from a number of employees. I met privately with Hill and told him he was a fucking jerk-off, but that I was prepared to accept him, providing he stuck to Sales, and developed product appreciation in an evident and detectable manner. Excited over his new designation as "Vice-President," he agreed. I made a mental note that has never been altered. People who seek titles are the last to deserve them.

In November, "KISS" drew a crowd of 8000 at Delta College with a $5 admission. Between my booking and the date, their first release had sold a million copies in its first few months and they were on television all the time. We had stopped selling tickets a week before the show.

I picked them up at the Tri-City airport and we headed for the gig, smoking several joints on the way. They were out of make-up and were playing "Name That Tune" with each other. I joined in and stumped them all with "The Theme from Navy Log." They had just seen "Texas Chainsaw Massacres" the night before and had been impressed and inspired. We drove past a large, cement, windowless building and they asked what it was. I had no idea, but told them it was the "Michigan School for The Blind." I had them for about three seconds. Gene Simmons then chuckled and called me an asshole as a few of the others fired up some hash. KISS gave a great performance. They exceeded my expectations many times over in becoming, arguably, the greatest rock "show-group" of all time. Get the "Firehouse!"

On December 19th, I presented Jim Dandy and "Black Oak Arkansas" at the I.M.A. The group cost $10,000 and, with percentage and expense considerations, I made around $50. The margin was disappearing. I was not allowed to open with a Flint or Michigan act. Any future concerts would have to be carefully structured and craftily booked with minimal risk. For the first time since 1969, nothing was planned for Christmas Night at Sherwood Forest.

Another New Year's Party at the Cavanaugh's ushered in '75 with clamor and class. B.C. got stuck crawling down a laundry chute. Goodbar accidentally locked himself in a broom-closet with two female WTAC employees and had to pound for release, an experience, I pointed out, with which he was undoubtedly quite familiar. Some guy no one knew had brought along three beautiful young ladies whose names he couldn't recall. Someone got their van stuck in the backyard a little before sunrise. Sandtrap Manager Mike Kahn dramatically produced a large tray covered with baking powder drawn into lines, which he immediately "accidentally" tipped-over. He tried to pretend it was spilled contraband covering the beer-soaked, whiskey-stained, hardwood floor. B.C. warned him about being sacrilegious. Who could have a better night? Well, I could. And only four weeks later.

CHAPTER THIRTY-TWO

MUSIC OF THUNDER

It was the best concert. This is surely a matter of personal, subjective taste. But, they were really on that night, and played for an uninterrupted three hours and 45 minutes with precision and perfection.

I had been curious as to how closely they could duplicate their heavily produced studio sound. It was surpassed in every instance. I was concerned they might be a little fatigued from their long road tour and/or excessive consumption of various substances rumored to offer relaxing measures of succor and solace during travels. I had worried for naught. I was anxious about seating arrangements. Atlantic Records had come through when it counted. Eileen and I were sitting in the center of the front-row.

It was at exactly 8 p.m. on Friday, January 31 of 1975, that the lights at Olympia Stadium in Detroit dimmed and four tall figures strolled confidently onto the stage. Launched with a thunderous explosion of sound, the mighty Zeppelin took flight.

Led Zeppelin had been formed nearly seven years earlier in July of 1968 by guitarist Jimmy Page, who had just left The Yardbirds. Page added singer Robert Plant, and drummer John Bonham from the little known British group "Band of Joy," and completed his assembly with a leading British session musician named John Paul Jones as bassist and keyboard player. Led Zeppelin had quickly stormed into the forefront of Heavy Rock with the release of their first album.

The band's name had been suggested by Flint car-sinking expert Keith Moon of the WHO. As was true of WHO, Led Zeppelin had always been essentially a musical trio with Robert Plant mainly limited to vocal contribution. That the sound had always been as big as it was, with only three primary players, had always been an awesome realization.

I had always believed there were a number of consciousness levels accessible through and evident within Led Zeppelin music. Zeppelin's primary definition and function as a "Rock 'n Roll Band" was surely beyond dispute. They obviously offered an enormously evident primal beat, powerfully throbbing throughout their more high volume efforts with unfailing presence and distinction. They were incredibly tight as a unit and could sweep through dimensions of intensity with singular thrust and total command. Their highly accomplished use of acoustical instrumentation offered yet greater focus, depth and unique musical originality. Even on the surface, it was obvious how the group generated mass audience appeal.

Deeper yet, I found them supremely spiritual. Through Led Zeppelin, I sensed a timeless essence had found expression and release.

In the ancient blood of some flow the genes and genius of masters, teachers, physicians and priests from a time when Druids walked the land and long before. Celtic mysticism enveloped the night. With both conscious and subconscious awareness, masterful words unveiled an absolute reality, both universal and beyond. Lyrical poetry and sweeping imagery spoke of many parallel worlds, all joined. With soaring sexuality, flesh and spirit became as one in an exuberant celebration of timeless existence and spaceless exaltation. In Led Zeppelin, rock music offered eloquent articulation of the unknown as merely unrecalled, expressing passionate human desire in both physical and metaphysical terms. I remain amazed that this singularly unique transcendence has never been fully appreciated, nor extensively explored.

Even before the Celts and their Druids had come Tuatha De Danann. People of the Goddess. Children of the Light. To Olympia came Led Zeppelin. Ceol Toirni. The Music of Thunder.

Excuse the heavy here, but we're dealing with Zeppelin.

From "Rock 'n Roll" (been a long time since I did "The Stroll") through a final encore with "How Many More Times?" Zeppelin never stopped. As a psychogenic aside, I watched the entire performance completely straight. We had charged down to Detroit from Flint with little time to spare. My stash had been inadvertently left behind in the rush. It was just as well. I would have mind-melded into the amp circuits. In addition to all of their most familiar material, the group introduced large segments of a soon-to-be-released double-album. It was thus I first heard much of "Physical Graffiti" with virginal ears.

That night in Detroit, I was ruined for life. The measure of excellence established on stage by Led Zeppelin was so far superior to anything I had ever heard before, it automatically became a new standard with which all to come would be subjectively compared. As of 2002, "The Song Remains The Same."

In March of '75, I visited Delta College again with "Styx." "Lady" had established them as a rising national act. We filled 6000 seats.

On Easter Sunday, we presented a rare Sherwood Forest concert with Bob Seger. Bob's new "Live Silver Bullet" album, recorded at Cobo Hall in Detroit, was about to be released, and would finally break him all the way nationally, putting him up there with Alice. Although most of the material represented old Michigan hits, it was all brand new to the rest of the world. After more than ten years of public performance, he was about to become an overnight success. It was Bob's last appearance at Sherwood, and one of mine as well.

WTAC's Flint ratings remained stable, although WHNN-FM in Bay City was now tearing up the Tri-Cities with their own FM Rock format and impacting heavily on our listenership to the north. Shit. Goddamn Armstrong.

37-CAVA

In September, I brought Bob Seger to Delta College. He sold-out the house with 8000 in attendance. It would be our last time working together. He was heading for the stratosphere, and would shortly be commanding $100,000 nightly guarantees. No one had ever deserved it more.

An Ann Arbor booking agent had invited me down for a concert at University of Michigan's Hill Auditorium. A new artist had just been released on the Columbia label, and word was out that something special was happening. I agreed, after seeing Bruce Springsteen and his E-Street Band. Bruce was on the covers of both Time and Newsweek within a month.

On the first of October, new owners bought WWCK-FM, along with WCZN-AM. They were from the Toledo area and owned WIOT-FM, which had started making major waves in that market. They intended to take Flint by storm.

CHAPTER THIRTY-THREE

BUYING TIME

Reams Broadcasting was owned by Frazier Reams, Junior. Frazier was a former Ohio State Senator and had run for Governor in 1968 on the Democratic ticket. He lost to the ever popular Jim Rhodes and decided to devote a career to broadcasting, buying the Toledo stations from his father, a former Ohio Congressman and Lucas County Prosecutor. Frazier's Dad had put the Toledo AM on the air on April 10, 1938, and the FM in October of 1949. Had Frazier been elected Governor of Ohio, he would have been holding office instead of his opponent when Rhodes called in the Ohio National Guard at Kent State.

Frazier Jr. had also purchased WKBZ-AM in Muskegon, Michigan. He liked the area, and had often traveled through Muskegon heading toward his summer cottage at Harbor Springs on Grand Traverse Bay in Lake Michigan. To buy the Muskegon station, he also had to purchase an AM/FM combination in Cumberland, Maryland. He quickly spun the pair off due to geographic inconvenience. It was not on his way to anything interesting.

Frazier had entered into partnership with Jim O'Donnell, a former General Manager of Toledo's WSPD. Jim owned a little piece of Toledo, but would share equally in the Flint stations. O'Donnell was the actual operations person and tried to impress the Flint community with his partner's impressive political credentials, referring to Frazier around town as the "Titular

Head of the Ohio Democratic Party." I started telling everyone that WWCK-FM had been purchased by "Tits," having never met the man. I had yet to make Mr. O'Donnell's acquaintance either, but felt I should properly introduce myself.

One of the first things WWCK's new ownership had done was radically slash their rates for concert advertising, and offer anything required for station involvement in live rock presentations. This was an excellent move on their part and one which could cost WTAC heavily— both in advertising revenue and future promotional opportunities. It was time for a neighborly visit.

I phoned WWCK's General Manager, introducing myself in the friendliest of fashions. I asked when Mr. O'Donnell might be in town and suggested that the three of us get together and discuss my purchase of commercial advertising on their station to promote "Peter C. Cavanaugh Concerts" on WWCK-FM. The GM almost shit. He certainly knew who I was. They still had that dartboard up in their studio. WTAC's Program Director becoming a client and buying time on their station? The potential credibility factor with other clients was huge.

A meeting was quickly arranged for the following afternoon. Jim O'Donnell was specifically driving-up from Toledo to be in attendance. I had done considerable research on the Reams organization and specific characteristics of major players. Mr. O'Donnell was certainly Irish, and I was counting on that fact, since the very best bullshit can only be verbalized.

Owing to the fact that I had become much more versed in FCC law than I would have ever preferred, as a result of our Spiro Agnew Letter, I was particularly familiar with various interpretations of Commission policies relating to station involvement in conjunction with the promotion of live events. I had obtained actual copies of proposals made to other area promoters by the new management of WWCK in writing. I was ready to rock.

Wearing my standard black leather jacket, jeans and T-shirt, I pulled into the WWCK parking lot for the first time in daylight. I walked toward the building with a look of grim resignation, surrendering to the inevitable. Met at the door by Mr. O'Donnell, I was ushered into their General Manager's office, which had once belonged to the Methodist Bishop of Flint. They brought me coffee and donuts. They asked about my family. They just couldn't have been any nicer. I told them I was prepared to cut a deal on the spot and seal it with a check for $1000 in advance if terms were right. I clearly sensed erections. Jim talked for over 30 minutes and I asked a series of innocent questions. I was assured about any number of things and obtained important commitment in several key areas. It sure sounded good to me.

We shook hands and I handed Mr. O'Donnell my $1000 check. He examined it carefully. He smiled. He turned it over and saw the entire reverse-side covered in astonishingly small print. He read it suspiciously. He frowned. I had gone to great lengths in attempting to cover all bases and had succeeded in addressing all central issues. There were several major stipulations which endorsement of the check would certify. Nothing was mentioned that hadn't already been guaranteed in our talk. Why the hesitation?

"What's wrong?"

There was silence.

"The money's good!"

His manager looked confused. O'Donnell looked plenty pissed.

Jim's acceptance and endorsement of the check would have handed me his family jewels on a platinum platter. He had told me many things in his enthusiasm to bring my business on board. All I had asked is that he sign a statement attesting to his veracity, albeit unconventionally drafted on the back of a check. He promptly returned the check and left the room. I asked Mr. Manager to bring him back immediately or really get fucked. He passed along the message, and Jim returned.

I congratulated Mr. O'Donnell on his new opportunities in Flint and discussed FCC guidelines as I understood them. I was speaking as an individual entrepreneur, not as WTAC's Program Director. I outlined a letter of complaint I could instantly draft to the Commission based on information I had already obtained, which existed completely independent of our little meeting. Of course, I would reference our conversations as well, even fully expecting he would completely deny many aspects. Mr. O'Donnell asked me what I wanted. My proposition was an even playing field, which I described in great detail. Agreement was reached. Obviously, I would not be advertising on WWCK. I thanked both gentlemen for their time and courtesy and took my leave. I had made a large impression, yet would not recognize its real importance for another four years. Meanwhile, WTAC rocked-on with more restrained competition. R. Nottingham received a full report and was quite pleased.

20 WTAC staff members and guests journeyed with me in December to Detroit's Cobo Hall for a spectacular performance by The WHO. It was the first time I'd seen them since the Bristol Road Holiday Inn. They were magnificent, and had set up rear stadium speakers for full multi-channel effect during their "Quadrophenia" segment. It was outstanding and I did remember to bring my smoke along.

1976 was to be the United States of America's Bicentennial Year. Bringing it in called for special celebration. With my brother Paul and his soon-to-be-wife Cindy visiting from Syracuse, we all journeyed to the new Silverdome Stadium near Pontiac to finally see Elvis Presley. He was in fine voice, but his pants split during the second number and there was a brief pause required for necessary replacement. It had been 20 years and over 100 pounds since we first heard "Heartbreak Hotel." We watched him with sad excitement. He had been the first, and wouldn't last.

The main thing on our early WTAC 1976 agenda was a long-shot. We wanted our own Flint FM station.

I had spoken with Joe Windsor on many occasions about technological inevitability. "AM Rock" was on borrowed time.

The FCC had approved a new FM frequency for Flint. There were many applicants, but I felt that Fuqua should take its best shot and go with an "experienced broadcasters in the market approach." It was the sort of opportunity we had to go for. The investment was minimal compared with the possible score. We were competing against three other major opponents for the license. It was eventually won by a local black group.

Michael Moore came by the station in February and I helped him put together some production for his "Davison Hotline." Michael enjoyed the distinction of being the youngest elected public official in Michigan state history. He had become a member of the Davison Board of Education at the age of 18, offering to annoy the establishment as his most specific campaign promise, and surprising many with his win, including himself. He had established the "Hotline" as an intervention service for teens, and had started publication of a "Hotline Newsletter" which was gaining wide circulation.

Michael and I had met several times before at Township Meetings when officials were trying to put both of us out of business for separate, although similar, reasons. A common enemy establishes instant alliance. Michael was Irish too. He was at one time on his way to the priesthood, and eventually might have been Bishop of Buffalo, were he not asked to leave his seminary. He had been listening to a transistor radio, under his bedsheets, as the Detroit Tigers eventually beat Saint Louis in the 1968 World Series; such nocturnal activity was forbidden. Michael felt he would have been better regarded for simply masturbating to Playboy by flashlight or candles. He testified this was a pastime not completely unknown in theological environs.

337-CAVA

CHAPTER THIRTY-FOUR

LONG WAY TO THE TOP

As exciting a year as The Bicentennial was from a national perspective, things had settled down to happy humdrum at WTAC in Flint. The station continued to maintain position against upstart WWCK-FM, even with their new ownership. In February, I attended a "Radio and Records" Convention in Atlanta, which is primarily memorable from the absence of clear memory.

"Radio and Records" was the new hot weekly trade publication. Record company suites were lavishly stocked and stacked. A number of us walked from the Convention site at the Peachtree Hotel to the Atlanta Underground against all advice. It was reputedly through the worst part of town. No one came near us, our behavior being too bizarre and boisterous to invite even malicious intervention.

We saw "Junior Walker and the All-Stars" at some dinky little bar, and visited what seemed like at least a dozen strip-joints, being asked to leave almost every one. A pistol-packing Southern friend shot-out at least a dozen street lights and killed a giant "Mr. Peanut" statue with three to the heart. It must have been the worst part of town. We didn't see a cop for hours, and only then to politely ask directions back to the hotel. That a fine time was had by all, is my best general summation.

The Sunday concerts at Sherwood Forest were now a thing of the past. Although local Rock 'n Roll bands were in plentiful supply, major drawing power was virtually non-existent. Audiences still remained only interested in seeing their favorites. These were now exclusively available in 5000+ capacity halls. I filled my weekend schedule with high-school dances, wedding receptions and other appearances which provided a steady income stream with no financial risk, still tripling my radio station salary. I was back at Sherwood Forest in June for a private Southeast Michigan Fraternal Order of Police Party, having become their regular disc-jockey for the annual affair. It was always scheduled from 9 'til 1, but would normally end just before dawn. I knew most of the officers and could be counted on for absolute discretion.

Our big WTAC Spring Promotion was giving away a "Coca-Cola Denim-Machine," which was really a prototype for glamour vans of the future. The cocksucker had everything. It was valued at over $30,000 when a brand new Cadillac could still be yours for under $15,000. We staged a Super-Drawing for the final winner at Flint's Small Mall on South Dort. Over 5000 people showed-up— most since Bob Seger had agreed to personally conduct the drawing at my request. Bob drove himself up from Detroit and we rendezvoused in the parking lot of the same Holiday Inn on Bristol Road that had housed The WHO. I whisked him to the drawing and back in under 30 minutes. He hated that sort of bullshit, and had agreed only as a personal favor for which I remain deeply appreciative.

Although Robert Nottingham Hill and I continued to maintain a working relationship, things were becoming strained with other staff members. Air personality Pete Flanders resigned, primarily because he couldn't stand the man. "The Cat" had established a successful disc-jockey service with several of his own employees and could afford departure. "Who needs the headache?" pondered Flanders.

Tom Roberts, an outstanding performer, accepted a position in Knoxville, Tennessee, rather than deal with "the asshole" any longer. Tom took the time to hide dozens of little notes all around the building which were still being uncovered years into the future. They said things like "R. Nottingham Hill Blows Goats" and other uncomplimentary allegations. Hill was becoming universally despised. Sales people were quitting, clients were complaining, and union members were discussing a variety of collective notions. Sullen management has always been organized labor's fastest friend. '76 gave way to '77 with barely a bang, then the bucks started really rolling in.

A sudden boom in the national economy was reflected in massive overtime for Flint auto workers and, as was always true in the past, local business exploded. WTAC was sold-out and monthly billings soared. The station had never done better financially, and Fuqua Communications was delighted. Robert Nottingham Hill took virtually sole credit and felt enormous job security. He determined it was time to set a few things straight.

One Friday morning, I left the air and went to breakfast with several record people I had known for years. Ours had become a personal, as well as professional, relationship, and I felt no particular rush to get back to the station. After a long and casual meal, they expressed disbelief that an "X-Rated" theater had just opened in the heart of downtown Flint. Lest my credibility be damaged, I felt obliged to bring them there. We spent 45 minutes or so verifying the fact that the film being shown did, in fact, deserve "XXX" designation, and then returned to the station. They bade me farewell in the parking lot, and headed-out for Lansing and Grand Rapids. I entered the building and, walking toward my office, glanced at "the spindle" atop our receptionist's desk.

"The spindle" was where phone messages were left for all. Normally, it would contain a dozen or so little pink "notation slips" marked with appropriate information. This day, along with regular messages, there was one from R. N. Hill to Peter Cavanaugh, written in bold, angry slashes. It told me that I was never to again leave the building without his permission during regular office hours, and that he was furious with me for having done so. He informed me that there would be no repeats. Or else. Mother Fucker.

Thursday, March 17, was an unusually splendid St. Patrick's Day. Joe Windsor had agreed to fly into Flint and meet with me the following day.

The next morning, I signed-off my final program on WTAC. The last song I played was "Houses of the Holy" by Led Zeppelin. I met with Mr. Windsor for five hours. At 5:25 p.m., an abundantly confident R. Nottingham Hill became aware of Joe's presence in Flint. At 5:30, he was fired. I was appointed Vice President and General Manager. It had never been a position I had sought, but one that I would accept. It was a heavily qualified victory. I was the "boss," but at great loss. After twenty years in radio, I was off-the-air.

Mr. Windsor left town and I had a number of meetings at my home over the weekend with staff members. I had decided to allow Hill decent time to remove personal effects from the building. On Monday morning, I arrived at the station to find Mr. R. Nottingham still occupying the General Manager's office. He informed me that he would be out possibly by the end of the week. I told him he had 15 minutes. At the end of that time, he and anything his still remaining would be thrown in the trash. He left immediately.

I appointed Bob Vanderweil as General Sales Manager and Jay "Jammer" Johnson became WTAC Program Director.

Bob Vanderweil was not only our best producer, but the finest naturally-gifted salesperson I had ever met. He had been a driver, then union-organizer, and finally a member of management and Vice President with Vernor Ginger Ale in Detroit. The company was sold, and he was discarded in the aftermath. He was in his early fifties, and had been hired in 1969 to sell advertising for WTAC at a guarantee of $100 a week against a fifteen percent commission. For his first six months at WTAC, he didn't even have his own desk. Bob would say, "All I know about radio is that it gets louder when you turn it up." He was a tough, gnome-like Dutchman with a thick mustache and a heart of gold.

After one year, Bob was the #1 biller at WTAC. Following another few years, Bob was bringing in such an astounding amount that his personal income greatly exceeded that of the General Manager. This was a fact in which Charlie Speights had taken great pride, and which R. Nottingham Hill openly loathed. I had always greatly admired and respected Bob. His sales technique was that he had no fixed method. He just made friends and influenced people, without ever really thinking about it. I was one of his accounts at the station for concert advertising. At every Wild Wednesday, Vanderweil worked the gate, refusing to accept any compensation. He did that sort of thing for all his clients. Late one night, after many drinks, I seriously asked him what his secret was in breaking every sales record in the history of Flint radio. He didn't hesitate in providing an honest answer. "It's all the things I do for free," he said. "The things I do for free!" Trade magazines would later echo with fanfare over "Value Added Selling." Bob provided exactly that with natural flare.

Vernon Popovich had started his radio career in Port Huron, and sent an audition tape to WTAC in early 1974. I received dozens of such tapes every month, and would listen to them all, most for less than ten seconds. When I put on Mr. Popovich's tape, I played the entire five minutes. What? Huh? The guy sounded sensational. He had an extremely resonant voice and exceptional announcing skills. We had an opening on the "All Night Show." I called Port Huron, and arranged an appointment with him for the following afternoon at WTAC.

When Vernon arrived, a number of staff members rolled their eyes as he walked through the building. What a straight-ass. He was wearing a suit and a tie and had really short hair. He looked like an accountant. I closed my office door and we talked. He was from the Detroit suburb of Lincoln Park, had gone to "radio school," and had successfully obtained his first job in Port Huron. He was looking to move-up, but there was one stipulation given. Popovich looked at me intently. He wished to tell me way up front that he would leave any station that gave up Rock 'n Roll. That's all he ever wanted to play. That was more important to him than shift-time, salary, call-letters or working conditions. I hired Mr. Popovich on the spot. We changed his name to Jay "Jammer" Johnson.

"Jammer" was so damned good, I shot him right into afternoon-drive after just four weeks. Vernon quickly became "Jammer." Out went the suit and tie. The hair grew long, not only on his head, but facially as well. "Jay Johnson" soon sported a great mustache and full "Jammer" beard. He combined talent with vision. There was no doubt he could become an extraordinary programmer.

"Jammer" and I would shortly attend a "Radio and Records" Convention in Dallas. It was there at a cocktail party we met Dr. Timothy Leary. Here was another Irishman just hanging around. I asked him if he would care to step outside and smoke a doobie with us. He was happy to do so. I had saved some special smoke for just such an occasion. It was almost hallucinogenic.

A third absolutely key employee in my new administration was not a member of management, and had almost been fired several times by my predecessor for insubordination, bad manners and continual rudeness. R. Nottingham Hill had refrained from termination, only because of raging insecurities brought forth in confrontations with this terrible employee (as he had noted in her personnel records), and a reluctance to interview other "ethnics" in searching for a replacement. R. Nottingham had also officially documented an instance when she had been violent toward him by throwing a pencil, the point of said object having become temporarily imbedded in his leg below the knee.

Bernice Fordham was WTAC's black receptionist. "Miss B." was the coolest. She was the smartest. She was incredibly street-hip, acutely perceptive, and wonderfully aggressive. She had two sons at home, of whom she was most proud and a husband named Tyrone, of whom she was not. They were in the process of divorce. Miss B. and I had always hit it off. We continually compared notes on life in general and the radio station in particular. I had come to value her friendship, and trust her judgment.

On my second day as General Manager, I was heading to work on Hill Road when I noticed Bernice's old Buick pulled off the road behind a Grand Blanc Township police car. There were two officers standing there with Miss B. She was handcuffed from behind. I slammed on my brakes, leapt out of my vehicle and jumped right into the middle. She had been stopped primarily because she was a black woman. The police had run a spot-check, and were arresting her. I was nose-to-nose with a red-faced, fat-necked, uniformed prick. I found myself screaming at the top of my lungs.

"You're fucking arresting her for what? Prick!"

Admittedly, wild anger momentarily ruled-out common sense, or even the slightest pretense of courtesy or respect. The handcuffs and their manner of application had done it. I was told that it was none of my business and that I would be arrested at once if I didn't leave immediately.

"Arrested? Fuckin' arrested? Asshole! Cuff me from behind! Maybe you just save that for black women?? I wasn't lost enough in fury to ignore certain cards. I played them all at once.

"I'm with fuckin' WTAC and this is our receptionist, Bernice Fordham. If you don't tell me what she's fuckin' doin' with those fuckin' cuffs behind her back, I'm going to ask the same fuckin' question on the fuckin' air in exactly three fuckin' minutes! Start countin'!" The other officer reminded me that I knew him. Shit, I did. The gear-shift was automatic.

"Hey, sorry for the screamin', but this is a fine lady. She's my friend. What's the deal?"

I was told that Bernice was stopped for a so-called "routine check," and that a Bench Warrant had been issued for her in the City of Flint. Tyrone owed $12 in Income Taxes. They had filed jointly. She was busted in his absence. I spoke further, and with restrained heat. The handcuffs were removed. Since they had already reported Bernice as apprehended, I followed them downtown to Flint City Hall. Things were expedited. I paid the $12 and a $10 late penalty. Miss B. was released. We retrieved her car, and went to work.

Later that morning, the Grand Blanc Township Chief of Police arrived at the station to offer profound apologies. I asked Miss B. to join us. His boys had been right, but wrong. She smiled. That same afternoon, Miss B. received a dozen red roses from the arresting officers. She smiled. At the close of business, a fifth of premium Chivas Regal appeared on my desk with a note from Miss B. It said, "Thanks!" I smiled. We worked together well. She was my eyes and ears. Nothing escaped attention.

I felt being a General Manager was nothing much. Although I was putting in 12-14 hour days, it never seemed like "radio." I had always thought of "radio" as wearing headphones and broadcasting. Anything else I had ever done seemed a prelude or postscript to an air shift. It was like being the "President of the Student Council" again. Joe Windsor had brilliantly summarized my responsibilities with three simple instructions:

(1) Protect the license.
(2) Keep up the rates.
(3) Collect the money.

Interestingly enough, as proven through time, that does cover just about everything.

The Spring 1977 Arbitron for Flint was released in early July. For the first time in history, WTAC-AM was beaten by WWCK-FM in total listenership. WTAC dropped from an 8.8

percent share to a 6.0 percent. WWCK had risen from a 5.1 percent to a 7.3 percent.

Fuck.

We had successfully beaten FM Rock for over five years, holding on to our contemporary franchise far longer than most. Even the renowned CKLW had fallen victim to WRIF-FM in Detroit two years before.

This was no consolation.

Then, Elvis was dead. The King of Rock 'n Roll passed away on his Memphis throne August 16th. WTAC produced a "Tribute Program," but we only played tunes from the Sun Records era, and his first two years with RCA. The first cut we aired after news of his death arrived was "Mystery Train."

Elvis had changed my life. The first record I ever bought was "Heartbreak Hotel." I remembered playing it over and over again in wonder, intently focused on my bedroom mirror, frantically imitating his moves. I'd seen him on "The Tommy Dorsey Show" and on Ed Sullivan. I vividly recall contemplating the challenge of ever explaining to future generations his impact and inspiration. For a 14 year-old kid, this was a reflection even more curious than the one in the mirror. I did quite poorly. All my daughters thought Elvis Presley was a fat, tired, ugly old man.

The only truly outstanding and personally rewarding musical moment of 1977 came December 5 at the Capitol Theater in Flint. It was my last "Peter C. Rock 'n Roll Presentation."

I had become very enamored with a new band just before I left the airwaves. Ron Counts, representing Atlantic Records, knew my taste in music, and had brought me an advance copy of their first release. Going nuts, I programmed almost every cut, especially one that sounded as though the lead-guitar had been replaced by a bagpipe. I told Ron that it was the best new product I had heard in years. The music was clean and raw; direct and basic. WTAC was the first station to play the band in America, and the album had sold more copies in Michigan than anywhere else in the country as a consequence. When the group announced their first U.S. tour, I called Joe Windsor. Although I had agreed to abandon any future personal promotional efforts as part of my ascension to the new highly-paid and well-compensated General Manager's position, I had to bring this group to Flint. I told Joe that I would do it as a benefit performance, with all proceeds going to Michael Moore's Davison Hotline. Joe asked me to promise it was a one-time request. I did so without remorse. This was how I wanted to end it.

I wanted to do "The Best of The Old with The Best of The New." I decided to contact the old MC-5, who had briefly reformed, and use them as the only opening act. They agreed. The "Best of The New" were picked up at the airport in Flint early in the evening. No sooner had they all piled in my car, than someone fired-up something in the back-seat.

"You want a 'it, Mate?"

Sure. Why not?

It was a Winston.

These were boys from Australia. To them, an American cigarette was something to be shared. I took a "'it," and passed it back.

A major snowstorm had moved into the area earlier in the day, and it took 45 minutes to reach the downtown area— at least double normal travel time. Roads were becoming blocked by snow and attendance had been limited by conditions to less than five hundred. The group was still virtually unknown. Who cared? I knew the night would be historic.

MC-5 performed a superb fifty-minute set. Our Australian visitors sat in the theater and were dazzled. There was a brief intermission for equipment change, then I killed every light in the theater. Everything was jet-black. The theater was utterly dark and ominously promising.

It started with a single, pounding, thundering bass note; droning in constant repetition. Dum-Dum-Dum-Dum-Dum-Dum-Dum-Dum-Dum-Dum-Dum-Dum.

BAAAAAAAAAARRAAAAAANNNNNNNNNNNGGGGG!!

The screaming lead-guitar came in out of nowhere. It was "Live Wire." Four spotlights instantly flooded the stage, all focused on and following a remarkably-strange, rapidly-moving, seemingly-possessed apparition. He wore knickers. He was dressed as a proper English schoolboy with necktie and knapsack. His head bounced as though about to become disengaged. He ran back and forth in circles around the other players, the intensity building and volume rising with every stroke of the guitar. He was barely out of his teens. His name was Angus Young. His high voltage band had been christened in reference to alternating and direct electrical currents, both common in familiar housing "Down Under." It seemed a nice name. AC/DC had come to Flint.

They played for over 90 minutes. The audience wouldn't let them leave. The MC-5 watched in wonder. AC/DC's final encore was the "bagpipe" song, the bagpipe being a guitar effect obtained through processing. Bon Scott belted-out the title.

"It's a Long Way To The Top If You Want To Rock 'n Roll!!"

I paid them $1000 in cash. They wanted to try some "Arby's Roast Beef," so we stopped at the nearest location, still open despite horrible weather. They bought packs of cigarettes by the dozen and emptied-out several brands from a machine. They loved the Arby's sandwiches, both for food and as projectiles. Since we were the only patrons and had tipped heavily, there was no hassle. I dropped them off at their hotel and extended sincere thanks. My last concert had been among the very best. They were equally appreciative. Their U.S. appearance had gone well. They had enough American cigarettes for weeks to come, no matter what.

A few months later, the boys were back in town. I traveled to a Detroit suburb and caught AC/DC opening for Ireland's Thin Lizzy at the Royal Oak Music Theater. The Aussies were most excellent, but I noticed marked sound mix peculiarities near the middle of their scheduled set. Things were becoming unbalanced, first upon my ears and then before all eyes. Out of nowhere, several security guards rushed onto the stage and attempted to conclude the performance. It was all fiercely fast. Suddenly, the music discordantly ceased. One uniformed enforcer made the tragic mistake of grabbing Bon Scott's arm. A violent head-butt sent the uninvited transgressor flying backward, then down and out. Chaos reigned. More police poured out on the stage. The group formed an immediate protective circle, rapidly expanding as AC/DC proceeded to kick super-serious ass. Even several members of Thin Lizzy joined the fray in unrestrained Rock 'n Roll reinforcement, advancing upon the uninvited intruders from behind. Feet flashed. Fists flew. Foreheads filled faces.

A phalanx of record company and management personnel somehow introduced themselves into the midst of the melee and separated participants, much to the relief of those few authority figures still unmarred. Confusion was abound. It was clear the group had no idea what had triggered so unpleasant an incident. The band members had reacted with instinct, not intent. It turned out to be a noise thing.

Neighbors near the theater had been complaining. The City of Royal Oak had passed a local ordinance proclaiming any sound level over 100 decibels as noise, and therefore a nuisance. An official "Decibel Deputy" had arrived on the scene and, standing next to the AC/DC sound board at the very back of the building, had clocked the lads in at 125 and climbing. Their sound man, responding to a tap on the shoulder and barely hearing the word "loud" screamed into his ear, joyously responded; "Ahhhh, yeah, man. And we're just startin' to cook!" There was a firm punch for attention delivered on the audio technician's back. The "Decibel Deputy" was dropped with a heel to the heart. Three security police dragged the offender off the monitor platform and, assisted by several others, effected arrest. This is where the sound mix got screwy. They ordered the performance to stop. That's when the stage went wild. The crowd was now in total uproar. Miraculously, calm heads prevailed. Charges forgotten, technician unfettered and sound restored, the group returned to their set.

I sent a formal telegram to the group the following day apologizing for all the "dainty little ears" they had encountered in our fair Michigan. They responded with a note expressing appreciation for my support. The "Battle of Royal Oak" had ended with encores.

The war for Flint listenership was now at fever pitch.

CHAPTER THIRTY-FIVE

DECISIVE ACTION

For the next major ratings period, WTAC pulled-out all the stops. Nothing was overlooked. We posted billboards all over town and ran television campaigns.

I created an updated version of a spot I had produced several years before, which had won a number of Gold Ad Club Awards in the "Television" category— the only time a local radio station had achieved such distinction. It had featured 152 edits in thirty seconds, synchronized to the closing beats of "Boogie With Stu" from Zeppelin's "Physical Graffiti." I had my MTV six years before it ever hit cable.

WWCK couldn't touch our promotions. We offered 10 days on the road with Alice Cooper and flew a couple to London, England, with Bob Seger for his European Debut at the Palladium. We gave away 300 seats in a special "WTAC Section" at Pontiac Silverdome for Led Zeppelin. There was exciting contesting, innovative prizes, and excellent listener involvement. The station library was trimmed to only the most proven material. Air presentation was impeccable. We were awake and ON 24 hours a day.

We got killed.

The morning the Spring '78 Arbitron was released marked the worst day in my entire professional career. WTAC dropped from the 6.0 percent to a 5.4 percent share. WWCK had rocked and rocketed from their 7.2 percent to a 12.5 percent. They had not only trounced us, they had maimed us better than two-to-one.

FUCK!

I was in agony.

I called Joe Windsor, the worst news always to be delivered as quickly as the best. I gave him the numbers, and expressed my sorrow and frustration. I admitted I had no answers and offered my resignation. He told me I was silly, and to take the rest of the day off. He said we'd talk the following morning.

He called the next day shortly after our offices opened. He said that he'd checked-around. WTAC was still doing better than most other AM operations with a Top Forty format. He reminded me that I had predicted years before that FM superiority would finally win the day. He had thought I was wrong at the time. My point had now been proven, albeit in a personally painful manner. Joe Windsor then gave me the best advice I had ever received.

"Peter, you learn a lot of things in the military."

Joe had landed in Italy during World War Two and had fought his way through Sicily and up past Rome. He was transferred to the German front, and had scratched and clawed all the way toward Berlin. I had gone back along with him several late nights over copious quantities of memory-enhancing Scotch. Mr. Windsor was a superior story-teller, and I had always found myself fascinated by his war stories. The guy had been there. What's more, he had married a General's daughter. I was certain he had the answers to our dilemma. Alright!

"Peter, listen carefully."

"Yes, Sir!"

"When you're in the military and you're commanding artillery fire, you have to keep adjusting trajectory on your target."

"Yes, Sir."

"You change your azimuth and your zenith, and you keep firing until you hit it!"

"Yes, Sir."

"But, sometimes, that just won't work. There are times that come when, no matter how much you try or work or care, that target still can't be hit. And what you do then in the military is what you need to do right now at WTAC!"

He had me breathless. And clueless.

"What's that, Sir?"

"Resort to initiative, and take BOLD, DECISIVE ACTION!!"

With those words, he hung-up the phone.

I was shaken. I was stunned. I was inspired.

I spent the next several days in severe meditation. Joe was right. Things just weren't working, and had to be changed to something which would. My job was to be creative, and determine a new type of programming weaponry. Then, I was ordered to attack boldly without fear or hesitation. Damn. Whatever we did, we would take no prisoners. I decided to review every reality.

We were pounding out heads against a pure Rock 'n Roll wall. As much as I loved the music form, I had to admit it sure sounded better in FM stereo, and to think otherwise was foolish. Although WTAC had leaned much heavier into rock than most Top Forty stations, at least half of our music in daytime hours still properly fell into other categories. If a song was selling singles, you could hear it on WTAC. We could not deny the continuing dilemma, only partially addressed years before with the WTAC Underground. It was the same problem, magnified through time.

An AC/DC barn-burner might be segued into "I Write the Songs" by Barry Manilow. I, in earlier times, had more than once unkindly introduced the title as "I Ride The Dongs." "Black Dog" by Led Zeppelin might be followed by Debby Boone and "You Light Up My Life." "Evergreen" by Barbra Streisand would give way to "Smoke on The Water" by Deep Purple. "Close To You" by the Carpenters would disappear under the opening strains of the Beatles' "Revolution."

Top·Forty had always tried to be almost everything to just about everybody. FM AOR (Album Oriented Rock) was specifically aimed at a well-defined audience. In addition to technical superiority, it offered exclusive configuration. WTAC needed to do the same, but in a different way, toward a massive group with common, singular tastes. It was time to detect, select and direct.

I reflected upon what had always seemed to make sense in broadcasting, and what had not. We needed to leap-frog conventional wisdom and throw-out all the old rule books. Many had already been discarded, but it was time for zero-based programming. Nothing was sacred, and everything fell under strict and objective analysis. Jay "Jammer" and I spent several weeks considering even the wildest of thoughts. We finally determined that we would proceed into a completely energized format with music selection determined by both familiarity and tempo. We would also move ahead with a quintessential definition of "Rock 'n Roll."

Early Rock 'n Roll had been derivative of both black and white musical influences in virtually equal proportion. Even Woodstock had featured Sly and the Family Stone taking everyone "High—ER" as the seemingly toothless Richie Havens had flapped his gums in praise of "Pppfreedum." However, formatic compression had already initiated a pronounced racially-based separation.

White Rock Radio had begun excluding almost all black artists with certain notable exceptions such as Jimi Hendrix and Chuck Berry, who had always primarily appealed to white audiences in the first place. Gone were all the Motown sounds and Aretha and the Isleys and Curtis Mayfield and Otis Redding. "Black Radio," always traditionally ethnic, was only available in Flint on an AM-daytimer (WAMM) and the new Black, 24 hour FM (WDZZ) would not sign-on for well over another year. The black population within the city of Flint stood at 35 percent and growing.

A Scottish group calling themselves "Average White Band" were selling millions of copies of soul-based music around the world. "Disco" had absolutely gone through the roof with "Saturday Night Fever" and the Bee Gees had convinced millions of long-haired American white boys they "should be dancin'." Look at all the pussy John Travolta got in that movie. Sheeeit!! You could see the phenomenon in every major Flint bar. It was "The Beat," man, "The Beat."

As all major radical moves should be, the "New WTAC" was a model of simplicity. Anything "slow" was pulled from the air. Anything without a danceable beat was dropped. Everything that made musical sense and was instantly accessible (i.e., "familiar"), would be included. Most important of all, our library was absolutely color-blind. The mix of white to black turned out to be fairly even. Energized dance music was run under every talk element on the station, including newscasts. These were trimmed to two minutes of headlines. All WTAC jingles were discarded in favor of call-letter "shouts," with both "white" and "black" versions rotated. All songs were coded for balance and blend. It sounded great and I put Miss B. on the air with a Saturday morning show. I even enticed Pete Flanders to return for weekend exposure. His theme was Wild Cherry and "Play That Funky Music, White Boy!" Pete was glad to oblige. I didn't need to wait for the ratings. The phones had gone wild.

I extended our concept into station promotions and live appearances. In cooperation with the City of Flint, WTAC ended the summer staging a massive "Disco-Rock Extravaganza" at the IMA Auditorium. Miss B. danced on stage with WTAC Account Executive Thalia Diebler, a blond-haired, blue-eyed, Nordic beauty. The crowd went crazy. 6000 packed the arena with an even split in racial composition. It was a wild night of exciting entertainment and absolute harmony.

A number of blacks approached me with testimony regarding their renewed allegiance to WTAC. Several mentioned having seen me at all the James Brown Shows that had come to

Flint through the years. I always arrived early, found a seat down front to stand on, and tended to be unique in complexion under such circumstances. James was certainly a major part of the "New WTAC." Good God.

Although the "New WTAC" had greatly shifted musical accent, a number of basics remained the same. Everyone pushed in the new direction with uncommon zeal. We all shared a sense of urgency and commitment. Production values reached new heights, and contesting was wilder and crazier than ever before. We moved further into "theater of the mind" conceptual presentations. Everything we did had to be bigger than life.

On Halloween, we broadcast a real "Seance" from a "Haunted House." We used actual "witches" and "mediums," or at least they thought they were, and would convincingly testify to the fact. They brought back Jimi Hendrix, Jim Morrison and Janis Joplin. How could I be more pleased?

For Thanksgiving, we arranged a "WTAC Turkey-Shoot." Listeners would phone-in to play the game. When they got on the air, dramatic audio staging would run in the background. You would hear all the turkeys gobbling-away as you picked your weapon; a rifle, a cannon or an atomic missile. You would then say, "Fire!" Depending upon selection, chaos and carnage would reign supreme for three to ten seconds. The "atomic missile" choice offered most prolonged mayhem. At the end of the sequence, the turkey might agonizingly croak one last, pathetic, gurgling gasp and loudly thud to the ground, which meant a frozen turkey had been instantly won. Or it just might victoriously screech a "na-na-na-na—na-na"-type turkey-jeer, which meant that you'd missed, and wouldn't get a thing. The turkey surviving the atomic missile blast was always the source of substantial personal amusement. I did receive several complaints from animal-rights people about the "Turkey Shoot," and had to point-out that they weren't real turkeys, which seemed to make absolutely no difference to them.

For our '78 Christmas Season, we invented the "WTAC Magical Legend of the Christmas Cuckoo." According to us, an old Bavarian wood-carver had long-ago created a special, magical cuckoo, which came to life only during the Holiday Season and was flying over Flint with gifts and prizes for WTAC listeners. If you called and were chosen, we'd have him fly over your house. You would have to look up into the sky to see him. The WTAC Christmas Cuckoo would let loose when you said, "Drop-it on me!" A long, dramatic "dive-bombing" sound would follow. Many times, you might receive great gifts, including expensive watches, diamond rings or color television sets. Other times, you would hear just a loud, splashy splat sort-of-noise. That meant that you lost, and had been hit with something other than a prize. I thought it was all quite fun and offered a refreshing change of pace from normal seasonal smarm.

On New Year's Eve, we presented Miss B, very live and in-person, broadcasting "Miss B's WTAC Soul Countdown" of the year's best dance music from the hottest Disco in town. It was packed to capacity three hours in advance. She finished at the stroke of Midnight. We then switched to Jay "Jammer" Johnson broadcasting live at Flint's biggest Rock Bar 'til 4 a.m. with his "WTAC "Jammer-Rock" Spectacular." Lines around that club were two blocks long.

Our first surprise came with the release of the DETROIT Spring '79 Arbitron. Major markets were always released first. WTAC in Flint was #5 in Adults (13-34) and #3 in Teens in the fucking Motor City!! What??? We had never shown-up in Detroit ratings. We couldn't believe it.

The Flint report was issued one week later. We had climbed up to a much healthier 9.2 percent total audience share, even as WWCK had edged back from their 12.5 percent to a 10.5 percent. Moreover, we beat WWCK in teens, in young adults, and even in total listeners from 7 'til Midnight. WTAC had also increased adult count by nearly 50 percent over the previous "book."

A headline article in the Detroit Free Press cited WTAC's penetration into the Detroit market, precipitating major local newspaper and television coverage. Radio trade magazines ran articles on WTAC being the only AM facility in the country to successfully reverse previously FM-held dominance in teens or night listening. They mentioned our "unique contemporary fusion format" as an "entirely innovative approach in modern broadcasting."

The first person I called with all the excellent news was Joe Windsor. He offered sincere congratulations, and jovially stated, "My battle plan worked!" He then hung-up the phone.

I was well aware that WTAC's amazing showing in Detroit was caused by extraordinary station listenership in Lapeer County, which, although directly adjacent to Flint, was part of the "Detroit Metro" ratings sample. Our signal was weak to the south, and barely reached Detroit proper. Who minded? It made great press. Similarly, we were proceeding through a limited window of opportunity. I anticipated WDZZ's pending sign-on as a problem for our "fusion format." Our new audience composition was 30 percent black. Still, we were extraordinarily hot for the moment and took full advantage of our renewed strength with advertisers. Station revenue rose proportionately. I also got a raise, and was corporately upgraded to President and General Manager of WTAC. The last one to hold such title was Thaddeus Murphy.

CHAPTER THIRTY-SIX

T-BIRD LOUNGE

My professional life had become primarily dedicated to various executive responsibilities lacking show-biz flair. "P&L's," budget-planning, sales-recruiting, marketing sessions and agency calls with our radio representative firm in Detroit, Chicago and New York took up most of my time. Staff memos, problem-solving, and constant organizational coordination also filled my schedule. I also became quite active in community affairs and was appointed to a number of charitable boards. Participation in the Flint Area Advertising Federation consumed a certain amount of my average month, and daily department head meetings also became part of the routine. Much of this may seem tediously boring. Might I assure you that it was. I believed in balance.

The T-Bird Lounge was on South Lippincott between South Dort and South Center Road, right near the railroad tracks. It featured local rock groups, and catered to bikers. Unspoken rules of conduct were rarely ignored, and then only for the briefest of interludes before fierce enforcement restored calm. Even though notorious by reputation, The T-Bird Lounge never saw police officers cross the door. All problems were quickly resolved internally. The crowd knew every narcotic and undercover agent within 200 miles, also being able to spot outsiders with a single, measuring glance. I was not an outsider.

I was now a clean-shaven, short-haired, white-collared, three-piece-suited executive. I had known most of the clientele for many years. For pure personal pleasure, extraordinary conversation, genuine brotherhood and excellent Rock 'n Roll, it was always the T-Bird Lounge, my home-away-from-home. I never worried about seeing other members of the Flint business or broadcasting community within the walls of the establishment. Even when invited, they would not come. They found it a scary place. One man's hell is another's heaven.

"Pass the whiskey, Roy Boy, and fire-up another one! I think I see Jesus!"

Lines of coke on the T-Bird bar were as common as cocktail napkins elsewhere, but then cocaine was everywhere in Flint in the late '70s. I had snorted with clergymen, stockbrokers, attorneys, judges and police. Its usage crossed all social, racial and demographic boundaries. It was fashionable and becoming fundamental. Flint was a money town and home of the highest paid factory workers in the entire industrialized world. The prevailing attitude of the day was that cocaine was as harmless as marijuana. We all knew how we had been deceived in our younger days about that. In entertainment circles, coke was the real thing. Convention suites would commonly offer sugar-bowls filled to the brim or, for the more skittish, an ounce or two conveniently available on toilet-tops in bathroom stalls for private consumption. No one ever worried about theft. There was too much around for that. In a few years, attitudes would shift, with sharp distinctions drawn.

I considered my own use recreational in nature, and restricted expenditure to discretionary sums accrued in my "Peter C. Rock 'n Roll Presentations" fund. Eileen received my weekly paychecks for family-funding and I was given an allowance, which, through time, would accumulate in my relatively dormant account. Every so often, I'd dip-in for a few hundred and stay awake several days. I thought of it as maximization of vacation time. In many ways, it was.

WTAC maintained a drug-free status, as far as usage on the property or within the building were concerned. Professional propriety means protective perspective. Everyone understood my thoughts on the matter. Other radio facilities were much more casual in approach, and it was widely known that some stations operated on a wide-open basis, as did a number of major record companies.

Another cardinal rule at WTAC was avoidance of anything remotely resembling "payola." Through all the years I was Program Director, all records chosen for broadcast were selected based on musical merit alone. All adds to the station were determined with established criteria and weekly lists were submitted to Fuqua Communications and our Washington attorneys. Everything was available for inspection. I had been particularly sensitive to potential accusations regarding conflict of interest due to my promotional activities, and had established guidelines in conjunction with my appointment as Program Director. I had turned-down many opportunities to receive favors as a matter of basic business. I didn't want to owe strangers. Why put your balls in a meat-grinder? Besides, as Coach Woody Hayes once said, "If it's easy, it ain't worth a damn!" Go, Ohio State.

Specifically, all the record promoters knew that any offer of cocaine to any member of our staff would result in being banned from the building. A call would be placed to their corporate President explaining why. There was too much at stake, and I deeply resented thoughts of subversive, external corruption. If anyone was going to corrupt employees, it would be me. In early November came a heart-stopper, but not one drug induced.

It was not uncommon, as I walked around the WTAC complex, to occasionally stop at our United Press International news machine and review incoming stories, an old announcer habit. It was nothing short of remarkable that I happened to wander by the machine at the exact time a story with the heaviest personal professional implications broke on the wire.

It was a bulletin out of Atlanta, Georgia. It announced the pending sale of all Fuqua Communications broadcast properties. Although the primary focus was on Fuqua's television stations, it also referenced WTAC in Flint. I had no idea a sale was even being considered. I tore the story off the printer and raced to my office. I called Joe Windsor. He was astounded. I sensed he was also blind-sided. He asked me to read the story again. He said he'd call me back. Minutes later, he did. There were complications.

Although the story said that the Fuqua stations had been sold, actually only the television stations qualified for this description. The two radio stations, WROZ and WTAC, were now immediately on the market. I knew the whole thing had to blow for Joe. The announcement effectively sounded taps for the entire Communications Division. At least I might have a bit of borrowed time before my future was so clearly evidenced.

Part of my job responsibilities now involved helping to peddle the station, and potentially put myself on the unemployment line. AM stations were now not the hottest action around, since FM was where the smart money headed. I assisted in putting together appropriate materials for prospective buyers. They certainly weren't going to be lining up at our door, wallets in hand. A number of potential players came floating though. Some were serious, and most merely curious. They were all handled with courtesy and attention. One could never know.

Joe Windsor called on a Tuesday afternoon. He had set up a meeting for me with someone looking for a more powerful AM facility in the Flint area. WTAC's northern signal also appealed to this new prospect. He liked to hear his stations while traveling. He was a multi-millionaire with serious intent. I was to meet the following afternoon in Brighton, Michigan, with Frazier Reams, Junior, the owner of WWCK-FM. I would again be calling on the competition. This time they held the check.

We met at "The Canopy" in Brighton, a reasonably upscale

restaurant just off US 23, north of Ann Arbor. I was immediately relieved.

Frazier Reams, Jr., was not at all what was expected. He was a refined, gracious, man. Frazier was in his mid-fifties with white hair and noble bearing. He bore a measure of resemblance to Peter Graves of "Mission Impossible" and now "Biography" fame, brother to James Arness of "Marshall Dillon" repute. Later, I would see Frazier mistaken for Senator John Anderson when the latter ran for President. I believe Frazier even signed a few autographs, rather than make the petitioners feel foolish. He used his own signature, a bold "FR2." No one complained.

Mr. Reams was quite candid regarding his intent. His Flint AM was licensed to broadcast during daylight hours only, and with a signal enormously inferior to that of WTAC. WTAC would offer a significant upgrade in power and strength, and would contribute meaningful ratings points, which could be sold combined with WWCK-FM. As is usual in such circumstances, there was no specific discussion as to my own status, should a successful sale be negotiated with Fuqua. Frazier did, however, reference my meeting with Jim O'Donnell a number of years earlier. He suggested that his Chief Operating Officer had been quite favorably impressed; although, due to circumstances of the moment, reluctantly so.

Frazier and I also reviewed implications of WDZZ-FM's sign-on, which had taken place three months earlier. I had sent Vern Merritt, the station's new General Manager and Co-owner, a floral arrangement to mark the occasion. It welcomed him and his staff to the Flint broadcasting community. I was the only competitor to have acknowledged their arrival. I expressed to Mr. Reams my conviction that WDZZ was doing fabulously well with Flint's black population, and had already rendered WAMM obsolete. I was also quite certain that WTAC's fusion format would also be negatively affected by the new operation, but that WWCK would actually benefit from further proof of FM viability in the market.

I presented Frazier with typical facts and figures relating to a general overview of WTAC, and answered all questions asked. I felt the encounter had gone very well and reported this later in the day to Joe Windsor in Georgia. Joe told me the following afternoon that Frazier had been very pleased with our meeting. Joe mentioned that Frazier was engineering changes within his own ranks, and would be getting back to us once certain matters were finalized.

The 1979 Holiday Season was filled with typical festive frolic on-the-air and behind the scenes. January was the first month in a brand new decade and WTAC remained for sale. I was somewhat surprised when Frazier Reams, Jr. called me in late February for another meeting. Normally, protocol dictated that further exploration on a purchase would be channeled through Joe Windsor in Georgia.

Frazier and I met again at the Canopy in Brighton. His direct approach then made complete sense. He was still unsure whether or not WTAC might make an interesting acquisition, but he was certain about me. He had dissolved his partnership with Jim O'Donnell, and was about to restructure the entire organization. With Joe Windsor's blessings, I concluded nearly 14 years of employment with Fuqua Communications as I joined Reams Broadcasting and WWCK.

My first programming meeting with the "105 FM" announcing staff was unexpectedly exhilarating. Their average age was almost a full generation lower than counterparts at WTAC. I was reminded of my earliest days at WNDR. I was presented with the "Peter C. Dartboard" and a pound of baking soda marked "Rock 'n Roll." They awaited my response. I thanked them for their exceeding generosity and ran it all down. I waved the package of baking soda high in the air and told them they had stumbled on an accidental, but brilliant illustration of where we were, and where we could go. The label said "Rock 'n Roll," but everyone knew the contents were a joke. WWCK would call itself "Rock 'n Roll," but wouldn't be a joke.

I stated that I would treat them fairly, expected their professional and personal best, and that we were taking ourselves to a pinnacle. I guaranteed that their efforts would be handsomely rewarded, and that WWCK would become the highest rated FM Rock Station in America. I promised them national notoriety and individual recognition. They trusted me and believed in themselves. In less than two years, everything came true.

CHAPTER THIRTY-SEVEN

BUFFALO DICK

WWCK programming was shaping up nicely. Program Director Tim Seigrist was handling responsibilities with new focus and clarity. Tim had stumbled a bit early on. I had obtained 100 tickets for one of Bob Seger's four sold-out Cobo Hall appearances in Detroit for a major station promotion. I had rented coaches for a Saturday night, and most of our WWCK staff and 68 lucky winners were planning to be on the exclusive "105 FM Seger Buses" to the concert. I had the tickets sent to Tim, which he reported were carefully counted and placed in his desk drawer for the big event. He called me in absolute panic early Saturday morning. The tickets had remained safe and secure. He had only then noticed they were all for the prior evening's performance. I called Punch Andrews, Bob's manager, and regretfully explained our plight. He told me not to panic. Two long rows of seats were added directly in front of the stage for our attendance. Only prior relationships had saved us from disaster. Tim and I spoke briefly about not "assuming." It was a conversation never repeated.

All of our WWCK station tickets were very much in order, with excellent seating arranged for another rare Detroit performance by Led Zeppelin in early October. The group was not to appear there, nor anywhere else again. Drummer John "Bonzo" Bonham died in bed September 25, entering Valhalla via vodka.

It was immediately announced that Led Zeppelin had accompanied him on his journey. The band was no more.

Jay "Jammer" Johnson had remained at WTAC and, in the face of WDZZ's ascension with black programming, had taken the facility in a pure rock direction. I had offered Jay the opportunity to make the move with me to WWCK. He had turned me down cold, observing that he would prefer remaining where he was as a real Program Director. That meant he would be calling the final shots following my departure. I was disappointed with his decision, but fully understood.

When Frazier and I determined that WTAC would not provide advantage proportionate to investment, certain competitive instincts came to the forefront. Although WTAC was operating with the same technical handicaps that had frustrated me for so long a time, it had become a nuisance. Every effort was made to force a format change on the facility. Meanwhile, "Jammer" became famous in the most unfortunate of circumstances with the most undesirable of consequences. It was horrid. Jay was handling a number of WTAC promotions personally. One of the more interesting tasks was selecting "Mud Wrestlers" for "WTAC Mud Wrestling Night" at an area lounge. They had to be over 18 and interested in getting dirty. He ran several ads in the Flint Journal soliciting "Mud Wrestlers." They were to send him pictures of themselves, and include some brief autobiographical information. Many entries came in. "Jammer" picked a dozen for private interviews in his office at the station. One young lady chosen turned out to be particularly well-endowed and playful in manner. Jay asked her if she had any personal photographs which might be more revealing. She giggled and responded that she did not, but wouldn't mind modeling if it might provide career enhancement. Jay generously and graciously offered to be of assistance.

She and a girlfriend accompanied Jay to his apartment. Out came the camera and off came her clothing. Clickity-Click-Click. Zoomity-Zoom-Zoom. Being a "trained photographer,"

Jay never touched her. She wasn't the only one posing. A few days later, he presented her with a full set of pictures, as promised. Goodie! Now she had a real professional portfolio. Yippie! She hid it in her bedroom closet. Her father found it there. He was enraged. He called the police. She was 14 years-old.

The police watched "Jammer" for a month. They also told the Genesee County Prosecutor's Office what was up. Word was passed to the Flint Journal. Stand by for NEWS.

I was attending a meeting of the Flint Ad Club when a Journal friend asked me if I knew about the big bust coming up. I did not. He whispered details. Returning to the station, I called Jay and shared the information. He thought I was kidding. We were competitors. I told him I wasn't and that, regardless of separate station affiliation, I still considered him a friend, and would help in any way I could. He thanked me, although expressing his opinion that my assistance wouldn't be needed since he hadn't really done anything. It was just a few pictures. Besides, she had signed a statement that she was eighteen-years of age. He still had it. It was written in pencil on the back of an Arby's coupon.

Although wildly hoping they had a real Chicken-Porno-King on their hands, and finding themselves bitterly disappointed that Jay had been so boring under surveillance, the police had to move. The Prosecutor was panting in hot anticipation of excellent electoral grease, and the Journal had already been plugged-in for maximum spin.

"Does he still have really long-hair? Excellent!"

"Is he still employed at that "Rock 'n Roll" Station? Sensational!"

Jay was arrested at 5:30 a.m. and hauled downtown. The newspaper photographers and television camera crews were ready and waiting. "Let's see those handcuffs, Jammer!" Clickity-Click-Click. Zoomity-Zoom-Zoom.

The official charge was "Contributing to The Delinquency of a Minor." It wasn't as good as "Sodomous Bestiality" or even

"Statutory Rape," but the long-hair and "Rock 'n Roll Disc-Jockey" angles more than compensated. What was lacking in content could be made up in form. Jay was front-page in the Journal and the lead-story on all TV newscasts. He was asked for his resignation at WTAC, and immediately tendered the same.

I found Jay the best street smart attorney in town, Jim Zimmer, who knew the moves. Additionally, his right foot was in a cast from a Rugby injury. Jim found limping about proved to be beneficial in evoking jury sympathy. Everything helped— especially when you had to introduce a pencil-marked, hot-sauce-stained Arby's coupon as crucial defendant evidence with a straight face. The judge was a part-time Nazarene minister. The six member jury panel were all of advanced age, and several napped through much of the trial. Only a key witness turned the tide.

She bounced to the witness stand wearing secure jeans and an even tighter T-shirt. It proudly proclaimed "Hi!" over a gigantic "Happy Face." She looked about 28. She stressed to the jury that she had told Jay she was 18, and he had never laid a finger on her. She said that her girlfriend had watched the whole thing and thought Jay was "weird." The Prosecuting Attorney made the dumb mistake of asking dramatically just what she meant by "weird."

"Well, 'cause he didn't seem interested in fuckin' us!"

There was an audible gasp from judge and jurors. She was excused. She waltzed toward the courtroom door, then suddenly spun around and faced the jury. She had their undivided attention. She smiled. She spoke.

"Have a nice day, everyone!"

She liked being liked.

The jury deliberated less than a minute. Jay was found "Not Guilty." I brought "Jammer" to WWCK and introduced him on the air. He read the news of his acquittal. He thanked everyone for their understanding and support. He then said goodbye to Flint.

WTAC went Country in less than two weeks. So did WWCK, but only at brief intervals and by most bizarre means. Jeff Lamb was the son of a famous Flint radio announcer named Bill Lamb. Bill was then working directly for Buick Motor Division, hosting a morning and afternoon show called the "Factory Whistle" on country station WKMF. It was a good job. Jeff was thus a second generation broadcast talent, although he had never yet been officially employed by any station. At 18, Jeff started playing records at disco establishments. He was quite the entertainer. He did magic tricks, jumped all over the place in animated frenzy, and told crazy jokes. He was an act. He started making tons of money, all of which he immediately spent on frivolous notions and passing fancies. You either loved him or hated him. I found myself in the former category, indeed seeing myself two decades before. We became friends.

Jeff also did "voices," and would hang around the station, spending substantial time bothering our secretaries and anyone else who might wander by. For Jeff, any audience was a good one. He would be ostensibly "visiting Peter C." Jeff would often be in the building for hours before finally reaching my office. He would perform for anyone in sight. Our cleaning lady thought he was another Johnny Carson. I couldn't figure out what to do with him. Then, I had a brainstorm.

My idea was to initiate "WWCK Saturday Morning Cartoons" on FM 105 with our normal music format in place, but with Jeff doing cartoon voices, instead of having a regular disc-jockey on-the-air. I thought it was ingenious. I spoke with Jeff and asked him to prepare a demonstration tape of possible voices for the exercise. He agreed and returned several days later, cassette in hand. He had spent considerable time in reflection. He told me that my "Saturday Morning Cartoons" idea was "stupid." I listened patiently. Gifted talent usually lacks tact. He had come up with something "much better" and guaranteed that I would "laugh my ass off."

The concept was delicately presented as "Buffalo Dick's Radio Ranch." It was a parody on the old Howdy Doody TV show for kids. Instead of "Buffalo Bob," you had "Buffalo Dick." In place of "Howdy," there was "Buffalo Chip" as primary side-kick. There was an audience of kids. There was an engineer named "Buffalo Peter," a homosexual policeman named "Officer Skip" and a spaced-out phone caller named "Raymond." Any number of guests would be passing through the show. The possibilities were endless. The content was double-entendre from start to finish, but in a remarkably clever way.

Instead of Saturday morning, "Buffalo Dick's Radio Ranch" was scheduled as a one-hour program Saturday nights at 10. There was an "Open," a "Close," and five "Inserts." Everything else was straight Rock 'n Roll music. Each "Insert" was a four or five minute comedy segment. All of "Buffalo Dick" was painstakingly produced by Jeff at home on his Dad's equipment. He did all the voices and used sound-effects, musical staging and creative enhancement with unbelievable skill. Jeff understood theater of the mind as only the son of a radio veteran could. He had grown-up listening to his Dad, watching him work, and studying the art. Jeff blended innate brilliance with experience far beyond his years. It was an unbeatable combination.

An opening instrumental track of "Who's Afraid of the Big Bad Wolf" would emanate across our airwaves as Jeff started each broadcast with the same disclaimer.

"It's time for Mom and Dad to leave the room, 'cause your old pal Buffalo Dick is on the air!!"

"Buffalo Dick's Radio Ranch" started in early October on WWCK. Listener response was magnificent. Ratings went sky-high. Billboard Magazine would judge "Buffalo Dick's Radio Ranch" a Gold Award Winner as "Best Local Programming/All Markets" the following year in national radio competition. Westwood One would syndicate the program on nearly 100 stations by 1982. Industry wisdom would have said the concept was too far out to ever work, which is exactly why it did. If it's really different, it always works. You simply have to go about it with complete abandon and perfect dedication.

CHAPTER THIRTY-EIGHT

RADIO FREE FLINT

The Federal Communication Commission suggested that a certain amount of weekly programming be devoted to discussion of community issues and other non-entertainment features. This was felt to be a meaningful demonstration of serving the public. In reality, it was nonsense. This is why Sunday mornings at many radio and television stations were cluttered with religious broadcasts, informational features, public affairs discussions, and other nostrums. If a station buried everything in a single block, they could devote the rest of their time providing what the public really desired, as opposed to what it was supposed to want. Sunday mornings were normally the trash-heap of the broadcast week.

"Might as well throw all the shit there, Burt!"

So they did.

We had to make things more interesting.

Michael Moore of Davison Board of Education and "Hotline" fame had approached the local Public Broadcasting Station about doing a program addressing matters of interest and concern to young people. The station, wishing to be safely hip, allowed Michael to write and produce several broadcasts. A number of guidelines were given. Michael wanted to talk about abortions, contraceptive devices, sexual freedom, law enforcement harassment and drug use. These were beyond the guidelines. The station wanted to inform, not offend.

37-CAVA

Michael and I had discussed the problem and had experimented with a program called "Radio Free Flint" on WTAC. It was recorded in advance, and ran very early Sunday morning. When I moved to WWCK, I decided to invite Michael along. Radio Free Flint moved too, except it was now broadcast live with open phone lines. Everything was approved for discussion and debate. From an FCC perspective, it was Public Affairs Programming. In reality, it quickly became the hottest radio talk show in Flint. It might be 8 a.m. on a Sunday when Michael hit the air, but our 12-line switchboard would light-up like a Grateful Dead crowd.

Al MacLeese was a columnist for the Flint Journal. I had read several superb pieces he had written, and had dropped him a note expressing appreciation for his wit and style. He had called me and we had lunch. He was a grizzled old time newspaper rogue, and was not unknown to heavily partake in liquid stimulants from time to time. I mentioned that Syracuse, New York, was my hometown. He mused.

"I remember finishing the last of my gin at five in the morning in the middle of the lobby at the Howard Hotel in Syracuse, while feeding what remained of my plastic Florida driver's license to a light-brown hamster hurriedly spinning his rusty wheel in a tarnished, old, copper cage."

This was all narrated without pause and in a single breath.

I received a Christmas Card from Al the following week. I've kept it ever since with other treasured memorabilia. There are but four handwritten lines:

> "Roses are dreary,
> Violets are sick;
> Did you kill Christ,
> You Irish prick?"

Al's column was called "MacLeese Unleashed." I envisioned a radio version on WWCK right after "Radio Free Flint" on

Sunday morning. I spoke with Al and then we both had dinner with his editor. The Flint Journal approved his participation.

In terms of chemistry, there was one additional perspective. Al MacLeese thought Michael Moore was an "ignorant punk" and Michael regarded Al as a "typically untalented Flint Journal slug." Both had often expressed their views in print. For what more could I hope? To bring heat to searing levels, I thought it would be nice for Al to make his debut at the end of Michael's show, and then feature Michael as guest on the radio version of "MacLeese Unleashed" for a few minutes. I carefully coached Michael on sensitivity, attitude and decorum. Al was a seasoned pro, deserving of respect and courtesy. Michael reverted to his altar-boy and Seminarian days, and couldn't have been any nicer. As soon as Al's program began and he was in charge, he called Michael an "asshole." There was no tape delay. Michael just laughed. Al was off and running.

MacLeese lasted for 16 weeks on WWCK and only retired from the airwaves when a Sunday morning broadcast became too much to expect from an old hamster-feeder such as Al. Hangovers were bad enough without sharing them with 10,000 listeners. The fact remains that he was as gifted a broadcaster as he was a writer. Sometimes, they just come and go.

With Al's departure, Radio Free Flint expanded to two hours. Michael continued the program through late 1985, even as he expanded the "Hotline Voice" newspaper into the "Flint Voice," which became the "Michigan Voice." Then Michael Moore left Flint. He was hired as editor of "Mother Jones" in San Francisco, a major radical magazine of national notoriety. Michael was too radical for the radicals. He published stories by Ben Hamper, the "Rivet-Head."

Ben was a Flint factory worker who had written about life in the shop for the Flint Voice. At my request, Ben had also appeared on WWCK doing "News in Your Face" as a regular morning show feature. The owner of Mother Jones had more than he could handle with Michael and Ben. There was discussion of Hamper's proposed feature article entitled: "Faces of Death"/"A Humorous Overview." It was a question of "sensitivities." Hamper got drunk. Moore got the boot.

Mike returned to Flint, and spent most of his time at the movies. He figured he should make one. He shot tons of film, then decided what to do. He worked for more than a year arranging, editing, chopping, adding and revising. The basic thread was a search for the Chairman of the Board of General Motors. Michael theoretically wanted to bring him to Flint for enhancement of social awareness. Roger Smith was always unavailable. Had he not been, it would have fucked everything up. Michael hoped his documentary might qualify for a shot with PBS or something. He entered the final product in several film festivals to gain exposure and recognition. No one could believe how good it was. Warner Brothers paid $3 million dollars for distribution rights. "Roger and Me" went on to earn over $20 million in global release. Later to come was "TV Nation" and "Canadian Bacon," John Candy's final film. "Downsize This!" established Michael as a successful writer in late '96. "The Big One" in theatrical and video release, and "The Awful Truth" on Bravo saw him safely into the New Millennium. Sometimes they just come and stay.

1980 had started with the death of Bon Scott of AC/DC in February and continued with Zeppelin's John Bonham in September. The year ended with the shooting of John Lennon in December. We presented twenty-four hours of tribute on WWCK. Michael Moore, Jeff Lamb and our entire staff combined forces to hold a Memorial Gathering at the Capitol Theater, followed by a silent, candle-lit march through downtown Flint. The theater was filled to capacity. We watched selected moments from edited Beatles' footage on the screen, and many speakers rose to offer their own thoughts and reflections. A microphone was placed on the stage, and members of the audience were invited to express their feelings openly and publicly. Many did so, with eloquence and passion. It was a very strange year, opening an even stranger decade.

CHAPTER THIRTY-NINE

SUNDAY SIXTIES

Flint Arbitron ratings were heading back up for WWCK, rising to a share of 13.4 percent from the prior 10.5 percent. WWCK was finally a solid #1 in the Flint market. Second place was occupied by newcomer WDZZ-FM. The black FM debuted with a 12.2 percent share. Every other station in the market was in single digits. WTAC had plummeted to a 3.1 percent. Research indicated that WWCK's audience was lily-white and WDZZ's jet-black.

WTAC had been the last Flint station to successfully combine large segments of both groups into a single audience. What had happened in Flint was occurring elsewhere as a consequence of FM's newly-found acceptance, and a fear-filled lack of daring. Programmers were becoming protective clones of clones, each regeneration more entrenched in defensive play.

Paradoxically, the proliferation of broadcast technology, instead of increasing mass communication, had exactly the opposite effect. Formats were becoming decidedly more discrete. The first separations divided white from black, and young from old. As time progressed, we would see demographic, racial and sexual segmentation becoming increasingly narrow.

In 1982, our AM station became WWMN ("Flint's New Woman"). It was brilliantly developed and expertly managed by Marsha Kloor, an outstandingly creative individual with whom I had worked at WTAC. Another "Five Alive," WWMN was only moments ahead of its time. The experiment was concluded in 1984. We had obtained industry-wide attention with the format, but potential was limited by our daytime-only, highly-restricted AM signal. On FM, it would have been a different story. Fragmentation was the future.

We now have stations programmed for young white males and middle-aged black females. Oldies stations are offered for the '50s, '60s, '70s and '80s crowds. There are groupings and sub-groupings and sub-sub-groupings into sub-sub-sub-groupings. Television has expanded from two or three to 60 or 70 or 170 channels. Then there's the Internet. It's all been a natural progression, and was bound to happen. Yet, one thing is undeniable. By direct proportion, the more options exercised, the more isolation obtained. Don't look now, but we've all been dispersed. The Global Village has become a lonely old town.

Among a number of programming adjustments during my first year at WWCK had come the introduction of a new Sunday morning feature. Although a certain amount of new music was being incorporated into our song rotations as time went on, it was becoming clear that our audience was far more interested in hearing more older rock music than recent fare. In rock programming, this was strange.

In the early days of Top Forty, once a song left the chart, it was rarely heard again. In the early '60s, most stations created an "Oldies" category to address this factor, and would feature one or two songs each hour from the classification. In the early '70s, the concept of "Recurrents" became common. "Recurrents" were tunes that were too young to be "Oldies," but too valuable to be dropped.

A sense of Rock Continuum was emerging. Certain material continuously led in musical popularity, regardless of age. There was also a pronounced nostalgia evident for "The Sixties," then only a decade gone. The majority of our WWCK announcers and listeners had barely hit puberty at the time of Woodstock and, Goddammit, they were pissed at what they'd missed. We decided to do a two-hour program called "Sunday Sixties" after "Radio Free Flint" concluded. It would feature music from the era, as well as thoughts, comments, observations and reflections offered in friendly narrative fashion by someone who had lived through those times in active, energetic pursuit of continual cultural enhancement and personal libidinal fulfillment. I hired myself as host.

"Sunday Sixties" was a form of executive therapy. It also attracted faithful listenership and a certain amount of controversy. In market studies conducted by a competing radio station, I was honored in being rated as the most highly recognized air personality in Flint radio. I was also the most liked by male respondents to the survey and most disliked by females, other than those under the age of 24. Basically, my overall scoring was identical to that of Rock 'n Roll as a whole. To be in the same company as Led Zeppelin was all I could ever desire.

"Sunday Sixties" was usually the end of my Saturday night. I also had a co-host. His name was "Roy Boy." Roy Guidry was (and is) a "crazy Cajun." He had come up to Flint from Port Arthur, Texas, and landed a job with "Generous Motors" in the early '60s. Roy had attended the same high-school as Janis Joplin. He was one of my Concert Associates, and had handled plenty of security detail at Sherwood Forest Wild Wednesdays. Scores of bad asses had learned propriety from Roy and his entourage. There had only been one close call. Some pecker-head had been throwing fireworks around in the crowd during the final performance of the night, so Roy and the boys had dragged him down to the lake and handcuffed him under a dock. Roy had left him "jes' 'nuf air to breathe, if he took li'l breaths." We had ended the concert and had headed out for breakfast. It was 2:20 a.m. I was in the middle of my bacon and eggs.

"Ahhhhhh, shit!"

"What, Roy?"

"I think we better go back to the park!"

"Why, Roy?"

"Somebody mighta drownded!"

The poor son-of-a-bitch was only semi-conscious. Since it was the middle of summer, with water temperature around 75, terminal hypothermia had been avoided. Roy slipped off the cuffs and dragged a forlorn figure out of the lake. The erstwhile pyrotechnic offender was unclear as to where he was, or how he got there. Roy Boy told him. Roy also said that he was lucky "bein' let-out early." Expressing gratitude, the contrite recipient of Concert Associates' justice squished-off into the night. Roy told me he'd be more careful remembering the sequestered on future assignments.

Roy Boy and I would leave the T-Bird Lounge around 3:00 a.m. and head for Billy Coleman's. B.C. always hosted "After Hours Cocktails" at his hideout on Flushing Road. We would drink a few more beers, smoke several bowls of hash, listen to loud music, and shoot rats running around the Flint River banks until the sun rose. It was then time to gather ourselves together and prepare for broadcast. We would have breakfast at Walli's and drink gallons of coffee. At the station by 9, we would spend an hour selecting music and scripting a few bits for the day. Roy Boy would also run over to the air studio and moon Michael Moore a few times whenever Roy discerned Michael was "gittin' too serious." We would hit the air at 10 a.m., ready to Rock.

Ostensibly, Roy Boy was our official "WWCK Rock-On-The-Road Reporter" and would give rambling, disjointed, surrealistic reviews of concerts recently held in the area— some of which he had actually attended. I would introduce him with great exaggeration. He would also do the weather, take phone dedications on-the-air, and read a few of the preceding Friday's closing Dow Jones Averages for the "Bi'ness Boys" listening. We would end each Roy Boy segment with a standard exchange, always involving what beverage Roy was consuming that morning.

"Hey, Roy. What's that stuff you're chuggin' today with that red thing floatin' on top?"

"Peter C., I'm drinkin' a "Kentucky Date!"

"What's a "Kentucky Date," Roy?"

"One sweet cherry and five fingers of "Old Granddad!"

Out of Roy's punch-line, which would always strive for maximum disgust, we would segue immediately into a high-energy rock song. It always worked. Almost all of our scripting time was devoted to drinks of the day. Everything else Roy did was best at its most spontaneous.

I also used "Sunday Sixties" to interview interesting people. I had Pete Flanders appear several times sharing memories of earlier Flint radio. Pat Clawson (with CNN at the time) was visiting his family in Michigan, and joined me one Sunday morning. Pat shared with our audience his experiences covering the crash of a commercial jet into the Potomac River just days earlier. He said most of the recovered bodies were frozen-solid in a seated position. Roy Boy asked Pat if he had any pictures. Even Charlie Speights, vacationing from Las Vegas, came on board while in town. Charlie and I received a call from a woman whom he'd known in the far distant past. It turned out that she was a regular listener to "Sunday Sixties." Charlie hadn't spoken with her for fifteen years. She invited us over after we left the air. She made us lunch. Roy Boy thought she had "real big titties." Roy and I left, but Charlie stayed for a week. Another "Sunday Sixties" character, although rarely allowed airtime, was our 18 year-old, WWCK dog-collared intern, Bill Larson. Bill was enamored with the whole Flint scene and, with a heart of gold, could be counted upon to sacrifice anything within his capability for Rock 'n Roll. He even gave his parents' $25,000 retirement stash to the manager of a relatively unknown band. Bill believed this group would be monster mega-stars in months. He thought he was purchasing 5 percent of the action. Not so. The manager ran away with his loot, but Bill finally gained a bit of long overdue recognition from the band in 2001, on page 86 of "The Dirt" by Motley Crue.

WWCK visibility was unavoidable in Flint. We had station

banners in every bar, and our air personalities were hosting movie openings, important community events, and every major rock concert in Flint and Saginaw. We were also top-rated in 18 to 30 year-old male listenership in the Tri-Cities to the north, an incredible achievement with our 3000 watts.

One of our newest acquisitions was the "105 Super Van," an outrageously loaded mind-blower. We painted it glossy-black with white-trim and red-lettering. We had been looking to obtain a station image vehicle for months, but needed to do so on a barter basis for budgetary reasons. A new employee named Nancy Dymond had achieved the impossible on her second day as an Account Executive in arranging the trade for our wonder machine. I couldn't believe it when she pranced into the station and waved the contract, thinking she must have misunderstood the impossibilities involved. A $40,000 vehicle for air time? That was a real long-shot. Nancy was surprised with my surprise. She told me she could sell. Guess so.

The "Super Van" went along to everything we did. It was in all the parades, and we even picked-up thousands of miniature footballs engraved with our station logo, that we would throw out of the top at High School Homecomings. No stone was left unturned, nor turn unstoned.

At the close of the 1981 United Way Campaign, we hung the "105 Super Van" 100 feet in the air with a gigantic construction crane over our WWCK billboard at the intersection of Flint's busiest two expressways, and staged a remote broadcast for 12 hours. We did it without advance notice or warning of any kind. All the heaviest of local dignitaries were hoisted-up for brief appearances. Doing it with the United Way provided permission otherwise unobtainable. Traffic was backed-up for miles. Pictures of the suspended van ran on the front page of the Flint Journal. Video was featured on all local television newscasts, and even carried in Detroit. Anchorwoman Karen Owens from Channel Twelve in Flint met and interviewed

Sean McNeill, who was now doing mornings at WWCK. They fell in love and got married.

We presented the "First Annual WWCK Rock-Off" at Flint's Capitol Theater. Finalists were selected after a month of on-air contesting. We ran it like a Spelling Bee. The production requirements were awesome. Each contestant had to identify a specific piece of music by artist and title. Everything had to come up in exact sequence. There were over four hundred separate elements included. It came off flawlessly in live broadcast. The team was getting really good.

It was becoming a challenge to make each new major station promotion bigger and better than whatever had come before. We decided to give away the world. "The WWCK Great Escape" offered an opportunity to win a trip for two anywhere on the planet. Listeners would call when solicited, and had to say where they wanted to go and whom they wanted to bring along. I thought that the second part would prove interesting and, in fact, it became the source of much advance contemplation in the minds of listeners. Hmmmmm. Who could they least afford to offend? Several finalists even chose the wives of others. Hey, we were talking anywhere with anyone. There would be plenty of time to straighten things out upon return. Rock 'n Roll!

We arranged to have the final drawing conducted on live television at Channel 12 in the middle of "General Hospital," where Luke and Laura were churning up viewership by the ton. I decided to have Price-Waterhouse supervise the exercise to certify legitimacy and authenticity and, most importantly, to offer additional dramatics. We had the entire air staff on hand, and even pre-recorded a two minute lead-in with everybody climbing into the "WWCK Super Van" and driving to the television station. Disc-jockeys were hanging off the roof and sides. I had set-aside $15,000 from our promotional funds to cover expenses. Our winners might be going to Australia or Russia or Hong Kong or Outer Mongolia. It didn't matter. We said anywhere and we meant ANYWHERE!

The moment of truth was at hand. We had a big barrel with all our finalists and their dream destinations marked on individual forms. The drum-roll began. The barrel was spinning. It slowed and stopped. A blind-folded Sean McNeill reached in the barrel and randomly selected our winner. It was a lady, and she and her Mother would be going to— Cape Cod! What? That's right, we said "anywhere" and she wants "Cape Cod." "Cape Cod" it is! Yayyyyyyyy!!!!!"

Although not exactly ending in the grandiose manner I had envisioned, our winner got her trip and we saved $14,300. I was glad we had conducted our drawing on live TV. Even so, with cynics everywhere, there were some who questioned the outcome. In future promotions requiring listener option, I would have our announcers suggest to contestants that they think BIG! Meanwhile, our "Great Escape" winner had a fantastic time at Cape Cod and wrote us a warm letter of thanks. I invited her out to the station and had her read the letter on the air. I then presented her with $1000 in cash. She almost fainted. I simply said that she could have chosen many other places which were much more expensive, but that she had been most thrifty in her selection. The $1000 was WWCK's way of saying, "We think you deserve more!" We realized another front-page shot in the Journal, and additional local television exposure. It was the talk of the town. We still had $13,300 left.

There was sadness in July with the death of Harry Chapin. Harry had enjoyed several major hits, including "Cat's in The Cradle," "Taxi" and "W-O-L-D," a song with which I particularly identified being the aging disc-jockey I was. Michael Moore had established a close relationship with Mr. Chapin through the years. Harry had appeared in a number of benefit performances for The Flint Voice at Flint's Whiting Auditorium and, in fact, was shortly scheduled for another when he was killed in an auto accident. He had appeared with me several times on "Sunday Sixties" and had struck me as a kind, responsible man. Michael hosted a special edition of Radio Free Flint over

WWCK the night of Harry's death in a program dedicated to his memory.

Flint now had two major 2000+ capacity entertainment lounges going head-to-head. They were both primarily offering, I would note, recorded dance music.

"The Mikatam" in Genesee was owned and operated by Tom Joubran, a Palestinian immigrant and self-made millionaire. Tom couldn't understand why everyone else wasn't getting rich in America. He would say, "Look at me. I rode a goat to the boat!" He also was amazed that no one else could seize opportunities as he did and profit accordingly. The truth was that few people could work 20 hours-a-day with the energy and drive that Tom considered a matter of normal routine. Sleep?

Tom owned laundromats, apartment buildings, pizza parlors, grocery stores and lots else. His first love, however, seemed to be "show business." He proved to be a gracious host, and extraordinary client. He brought a number of relatives over from the old country, and there were a few confusions from time to time. I was visiting Tom one night when we both noticed everyone being turned away from the door by a young nephew, who had been instructed to check for I.D.s. He was demanding passports.

Tom's primary nemesis was "The Light," an ultra high-tech establishment occupying most of the basement area in the Small Mall on South Dort. "The Light" was owned by a Cincinnati-based group and managed by a young Irishman named Neil Kearney, who took his responsibilities most seriously. Since each establishment was continually at the throat of the other in advertising and promotions, it was inevitable that points of dispute would sometimes arise, which I would be required to mediate and/or decide as manager of the radio station. Both "The Light" and "The Mikatam" regularly spent thousands of dollars on the station, often within a single week's time. They were thus premium accounts, requiring continual executive attention.

A disc-jockey from "The Light" had moved to "The Mikatam" and Tom was making it sound in his radio advertising as though "The Light" was absolutely finished. The new Mikatam disc-jockey had recorded a commercial wherein he told everyone how rotten "The Light" was, and how glad he was to be out of there. The manager of The Light, Mr. Kearney, was highly displeased, and demanded that the spot be pulled. After debating the issue, I resolved that The Mikatam should be able to run whatever it wanted, with The Light afforded identical liberty. The last thing I wanted to get involved with was becoming arbiter over issues of client copy. I'd always be alienating half our account list. Let freedom ring.

Mr. Kearney was dissatisfied, and attacked on all fronts. He pulled his entire broadcast schedule, instituted a lawsuit against the station, and was down at the Flint Journal trying to get them to do an exposé on WWCK mismanagement, all in less than a single afternoon's time. It seemed appropriate that we talk.

WWCK Sales Manager Ron Shannon and I traveled to The Light and met with Neil. I applauded him on the intensity and speed of his offensive. I suggested that, while not altering my position on the problem at-hand for a variety of reasons, I understood his anger. I offered to provide a number of free announcements the following week for The Light in a ratio of one non-paid commercial for each one purchased. I said that I was doing that because I appreciated his business, and felt that he had something coming as an offer of friendship. He immediately asked for two free ads for each one bought. I told him the ratio would remain as I had outlined, but that I would throw 10 additional twenty second "mentions" into the bargain. We shook hands.

We had several drinks. I then observed that I was quite taken with his initiative, aggression, commitment and loyalty to company. I told him to call me if he ever wanted a job in radio sales. He did so three months later. His first assigned account for WWCK was The Mikatam. He doubled its billing. Along with Nancy Dymond and Ron Shannon, I had one more exceptionally talented player on the roster. I would need them all.

CHAPTER FORTY

FLINT TO FLINT TO FLINT

Well, how could we follow-up on "The Great Escape"? Great ideas often come from passing thoughts exchanged in pleasant conversation. I was hanging out one night with our station attorney, Mr. Zimmer. We were at The White Horse, a tavern near downtown Flint. He was talking about law school and interesting things he had discovered on his way to the bar.

"Did you know there's an island called Flint?"

"Where?"

"In the middle of fucking nowhere. It's out in the goddamn South Pacific."

"Its name is FLINT?"

"FLINT!!"

Research the following day revealed that the island of Flint was part of the Republic of Kiribati. It was a three-and a-half by half mile coral reef in the South Pacific, existing totally uninhabited, approximately 400 miles north of Papeete, Tahiti. Discovered by American sailors in 1798, Flint was described as a "tropical paradise." The island surrounded a deep, blue lagoon with an average, year-round temperature of 77 degrees. It was ten degrees south of the Equator.

The promotion took two months to arrange. With cooperation from the U.S. State Department, The National Oceanic and Atmospheric Administration, The Republic of Kiribati,

The British State Department, The French Department of State, the government of French Polynesia and an extraordinarily resourceful travel agency in Venice, California, our "prize package" was complete.

WWCK would give away a "Trip to Flint!"

We first announced that we were about to introduce the greatest radio promotion in the history of Michigan, and it would mean journeying "from Flint to Flint to Flint." Everyone thought we were doing some sort of bizarre campaign for the Chamber of Commerce. After a week of teasing, the complete outline of the promotion was presented in a masterfully produced 15-minute announcement, which had taken over 20 hours to complete. Each step of the mission was introduced with sound effects, staging music and killer narrative.

The approach was quite simple. WWCK had discovered there was an island called "Flint" in the South Pacific. We wanted to prepare a "WWCK Time Capsule," filled with contemporary artifacts from Flint, Michigan. We needed a willing couple to travel to the island and bury the capsule beneath the sand where it would "await discovery by some future civilization who will know of us all through the incredible achievement of our winning couple." We also had an imaginary "WWCK Time Capsule" which we would hide "somewhere in our 105 FM listening area." We would give clues. Whoever eventually guessed the location would head for Flint. And what a trip it would be.

Our winners would be picked-up in the WWCK Super Van and driven to Metro Airport in Detroit, from which they would fly to Las Vegas for 24 hours of casino enjoyment, and a Master Suite at the MGM Grand. The next morning, it was on to Los Angeles for another 24 hour stop-over with studio tours and a visit to Disneyland. Then the real excitement would begin. There would be a non-stop flight to Papeete, Tahiti, via "Air Tunguru," and several days of enjoyment at the luxurious Te Puna Bel Air Resort in a private bungalow, adjacent to a natural spring-fed pool. After taking in the sights and sounds of Papeete and its surroundings, our couple would board the 54 foot schooner "Mimetaga," and be the only passengers aboard this special WWCK charter, heading romantically north with a professional, licensed crew to "The Lost Island of Flint."

The vessel would be piloted by the "legendary Captain Michel" who, through an interpreter, stated that he "understood WWCK's mission and philosophy with excitement and enthusiasm." After five days of voyage on the "Mimetaga," offering "private air-conditioned cabins with plenty of food, and refreshment of every kind," the schooner would anchor off "Flint" and all aboard would set ashore at dawn for a day of exploration as "Rock 'n Roll Robinson Crusoes" and complete their day at sunset by burying a genuine "Time Capsule" in the "eternal sand."

It was all real. The City of Flint went crazy. Newspaper and television coverage for WWCK was continuous during the entire duration of the promotion.

The eventual ratings of a 14.3 percent total audience share during the "Trip to Flint" period was not only the best in the history of the station, but the highest measurement by market share of any FM Rock station in the entire country. WWCK was voted "Album Rock Station of the Year" by the Burkhart/Abrams consultancy and Billboard Magazine. The "Trip to Flint" campaign won not only a "Gold First Place Addy" from the Flint Area Advertising Federation, but was determined by the judges to be "Best of Show," beating not only other local media efforts in all categories of entry, but also national Buick Motor Division advertising for the entire year.

Our "Trip to Flint" winning couple seemed to be ideal. They were both educated and articulate, and appeared thoroughly enchanted by their pending journey. They pledged total cooperation in calling-in reports and video-taping highlights of their adventure. She did her best to keep things together. It might have been better if he had not turned-out to be a raging alcoholic of vicious disposition.

I had asked the couple what their favorite beverages were so we could surprise them with a toast beginning their journey in our Super Van on the way to the airport in Detroit. He killed his pint of Jack Daniels before we hit the parking lot at Metro. What have we here? Just jitters?

They lost several thousand station-provided dollars of "spending money" in Las Vegas. It had been "stolen from their room." Sure. They were broke. I wired another two grand. They finally made it to Papeete, where our hero tried to sell their boat passage for cash. They were thrown-out of their hotel for various forms of misbehavior. All reports indicated he was regularly beating her. Screw it. I ordered the mission scrubbed and the couple sent home.

He went directly to the press and complained about the nightmare he had found in Tahiti with "machine-gun toting natives" and "Third World accommodations." I was quoted as saying that WWCK felt sorry that the couple had reacted so negatively, and that it was clear "personal issues beyond our control" had rendered the vacation disappointing. All in all, we got very fair and favorable local coverage.

The "National Globe" ran hubby's version. Our attorney told the asshole that we would sue for everything he had and tell the whole world the real story if he didn't shut-the-fuck-up. He agreed to do so. Soon after, word came that he threatened to burn down his house with wife inside. She had already gone to the police. The conversation was wire-tapped. Time in a Federal slammer awaited. Fuck him. All's well that ends well.

I had become President of the Flint Ad Club and was chosen "Businessman of the Year" by Flint Sales and Marketing Executives, a unique distinction for me and for radio. In April of 1983, Frazier Reams asked me to move to Toledo to accept appointment as Executive Vice-President and Chief Operating Officer of Reams Broadcasting.

CHAPTER FORTY-ONE

T-TOWN

I was extremely touched when the Flint Journal recognized my departure with a front-page story headlined "Goodbye, Peter C." The article by Dave Guilford tracked my history in the market since the "Beatle Days" almost 20 years earlier. It was more than generous with praise and positive comment. I'm sure I'll never live to see a finer obituary.

The reorganization of WWCK/WWMN was made relatively easy with the management talent available. I appointed Ron Shannon as Vice-President and General Manager, Nancy Dymond as Regional Sales Manager and Neil Kearney as Local Sales Manager.

From a corporate perspective, my elevation was perceived as the pirate frigate taking over the fleet. In spite of common ownership, Flint had remained organizationally isolated from WIOT/WCWA in Toledo. On my first morning in "T-Town," the only person I knew well was Frazier. Everyone else was a mystery— but not for long.

In terms of physical facilities, there were hardly any fair comparisons between Flint and Toledo.

WWCK/WWMN were housed in a rambling structure of undetermined origin and antiquated architectural design. It was a large garage with wings, located adjacent to an expressway in a district which had seen its best years far in the past. We often had floods in the rear of the building and broadcast equipment was functional, but hardly flashy. I had installed a new production studio during my tenure, and was fortunate in having young engineers who could fix anything and/or make do with what they had available. Technically, we sounded great on the air.

WIOT/WCWA and the corporate offices of Reams Broadcasting had just moved into Fort Industry Square, a string of old buildings which had been renovated and restored at a cost of some $35 million. We occupied the entire fourth floor of the largest section. Fort Industry Square represented the heart of a downtown Toledo undergoing fabulous change and renaissance.

We were right on the banks of the Maumee River, next to five acres of Promenade Park. Frazier was a partner in Fort Industry Square, and had participated in other new investments as well. In less than three years time, nearly $200 million dollars had been committed to construction and restoration projects in a five block area.

Our surroundings were upscale and expensive at Fort Industry. There was an extraordinarily appointed restaurant in the building called "The Boody House," named after a famous Toledo landmark. Beneath "The Boody House" was "Digby's," a lovely jazz bar offering excellent atmosphere, and copious supplies of alcohol. One didn't even have to venture outside Fort Industry to find generous drink and congenial companionship. Oh, my.

The Toledo Speedway had become a site of major outdoor rock concerts on a grand scale. WIOT was proud to host Bob Seger in early July with over 45,000 in attendance. He came in by helicopter. We spoke briefly backstage, agreeing we were both a long way from Sherwood Forest, he more than I. He received $300,000 for his appearance. It was the last authentic "Toledo Speedway Jam" until WIOT would present "Guns and Roses" in 1991.

I had been in Toledo two months when new competition broke into the market. A Bowling Green station moved their tower closer to the city limits and WRQN started rockin' the town.

They stole our WIOT morning team, and four company salespeople. One Account Executive who abandoned our temporarily floundering ship was a very uptight young lady who had been working with "Big Band" WCWA. She had taken great offense when, just after my Toledo arrival, I signed a General Staff Memo with the words "Rock 'n Roll!" This was an insult, she felt, to those not musically associated with anything more recent than early Perry Como. I ended my next Memo with "Swing's The Thing!" and she was temporarily mollified, but not enough to resist WRQN's siren call. Lucinda Bassett abandoned radio shortly after being reduced to playing tapes to clients from a phone booth in the pouring rain (WRQN not having paid certain bills) and started her own company. Lucinda's now made millions with her "Midwest Center for Stress and Anxiety" and I'd like to think writing "Rock 'n Roll!" that way, that time, is what jolted her loose.

On the Programming front, I found two guys who'd been together since high-school in the Milwaukee area working on a station in Kalamazoo. Bob Madden and Brian Nelson were greatly gifted. Bob was perpetually "up," and found the world exciting in every way. Brian was almost manic-depressive and the essence of dedicated cynicism. Their chemistry was perfect and they are today Milwaukee's top-rated morning rock personalities on WLZR.

We did a Toledo version of "Great Escape," except we chose the destination. I didn't want another Cape Cod. Our Toledo winners accompanied Bob and Brian to Australia for a week. They brought back excellent video which we used for post-promotional purposes. Bob and Brian were proudest of their camera-work offering prolonged focus on a flushing toilet. They proclaimed with elated wonder, "The water spins backwards!" Bob and Brian were always asking Frazier to buy them a pony.

Toledo General Sales Manager Bob Lafferty quickly replaced departed sales people with new hires of serious merit, including Tammy Kinzer. Tammy had worked with WCWA in times before, and had been lured away from Reams by the local cable company. She came back to WIOT, and was to set local sales records within weeks of her return.

All in all, we never missed a beat. WIOT ratings edged up to a 12.3 percent audience share, even as WRQN debuted with a 10.0 percent. I took great personal satisfaction in having successfully steered us through a potential crisis. Frazier was happy. His wife Susan was our Public Relations Director and, with serious political ties, could cut through substantial red tape within city bureaucracy. WEBN in Cincinnati had pioneered "Fireworks on the River" several years before. We expanded on the idea.

Our first "WIOT/WCWA Sky Concert" was held on Labor Day in 1983 as a conclusion to the "Toledo Festival of the Arts." It was pyrotechnics synchronized to music. In subsequent years, we would add the 4th of July to our schedule. Future productions would be executed on eight-track tape with sound effects, laser-guns and direct electronic-firing incorporated into our efforts. Giant speaker banks would line both sides of the Maumee. Estimated crowd size would increase to a half-million in attendance and even more watching live television coverage in the comfort of their homes. The "Sky Concert" fireworks became an ultimate corporate statement. Reams Broadcasting ruled the river as WIOT/WCWA took the town.

I attended an ABC Radio Network Affiliates Meeting in Palm Beach, Florida, and was elected Chairman of the Rock Network Affiliates Board. WIOT and WWCK both carried the network. I was quite excited with the opportunity to offer direct input into national programming plans.

Westwood One had dropped their involvement with "Buffalo Dick's Radio Ranch," due to content problems with some affiliates. I brought Jeff Lamb to Toledo, where I would try to launch our own Reams Broadcasting efforts to syndicate the show. We were now carrying "Radio Ranch" in Toledo and Muskegon as well as Flint. We had recorded our first "WIOT/ WCWA Fireworks Soundtrack" in Jeff's Toledo apartment. To further justify Jeff's salary, I tried him out as a disc-jockey on WIOT. It was awful. Without the character voices and conceptual opportunities afforded by "Radio Ranch," Jeff didn't know who Jeff was. We decided to concentrate on "Buffalo Dick," but I was facing problems finding adequate time to properly pursue the project. We needed someone who could both personally manage Jeff and sell the program coast-to-coast. An excellent candidate appeared on the scene who had expressed his interest and availability. Jeff and I waited at my house for his arrival on a sunny September afternoon. I received a call from my prospect. He had been stopped for speeding as he crossed into Ohio from Michigan and was stranded at the Sylvania Post of the Highway Patrol in lieu of $45 bond. He needed us to bail him out. Terry Knight was broke.

When Terry Knight and Grand Funk Railroad parted company in 1973, Terry had come out of the deal with approximately $10 million. He owned his own jet planes, hung-out with the stars, and had raced cars with Paul Newman. He had managed English model "Twiggy," and had become involved with motion pictures, Broadway musicals and varied investments around the world. He was one of the smartest and fastest players on the circuit. It got too fast and not at all smart.

Terry and I had spoken many times since he surfaced back in Flint shortly before my move to Toledo. He was honest in stating his predicament. He thought he might like to return to his disc-jockey roots and try an airshift on WWCK. That seemed unusual. I had discussed "Radio Ranch" with Terry, and how I felt it offered a natural opportunity with substantial potential. He was coming to Toledo to spend time with Jeff. We sprang him from the cooler in Sylvania.

Terry and Jeff worked together for two weeks. Jeff was waiting for lightning to strike. If Terry had brought Grand Funk Railroad from obscurity to world fame, "Buffalo Dick" could surely ascend with similar magnificence. Even part-way wouldn't be half-bad. Terry seemed more interested in the creative side of things, exactly what we didn't need. The product was already proven. We wanted networking, not circle-jerking. Terry decided he just wanted to write. We abandoned the exercise and wished Terry well. He asked me if he could borrow $1000. I politely declined.

Terry's fall was as spectacular and awesome as his rise. A meteor burns brightest only seconds before impact. Had Jeff and I witnessed final flame-out? We were not to know. Terry left Toledo and disappeared. Mr. Knight's whereabouts first remained an enigma, with rumors of participation in a Federal Witness Protection Program, but then came news he was living openly and happily in Yuma, writing books for little children.

Reams Broadcasting moved Jeff back to Flint in late November, and put expanded "Radio Ranch" efforts on a backburner. Jeff and I remained friends, and I promised him we'd work together again— a pledge which was honored seven years later when Jeff would host one of the highest-rated morning shows in Toledo history on WIOT with a completely different approach. Sometimes it takes a while figuring things out.

1984 started with attendance in January at the annual "Burkhart/Abrams Programming Conference" with Bob Lafferty, Ron Shannon and Susan Reams. It was held in San Francisco at the Fairmont Hotel and featured many wild, unusual highlights.

There was a special record company party at the "Starship Mansion" where Jefferson Airship/Starship had lived for many years. With the strains of "White Rabbit" thumping away in the background, Susan Reams met lead-guitarist Paul Kantner and asked him what he did. He dryly told her he "lived in the house," then proceeded to roll the largest joint in history of the world outside Kingston. He fired-up and thrust the monstrous mountain of marijuana at Mrs. Reams. Without hesitation, she courteously faked a toke or two and passed it along. She excitedly whispered.

"Peter. Peter! Is that a joint?"

Right.

"I'm not sure, Susan, but I expect we should go along with it."

"Well, I think we should too!"

Right.

"Right!"

Ron, being a former-musician, got carried away with it all and wanted to drive our tour bus upon leaving the mansion. He sensed the hills of San Francisco offered exceptional promise for motoring sport. Popular sentiment carefully expressed persuaded him to the contrary.

We were treated to a trip north into Sonoma Wine Country as guests of the rock group "Journey." Their private chef fixed lunch for us on a verandah overlooking the Pacific. Dessert was Hawaiian "Maui Wowie." What a thoughtful touch. Lee Abrams and I smoked our way down through Sausalito and across the Golden Gate Bridge at sunset. Incredible.

We were at a meeting the next day when James Brown walked into the room. The "Godfather of Soul" was appearing at the Fairmont, and had heard that some radio people were hanging about. He just stopped-in to say hello. Susan shook his hand and told him how much she loved his work. She later asked me who he was. She was under the impression she had been introduced to "James Bond." He certainly looked different off-screen.

We all returned home with the satisfaction that only hard work, sleepless nights, and diligent application of effort at a radio convention can bring.

I appointed Lafferty as General Manager of the Toledo stations.

Neil Kearney accepted the position of Vice-President and General Manager of WKBZ/WRNF in Muskegon. Frazier and Susan had just purchased an FM companion for the AM albatross.

Muskegon was the source of constant frustration. It was losing well over $250,000 a year, as was WCWA in Toledo. WIOT and WWCK were enormously profitable. It was imperative that losses be reduced to assure continuing prosperity. Neil seemed ready for the challenge in Muskegon, even as Bob was formulating new plans for our Toledo AM.

Within two years, Neil would sharply curtail Muskegon deficits and gain enormous managerial experience for a greater task ahead. Under his guidance, WKBZ would become the highest-rated AM station in Western Michigan and WRNF-FM would triple its listenership and become Muskegon's leading contemporary music outlet. Neil became active in the Muskegon Chamber of Commerce and staged 4th of July "Sky Concerts" on Lake Michigan simulcast on WKBZ/WRNF. Where'd he get that idea?

In Toledo, we decided to take another giant step in dominating the downtown riverfront. Promenade Park was not only right next to Fort Industry Square and our radio stations, but looked to me like a great place for concerts. ROCK 'N ROLL!

Starting in 1984, WIOT's Toledo "River Rallies" rocked the docks for the next decade with national talent and exceptional crowds. Six or seven major events were scheduled each season from Memorial Day through Labor Day. Admission was free-of-charge with beer sold. WIOT attractions presented included Mitch Ryder, Cheap Trick, REO Speedwagon, The Hooters, Bo Diddley, Loverboy, The Outlaws, Rare Earth, Todd Rundgren, Bachman-Turner-Overdrive, Eddie Money, Jason Bonham, Martha and the Vandellas, :38 Special, The Guess Who, Peter Frampton and many more.

I attended the 1984 National Association of Broadcasters Radio Conference in Los Angeles in September. It was brutally hot.

Following four days of meetings, I traveled south to attend another five days of sessions with the ABC Affiliates Group at the brand new Ritz Carlton complex in Laguna Nigel. It didn't suck. Eileen flew out to join me. The ABC Radio Laguna Nigel gathering took place before accountants grabbed the networks. The accommodations were the finest I had ever enjoyed. No expense was spared in assuring pleasant times for all. We were the very first occupants of the new structure and were treated like royalty by the hotel staff. They all wore neat little uniforms and kept coming up and asking if they could "refresh our drinks." In Flint I had become used to hearing "Whachurs?" It was all very nice.

Ed McLaughlin was a fine Irishman, and President of the ABC Radio Networks. I played bongos in the hotel bar with him 'til 5 a.m. one morning. Ed was to leave ABC after Capitol Cities took over. He "retired" to create his own satellite network, and took a run at Paul Harvey. When that idea came to naught, he found a talk-show host in Sacramento he felt worthy of "putting up on the bird." His discovery had been fired from a number of stations for "lack of talent," but Ed could spot a good thing when he heard it and trusted his instincts. Rush Limbaugh didn't disappoint him.

Saturday morning was to be the final big session at the meetings. Each network affiliate group was to come up with a campaign against alcohol abuse and present their ideas at that time before all assembled. As Chairman of the Rock Affiliates, I would do the honors.

Friday night we met to discuss strategy. This was an important item. There were rumors in Washington about possible restrictions being placed on broadcast advertising for beer and wine. Such action could cost the radio industry millions of dollars. We had already been seriously screwed with a ban on cigarettes. It was time to display responsible recognition of alcohol's dangerous potentials, and direct meaningful professional attention to Congressional concerns. Anything less could see us nailed anew. It seemed artistic to suggest we all get really drunk and deal with the problem as close to it as we could get. I was a popular Chairman. We ended the evening with a tequila duel. After 11 rounds, I called it a draw. I held up a napkin marked "R.O.C.K." It was the name of our network and I loved acronyms.

The following morning, we received standing applause from all after I summarized the masterful outline for our "R.O.C.K." ("Reckless Operators Can Kill!") Campaign. We realized heavy network play with our efforts, and later received several industry awards. The positive press was sensational. Ed McLaughlin sent me a personal note of congratulations, expressing his pleasure with our project. What made me the happiest was not passing-out at the podium during my presentation. Although functionally sober, I was deservedly in utter agony before a highly influential audience of inestimable professional importance, as a direct consequence of having once again yielded beyond restraint to undisciplined indulgence, far past any reasonable norm. Then again, I had come up with "R.O.C.K." only after that last tequila. And you never know what's enough until you do too much.

The Cavanaugh family had moved to Perrysburg, Ohio. Perrysburg is just south of Toledo, across the Maumee River in Wood County. Our "little girls" were no longer little.

Laurie, the oldest, had left for college at Central Michigan University the year we moved to Ohio. Colleen would graduate from Perrysburg High School the following year and attend Bowling Green State University, just down the road. Candace would follow in 1988 and journey south to Miami of Ohio at Oxford before completing Law School at the University of Detroit in '95. Our "baby," Susan, would leave for Ohio University in Athens in the autumn of '91. All four daughters were to attend different schools within the same collegiate conference. I had always encouraged unified diversity.

When Ronald Reagan made his successful bid for re-election in the fall of 1984, Perrysburg was the final destination on a whistle-stop train tour through Ohio. It had been arranged to capture a nostalgic sense of traditional American political campaign history. There were Secret Service agents swarming all over our tiny town. Reagan spoke only four blocks from my house. His last words were that Democrats always thought it was April 15th, but Republicans wanted every new day to be the Fourth of July. Right on cue, fireworks exploded in the distance, and a band struck-up "Stars and Stripes Forever." It was slick as hell. Paul W. Smith acted as Master of Ceremonies.

Paul had worked with me at WCWA and was then doing a morning show on CKLW in Detroit. Paul W. Smith had once made approach for a salary increase with the greatest line heard by me before or since, in the context of such a request. Paul had forlornly looked my way and said, "I want you to clearly understand that I'm not selfishly thinking about myself in this matter. What's at stake here is the well-being of my future wives." He got a laugh, but not the raise. Spending later years at WABC in New York and WWDB-FM in Philadelphia, Paul eventually replaced the legendary J. P. McCarthy as morning show host on "The Great Voice of the Great Lakes", Detroit's WJR.

Ron Shannon was leaving Flint. He had received an opportunity to become President of a broadcast group based in Little Rock, Arkansas. We both agreed on a choice as Ron's successor. Nancy Dymond would become Vice-President and General Manager of the stations, and the first female to occupy such a position in Flint radio. Nancy was once described by one of our more eloquent consultants as being "a curious combination of "Rebecca of Sunnybrook Farm" and "Ilsa, The Nazi-Queen She-Bitch." She was ecstatic over her promotion, but would shortly wonder why the hell she'd ever been so happy.

WGMZ-FM in Flint had changed format and call-letters from "Beautiful Music" to "Adult Contemporary" just before Ron's departure, and were seriously threatening WWCK's older listenership by offering a plethora of rock "oldies" in their music mix on WCRZ-FM. WIOG-FM in Saginaw was about to change tower location, and dramatically upgrade their signal into Flint. They were programming "Rock Top Forty" which would radically impact WWCK's younger demographics. Bitter competitive pressures were in the wind as our lovely Ms. Dymond took the helm of the "Good Ship 105."

Early '86 saw Lee Abrams visit Toledo in February when he spoke before a group of WIOT/WCWA clients, who were assembled at a special Advertising Clinic presented by Reams Broadcasting at the ever-exclusive Sofitel Hotel, which was very "French." We also featured Erica Farber from McGavren-Guild (our rep firm) and Tom Birch, President of Birch Radio Ratings. Tom had made significant inroads establishing his ratings firm as a viable alternative to Arbitron and, as far as I was concerned, he offered a superior methodology to the older service. All of our speakers were excellent. Tom and Erica had to leave town. Lee Abrams decided to spend time with us. Look out. The party lasted until 4:30 the following morning.

I went home to shower after first making snow-angels in my backyard. That I occasionally behave in such manner without audience is a particular point of Irish pride. I was at work by 8 AM. There was a small cut on my head, which Lee told me had come from a security guard's nightstick. I sheepishly reported this to Frazier, and later was informed by Lee that he had been kidding. Score one for Abrams.

I called a friend at the Sofitel and had them run a fake computer invoice for damages in Lee's room. The amount came to $5,987. When it was hand-delivered, I gave it to Frazier. He presented it to Lee with grave manner. Make that a tie with Cavanaugh.

Frazier and I visited both Cincinnati and Nashville.

Frazier was interested in adding new properties to the group. WSKS-FM was available in Cincinnati for $4.5 million. WSIX

AM/FM in Nashville was on the market for $8 million. Negotiations continued through the summer months. It seemed as though we would move on one or the other opportunity, given favorable terms and adequate financing. In September, Frazier called me on his car phone. He was buying both.

CHAPTER FORTY-TWO

EASY MONEY

A pause for review seems in order.

Financial speculation in the '80s has since become notorious, only later overshadowed by the dot-com and NASDAQ crashes of 2000. There were "Barbarians at The Gate" in many industries. Radio was no exception. Wild money was floating all about. Station prices were being driven upward by astounding ratios. It was easy money. In pursuit, we flew down to Cincinnati on Tuesday, September 23rd, 1986.

WSKS-FM was an anomaly. Her "sister station" was the powerful 50,000 watt WLW-AM. It was the home of the Cincinnati Reds. The combination represented a rare instance wherein the AM partner was outbilling its FM counterpart by at least 8 to 1. By the middle '80s, it was normally the other way around. Both facilities were operated by Republic Broadcasting. They were about to merge with Cincinnati-based Jacor Corporation. Jacor already owned WEBN-FM in Cincinnati, which meant that Republic had to blow-off their FM to make the deal work. The Federal Communications Commission only allowed a single entity to own one AM and one FM in any given market. Back then.

My original idea had been to rock WSKS-FM and smash it up against WEBN. WEBN was the #1 Rock station in Cincinnati. I was certain we could bring them to their knees. That was now out of the question. Frank Wood was the President of Jacor.

Frank had traded WEBN-FM for a significant share of Jacor stock and the corporate position. His father had founded and sold him the radio station. Frank had earned a Law Degree from Harvard University. He had not been disadvantaged. Still, there was little doubt he was distinguished by his own efforts. Circumstances had offered acceleration. It was made clear in final discussions that WSKS-FM would be available to Reams only if we agreed to take it Country. The last thing Frank needed was a bunch of dipshits from Toledo trying to fuck his pride and joy. Frazier agreed to the condition.

I met with Randy Michaels, who worked with Republic, and would become Programming Vice-President of Jacor following the merger. He would much later be named President following Frank's departure and corporate reorganization necessitated by financial discomfort. Randy's life was radio and he would go spiraling to the peak. Personal and professional existence were one and the same, with no distinction. He was architect of "The Beaver."

WSKS-FM disappeared and there it was: WBVE-FM. "The Beaver."

Randy recruited an entirely new staff in less than a week. He brought them out for a night of carousing at every significant Country bar in Cincinnati to "capture life-style focus." He rented a local recording studio and brought in a band. The jingles were real shit-kickin' jams.

"Weeeeeeyyyyyylllll. It's finally on the ray-dee-ooooh. Real Country Music. Beaver Ninety-Six-and-a-Haaaaaaaaayyyyyffffff."

They were inspiring.

Although Reams would not assume control until near the end of the year, Randy wanted to give us a running start. The fact that WSKS had been programming a form of "MTV Rock" was also part of the equation. It wouldn't hurt WEBN to make that go away immediately. The future was taking shape. Randy also had balls.

As part of our final talks, once the Country issue had been presented as a required prelude to purchase, I suggested to Frazier that we throw in a condition of our own. Republic had to guarantee an Arbitron performance in the Fall '86 Cincinnati ratings no lower than WSKS's then-current level of a 3.8 percent share. With a completely radical format change being undertaken even as the survey started, this would be a formidable task. Anything less would result in a lowering of the purchase price by as much as $.5 million. Randy didn't flinch and the deal was cut. He was to hit that number right on the nose. He, himself, hosted WBVE's very first few hours on the air. He reminded the competition that they might win some battles in life, but they "could never lick the Beaver." I still have that on tape.

From Cincinnati, Frazier and I flew straight down to Nashville.

WSIX AM/FM had been owned by General Electric, and sold to another group for whom price inflation would be savior. Operationally, they had pretty much fucked-it-up trying to save their way to prosperity. Both stations were Country, with most sales action on the FM. WSM AM/FM was the other Nashville Country combo. They were kickin'-butt.

We had a meeting with the Nashville staff, and I was impressed with the potentials I saw. Spending several days in the market, the only name I kept hearing was "Gerry House." Gerry had been at WSIX-FM and had switched to WSM-FM when he couldn't get a raise. He was now in Los Angleles at KLAC-AM, working with the legendary Scott Carpenter. Word was that he'd love to return back home, but it would be expensive to lure him back. I obtained some tapes and listened. He'd be worth every cent, being one of the best I'd ever heard.

Everything was starting to assume a profound surrealistic quality. Frazier and I discussed immediate priorities. We would sell Muskegon. It had never been a major profit center, and I wanted Neil Kearney to manage "The Beaver." We would also test the waters on a price for Flint. With new parameters of competition already impacting, it seemed a perfect time. We would also drop "Big Band" on WCWA, and move to a "'50s Oldies" format, which would generate audience more compatible with WIOT's listenership for sales purposes. We never discussed financing of our new properties. I would not presume to intrude on such matters. As far as I knew, Frazier might have more money than Leona Helmsley and Donald Trump combined, pardon the thought.

Not quite.

Frazier had arranged for "Certificates of Deposit" of $500,000 each for our purchases in Cincinnati and Nashville. These were like "non-loan-loans." If we didn't go ahead with the deals, the bank would spring for a million dollars in forfeiture, and Frazier would have to somehow make it good.

On the 23rd of December, we were driving to Cincinnati. We would close that morning on the purchase of WSKS, now WBVE. Simultaneously, the Republic/Jacor merger would be finalized in the same room. Timing was everything. It was all very exciting.

We were heading south on I-75 at eighty miles-an-hour in Frazier's BMW, radar detector engaged. We had just passed Dayton. Frazier spoke quite casually, as though discussing cows.

"Peter, there's something we should think about."

"Hmm?"

"I'll do all the talking."

"Hmmmmmm?"

"We don't have the money yet."

What? "We don't have the money yet?" I sure as fuck didn't have the money. I had about a hundred bucks on me and a Visa card. With luck, I might be able to cover lunch if I shorted the tip.

It was no time to panic. It never is.

The closing was scheduled for 10 in an elegant, oak-walled Conference Room on the 23rd floor of the Central Bank Building. The carpeting was several inches deep. A view of Cincinnati's downtown skyline was spectacular.

There were over 30 participants in attendance, mostly attorneys with individual hourly rates easily twice the contents of my wallet. Closing documents were everywhere. There was heavy, rich, energized tension in the air. The transactions about to be executed involved more than $40 million in properties. Excruciating care had been exercised in fitting every last piece into proper order. There would be no mistakes. It would be perfect. This was big-time boogie.

Frazier had decided to wait until the meeting started to drop his goody. He had a zestful spirit and loved surprises.

The shrieking silence defies description. For the only time in my life, I actually believe I heard hearts stop. No one said a word. One could not detect breath being taken. Frazier's eyes roamed around the table with a patient stare of perplexed wonder, as though something was curiously wrong with everyone else. The Treasurer of Republic finally loudly gasped and stood, moaning with chagrin and despair.

"Frazier, you told me yesterday you had the money!!"

"Well. I thought I did!"

Frazier had raised his deep, baritone voice ever so slightly on the word "did!" It seemed to shake the room. Within the somber, suddenly darkened atmosphere which prevailed, Frazier had effectively just told the Treasurer guy he could go fuck himself. Jesus. Time-Out.

As things were, Frazier had everyone by the balls. Nothing could proceed until the WBVE issue was resolved. There was no turning-back. Everything had been filed with the FCC. It had taken three months to get approval. Damn. With $40 million hanging in the air, any prolonged delay could cost a fortune. Shit. Jacor would be better off funding Frazier's purchase themselves. It was really the only sensible option. Fuck.

This all took about five hours. Frazier's only seriously expressed concern, continually repeated, was where we should dine that night.

They told him how it would have to be.

Not a problem.

They'd lend him the money for one hundred and twenty days at 15 percent interest.

That sounded fair.

He would have to sign with both corporate and personal guarantees and everything he owned anywhere as collateral.

Who's got a pen?

He would have to pay for all additional legal expenses at horrendous overtime rates sure to be incurred in preparing new drafts on a billion-trillion documents over the Holiday Season because everything needed to be finished before the end of the year for major tax reasons which Frazier certainly had known about and thanks-a-lot-you've-fucked-up-everybody's-Christmas-you-asshole.

Fine.

It was done.

I detected a barely discernible sigh of relief. I knew Frazier had finally found peaceful resolution in his mind. It would be shared. He leaned over and whispered in my ear. We would enjoy dinner that evening at the Westin, overlooking Fountain Square.

I called Neil Kearney at the WLW Sales Offices of WBVE and asked him to join us. Neil had already been in place for four weeks preparing for our transition. WLW's General Manager had told him it was rumored that Frazier had shown up without any cash. Neil had spent the day wondering if there were any late-night bartending positions open back at "The Light" in Flint. I told him everything had been arranged. For the moment.

If Cincinnati had barely made it, where were we with Nashville?

CHAPTER FORTY-THREE

EL SUCKO CENTRAL

Frazier and I spent most of January visiting banks. He confided that he was astounded raising the money for our new ventures had proven such a challenge. He was dead-serious. I suggested Nashville dreams might have to wait. We were looking for $12.5 million and the clock was ticking on our time-pressing, mind-distressing Jacor note. Cut bait? We'd wait.

Frazier had defaulted on the Nashville purchase agreement and another buyer appeared. They offered $8.2 million. They would bring back Gerry House and quickly own the market. $500,000 was now owed by Reams on the "Certificate of Deposit."

Obtaining funding may have been much easier, had we not pissed-away a half-million on absolutely nothing. That's the sort of thing that catches notice. Although their moment was yet to come, Beavis and Butt-Head went banking.

"Ummmmmmmm. We'd like to borrow $8 million?"

"Ahhhhhhhhhhh. It's for this radio station?"

"Errrrrrrrrrrrrrr. "Assets? Heh-hah-heh-heh-hah-heh-hah-heh."

We had turned-down $5.25 million for our Flint holdings shortly after signing the Cincinnati/Nashville contracts five months earlier. An advisor had informed Frazier he suspected Flint to be worth a minimum of 6 million. Then General Motors announced another series of massive lay-offs in Flint, and Michael Moore was in the streets filming "Roger and Me." Unemployment in Genesee County had reached 24 percent. WWCK's ratings were getting hammered by WCRZ-FM and WIOG-FM. Former listenership was about to be cut in half. Flint had become El Sucko Central.

In Toledo, WIOT had experienced a troubled time with the release of an Arbitron showing a 6.7 percent total audience share at the same time Birch Ratings had tracked us at a 15.3 percent position. Something was wrong. I reviewed all the initial data and called Arbitron. Their younger male sampling had been woefully inadequate in the Metro area. I demanded they recall the book. They told me I wasn't a subscriber and, "if I wanted to sue them, I could get in line." I charged to the front of the pack and instituted litigation charging Arbitron with "Racketeering" under Federal "RICO" statutes. In the Arbitron survey under question, it just happened that every Arbitron subscriber in Toledo had gone up and every non-subscriber had dropped down. Call it fate. When the facts are on your side, truth is never an issue. The next Arbitron measurement had WIOT back in double digits. It was where we belonged. We dropped our suit. The 6.7 percent hurt us, nevertheless. Agency "cost-per-point" computers are blind in their precision.

We found an "Investment Specialist" who knew her way around the barn. She radiated confidence, had excellent credentials, and gave great hope. She lived on Beacon Hill in Boston. That should have been a clue. She threw together a smokin' prospectus. Mirrors came from the replicate key on Lotus. She put together a $6 million loan with Rhode Island Hospital Trust and still had $2 million left to go. A venture capital firm in Boston was glad to kick in the last few bucks. What's $2 million between friends? They were incredibly warm, graciously understanding and charmingly attentive. Irish. Interest was only 25 percent a year. Frazier only had to pay 10 percent, if he wanted.

The other fifteen would simply be added to the principle amount— easier than falling off a cliff.

The deal was transacted only hours before Jacor would have seized all of Frazier's assets. We were on our way. Our "Investment Specialist" picked-up her check, too. $250,000 every few months keeps a girl healthy, wealthy and on the Hill.

We kept things going through the end.

CHAPTER FORTY-FOUR

A DEAD BEAVER AND NIGGER MUSIC

WWCK AM/FM was sold in December of 1988 for $2.25 million. The pair would be resold ten years later for over seven times as much.

Nancy Dymond was transferred to Toledo when Bob Lafferty jumped the fence with another four salespeople to become General Manager of WRQN. Bob had seen the writing on the wall. It didn't say "Stick Around, Sucker!" All five stayed less than two years.

Nancy brought Tammy Kinzer back from Boston as General Sales Manager. Tammy had left Reams to work in Chicago, and then had moved out East. Nancy and Tammy increased WIOT revenue thirty percent over the prior year.

WCWA's conversion to "Oldies" was a smash. AM billings jumped 40 percent.

Combined WIOT/WCWA radio revenue not only led the market in every category, but was a full 25 percent ahead of our closest competitor. In listenership, WIOT climbed to first-place, and became the highest-rated rock station in the country. Reams Broadcasting had achieved such distinction now in both Flint and Toledo.

Jeff Lamb returned and just did voices, while a gentleman named Mark Benson played disc-jockey on our WIOT morning show. Ratings rocketed.

Neil Kearney took "The Beaver" to the top for the first two

years of Reams' ownership. Monthly revenue went from $20,000 to $200,000 in eighteen months. The competition didn't stand still. WUBE grabbed the audience back with millions of dollars in promotional expenditure. WBVE's advertising budget had disappeared. All available cash was going to pay loan interest.

Frazier decided to sell Cincinnati. Joe Field of Entercom offered $5.8 million for the property. We signed the agreement in October of '89 and flew to Washington on March 12, 1990, to close the deal. Our broker told us we were catching the last stagecoach out of Dodge. Radio station prices were crashing everywhere. Mr. Field pulled out at the last minute, seemingly practiced at the act. Neil Kearney had already accepted a new position in Fort Wayne and was leaving. I had a dead Beaver on my hands. I would commute to Cincinnati every week for the next two years. It was certain that bankruptcy and foreclosure were just around the bend. I wanted to go out with a scream.

"Valhalla!

I am coming!!"

In a radical move approved due to pressing circumstance, I drove to Cincinnati without warning on the morning after Christmas '90 with a number of Toledo-produced "IDs," "Promos," "Comedy Inserts" and a CD library containing nothing but hard-core, screeching, screaming Rock 'n Roll.

At High Noon, I commandeered the studios without prior notice to the audience (all pretty much 35+ "Country" fans) and went straight from Buck Owens into six solid hours of an ancient and hypnotic classic from the late '50s. "They're Coming To Take Me Away" was repeated over and over again, backwards and forwards, on a tape loop. We ran some vaguely detectable audio in the background approximating snarls and growls of suggested evil incarnate. We generally offered the impression that the station had been taken over by alien invaders, who had seized the building with questionable intent. A deep, mysterious, tortured voice could be faintly heard beneath the din warning, "Don't call the police!"

Our WBVE parking lot was quickly surrounded by squad cars. After discussing the matter with the sergeants, I willingly agreed to add a broadcast disclaimer every 15 minutes.

"Ladies and Gentlemen!"

"Nothing is wrong with your radios!"

"There is absolutely no cause for concern, panic, terror or alarm!"

"But!"

"THE BEAVER has left the building!"

After six hours, we went directly into new call-letters "WZRZ-Z-ROCK!!!" and played four solid days of pure Led Zeppelin. WEBN's proud mascot was "The Frog." Every half-hour, we would execute "The Frog" by blowing him up, mixing him in a blender, dropping him in a grinder, drowning him in the Ohio, garroting him with piano wire, pulling-out his eyes with tiny fish hooks, sawing him into painful pieces or crushing his little frog nuts in a vise. It was all done with sound effects. Our production team creatively outdid themselves with wildly imaginative, savagely diabolical terminations.

There was a "WBVE listener comment line", which was recording observations on our Led Zeppelin music from former "Beaver Fans." More than half the calls profanely condemned our playing "all that nigger music." I hadn't heard such expression in relationship to rock since my earliest days at WNDR. We played many of the calls on-the-air between Zeppelin cuts.

After four days of getting the Led out, we linked with satellite. From that point forward, WZRZ blasted nothing but "Flame-Throwin', Ass-Kickin', Name-Takin'" Rock music. It was exclusively and narrowly aimed at a young male audience. On the proverbial scale of one to ten, if WIOT was an "8", "Z-Rock" was an "87." "Z-Rock" was programmed by Satellite Music Network in Dallas, Texas. It was a creation of Lee Abrams.

On the first day of change, we had wound up with headlines in both Cincinnati newspapers and extended television coverage of the format shift. There were a number of concerned meetings. Phone banks had been jammed. People had panicked. It all had been very disorderly. Riots could have broken-out. Farmers might have run through their fields. Mice might have been trampled.

The general consensus from the authorities was that I had broken no local, state or federal laws during the exercise. Still, I had taken things to the edge of the envelope. They were still getting calls. I was a naughty Peter, even if nothing had really happened with which they could prove the point. I met with authorities, and agreed to let them know ahead if similar things were ever in the offing. They were delighted and particularly happy with the brand new "Z-ROCK" T-shirt every officer received. It displayed the picture of a shark eating a frog.

Within weeks, "Z-Rock" owned Cincinnati in Men (18-34), even beating WEBN in total audience by the end of two months. I have the March/April '91 Birch Radio Report for Cincinnati in front of me even now. It says:

WZRZ—8.0 %

WEBN—7.9 %

That's an historic fact!

Tammy Kinzer had joined me from Toledo and was appointed Vice-President and General Manager of WZRZ. She turned the ratings into instant revenue.

My fondest "Z-Rock" memory is from the night of May 21, 1992. A young gentleman (of whom I happily approved) was marrying my beautiful daughter Colleen in Cincinnati on May 23. A group of his friends decided to give him a Bachelor Party. Since he and I were, and remain, on excellent terms, he asked that I be invited to come along. Although I would suspect deeply disenchanted at the thought of having to drag "Colleen's Father around," the group was kind enough to ask me to join them. I surely did so.

We met in an elegant Lobby Bar at The Omni Netherland in Cincinnati, where Eileen and I were staying. It was 8 p.m. I promptly ordered up "Kick-Starts" for the celebrants. "Kick-Starts" are a triple-shot of Jamesons Irish Whiskey, and a beer to wash it down.

We were soon all the very best of ageless friends.

I then gently suggested that I was certainly not attempting to plan out the evening for everyone, but we could cross the Ohio River into Kentucky, where the radio station was doing a promotion if there was any interest. I only slightly hinted of what might wait ahead. Since all were in an adventurous mood by then and open to anything, we headed for the bridge.

WZRZ was broadcasting from a gigantic barge floating on the Ohio and anchored to a docking area directly across the river from downtown Cincinnati. The night of the 21st saw over 4000 gathered outdoors on the deck. They were crowded in tumultuous assembly. It was "Z-ROCK BARGE NIGHT!!!" Live music was generously being provided at supersonic levels by a major Swedish rock band named "Shotgun Messiah." Most importantly, I had scheduled the official judging that evening of over 50 bikini-clad, nubile young maidens. These were contestants vying for the enviable and much desired distinction of being chosen "Miss Z-Rock Babe." The contest seemed analytically, if not politically, correct.

I took the microphone at an appropriate point in time. I anointed and appointed all my fellow Bachelor Party attendees as "Our Official 'Z-Rock' Judging Panel." I further explained that they would be spending their next several hours fulfilling this critical assignment, and that all contestants would be expected to offer complete cooperation to the judges in their difficult, laborious efforts to arrive at a winner.

It was then that my soon-to-be son-in-law and his mates began to enjoy themselves beyond restraint, although certainly maintaining marginal propriety. They weren't bothering with the beer anymore, taking their whiskey the warrior way. We collectively entered into the very best of an extraordinary time. This all took place under a full, bright, May moon. Temperatures remained soothingly warm well past Midnight. The majestic skyline of downtown Cincinnati soared in the background, its lights reflecting eerily across the dark, rushing waters of the mighty Ohio.

Much later, I arranged for transportation back across the river to the Omni. I obtained extra rooms. A dozen or so exhausted celebrants found restful sleep, many on carpeting, across chairs and in various tubs. I woke them all and hosted breakfast in the early morning, suggesting excellent virtues to be found in recounting the prior evening's events with tasteful editing for wives, girlfriends, or fiancées. It was a thought with which everyone enthusiastically agreed.

So it was I walked my radiant Colleen down the aisle the following day and gave her away with particular paternal pride in both bride and groom— a Princess and a handsome Prince who'd proven truly worthy of her lovely hand.

WZRZ had two months to live.

Reams Broadcasting had entered Chapter Eleven in July of '91. Frazier had hung-on much longer than anyone expected. He surrendered in January of 1992.

That Irish Investment Firm from Boston would take things over. They would receive 90 percent of Reams Broadcasting and would cover debts still owed elsewhere. Everything would close as soon as the agreement was approved in Federal Bankruptcy Court, and by the Federal Communications Commission.

A partner from Boston and I met the following week in Cincinnati. Understandings were reached. I would remain with Reams Broadcasting through ownership transition. Frazier Reams would also exit at that time. I would broker the sale of WZRZ-FM for a handsome commission. Nancy Dymond would stay with the new company as Vice-President and General Manager of WIOT/WCWA. We shook hands.

My last day at Reams was September 17, 1992.

CHAPTER FORTY-FIVE

ROCK 'N ROLL

1992 was the 100th Anniversary of my Great-Grandfather's death. He had left Ireland during The Famine Years in 1848 and had crossed the North Atlantic to the green fields of America. He rests buried under a fine Celtic Cross in a little churchyard just north of Syracuse. His name is engraved in sharp and bold lettering, still clearly distinct with a century gone:

PETER CAVANAUGH

My namesake's handwriting appears in an old, worn book on Irish History which was passed down to me. It was all Peter left us in memory. This is what he wrote:

Cavanaugh
Diocese of Fern
County of Leinster
Town of Ballyoughter
Irish Nobility
Evicted By The English
And Abandoned By God

I had left broadcasting after 36 uninterrupted years. I knew where to go. Eileen and I drove to Detroit and caught a flight to Dublin. We rented a car and traveled the land without itinerary or agenda. There was no need. There were spirits everywhere. We were led.

Peter is listed as the son of James and Margaret Cavanaugh, born in the summer of 1816 in Ballyoughter. The town has disappeared. It was located east of Enniscorthy, just south of Dublin in the Wicklow Mountains near the Irish Sea.

Peter was baptized July 15 of that year, according to parish records now miraculously preserved on microfilm at the Library of Ireland in Dublin. The fancy spelling of the family name "Kavanagh" with a "C" and a superfluous "u" can be attributed to the transcribing priest, who wrote in a most graceful and elegant hand. Before and after his stewardship of some thirty years, the whole bunch were "Kavanaghs." The priest had faithfully noted births, marriages and deaths in the small community during his whole time of tenure. It is a ledger covered with invisible tears. There are five pages per year before "The Famine," and five years per page thereafter. Many in our family died of hunger.

Peter made it to America. He was unmarried and in his early thirties. He found an Irish bride in the States. Their son John, my Grandfather, was born in 1854. It was John's son, Donald, who died on the radio. Our direct Cavanaugh (Kavanagh) line is traced to the middle of the Twelfth Century and one Donal Kavanagh, who had become very disenchanted with his father, Dermod MacMurrough, King of Leinster.

Dermod was the Irish King who first let in the English to help extend his power and control over the entire island. He is described as: "No hero, but a large, lustful, blustering, hoarse-voiced man, whose name had an evil sound in the ears of the Irish. He was the bad son of a bad father, one who chose rather to be feared than loved." In honor of his friend, King Henry II of England, Dermod thought he'd take an English wife.

King MacMurrough wasn't much for courtship. He kidnapped "Chelsea of the Willows," a beautiful English noblewoman, and dragged her back to Ireland in chains. He married her, and impregnation with a son to be named Donal, quickly followed. The lovely Chelsea wasn't a withering willow. She introduced further disrepute into the family picture by poisoning Dermod and burning him alive on their Wedding Anniversary. She torched him with a flaming log, revenge with phallic overtones. She told King Henry she was sorry and built an Abbey for penance. She was royalty and could cut a good deal. Eileen and I walked the ruins of the Abbey at sunset. Only crows cried welcome.

Donal had faced an image problem. Although the family name was later fully redeemed with great honor by Donal's son, Art MacMurrough/Kavanaugh; with a traitorous father and murdering mom, Donal felt major disassociation would be highly appropriate and refused to be called a "MacMurrough." He chose "Kavanagh" as a new surname in honor of his counselor and close friend "Kavan," a prominent Irish priest and confessor.

Discussing DNA and what have you, it is striking to note that Dermod and Chelsea's genes undoubtedly enjoyed constant and particular reinforcement in a most unique manner all the way through to "The Great Hunger," and Peter's passage to America. Ballyoughter was less than five miles away from Fern, the ancient Irish capital from which Dermod and his fierce warriors ruled and plundered. Our particular tribal branch, as verified by those parish records in Dublin, thus never seriously strayed away from home for over 700 years between Dermod's smoldering remains and Peter's farewell to the groves of shillelagh and shamrock. Dermod and Chelsea have just kept on sharing each other, all forgiven, in a hard, continuing compression, common for those of Irish descent. It's never been otherwise.

Dermod and Chelsea had arrived late in the true Irish sense of things.

The village of Slane is forty-five miles northwest of Dublin. On its ancient castle grounds have played The Rolling Stones,

Bruce Springsteen, Bob Dylan and U-2. On the Hill of Slane, Saint Patrick proclaimed Ireland to be Christian in 433 A.D. by lighting a paschal fire. The burial chamber at Newgrange is on the banks of the River Boyne a few miles to the east. It is over 5000 years old.

The Newgrange chamber is a huge, circular, man-made mound of white and black boulders, largely covered with earth and grass. It measures 240 feet across and is 44 feet high. An entrance overlooks a broad bend in the river. A narrow tunnel leads 70 feet down into the earth. Passage is slow. A central chamber contains three rooms, all openly facing into the center. Water has never penetrated into the surrounding rocks. Construction was by master architects. It was built for the ages. The spiral markings are everywhere. Their meaning is unclear.

A small opening over the entrance is aligned so that the sun's rays penetrate and illuminate the chamber with a fiery red glow only once each year at the exact point of the Winter Solstice. It is seen as a symbol of rebirth and renewal. The effect lasts less than twenty minutes.

Newgrange was not erected as a tomb. It is a womb. It is two thousand years older than Stonehenge. It is perspective.

Eileen and I spent some time in England and visited Stonehenge, too. We went through the Tower of London, and saw where Henry had his heads hacked and many Irishmen spent long, last years. The British Museum was overwhelming. All the heroes were conquerors and kings. There were spoils from many lands. We climbed to the top of Saint Paul's Cathedral and spent hours at Westminister Abbey. We went to Tussaud's "Rock Circus" on Pickadilly. All the rock stars are in wax. Eileen had her picture taken with Freddy Mercury. He'd been dead for months. There were security alerts on the London Underground all the time. We stayed at the Copthorne Tara in Kensington.

We returned to Perrysburg in late October.

There was no question as to my immediate intent. Ireland had shown the way. There was only one thing I would do for a year. Nothing. I've felt quite rested since.

I remain 5000 years younger than Newgrange and still stay in touch with Sister Cecilia from the old Cathedral days. An indication of her lasting influence came during a 25th year High School Reunion in 1984. It was the first time the Class of '59 had ever assembled since Graduation. It had been then that we boys were told to "never again darken the doors of the school" following a brief beer-soaked misadventure.

Sister Cecilia had driven herself to Syracuse for the event from the Mother House in Maryland. It was evident that passage of time had changed her only in small ways. I was delighted to discover for the first time that her last name was Connolly. Such things had not been shared in earlier times.

Also in attendance was Army Major John Haywood.

John had entered the service and qualified for special assignment. He had successfully completed officer training as a Green Beret, repeating several tours in Viet Nam, volunteering for each and every one. He had flown helicopters as a combat pilot, then committed his life to the military.

I saw him coming in the front entrance and greeted him with a hug. I excitedly told him Sister Cecilia was in the next room. John thought he could use a drink. After double-scotches, he moved into the staging area and greeted Sister. She hugged him, too. In Viet Nam, the closely encountered enemy had been ferociously unfeared. Sister Cecilia was quite something else.

Sister Cecilia had been most emphatic back in the Fifties that Elvis Presley, Chuck Berry, Little Richard, the Platters, the Diamonds, the Del Vikings, Bo Diddley, Duane Eddy, Georgia Gibbs, Jody Reynolds, Ronnie Hawkins, Fats Domino and the rest of those "bold, brazen things" were "Occasions of Sin." She knew this to be true because Father Shannon told her so and he heard confessions.

Sister Cecilia Connolly had lived in the convent next to Cathedral school with other Sisters of Charity. They were only allowed to watch Bishop Fulton J. Sheen on television. Collective exposure to the newly emerging world of visual communication had been thus limited to 30 minutes each Tuesday night at 8.

A brilliant woman, trusting with unequivocal determination the tenets of her Church, Sister Cecilia saw nothing but dangerous rebellion in the new music of youth.

But I believed in Rock 'n Roll.

On the surface, this indigenously American music seems all about an uncomplicated, ageless desire to "feel good."

It's a natural sort of thing.

Like sex.

Looking at sex from a purely mechanical perspective, it's silly. Ecstasy ignoring embarrassment. What a juxtaposition. We follow powerfully transcendent instinctive inclinations and, in unqualified surrender, gain ultimate pleasure.

So might the enjoyment of certain sounds emerging in particular patterns featuring specific combinations of varying frequencies at appropriate amplitude offer suspect satisfaction, but only to those not blessed. Never, if it's in the blood.

It has been my experience that Rock 'n Roll Music and personal liberty are inseparable. Those who oppose one, will invariably oppose both.

Radio in 2002? Corporate consolidation has stalked the land. Late in the first Bush Administration, our FCC doubled prior ownership restrictions on radio stations, allowing the acquisition of two FM and two AM licenses in each broadcast market by a single entity. Don't blame Republicans. The 1996 Telecommunications Act, signed by President Clinton and supported in Congress with near bipartisan unanimity, doubled things again. Many companies came to own eight radio stations in a single city, and these corporations were purchased by even larger groups, which operated hundreds of outlets in dozens of states under singular organizational control. Randy Michaels is now President of Clear Channel Communications, directing well over a thousand properties. He's the very biggest.

Senior management radio positions were reduced by well over 60 percent in the first two years. The savings were incredible. Serious formatic competition has been eliminated in many instances, with former promotional dollars now flowing to the bottom-line. Cash-flow is superb.

Commercial rates are climbing, and advertisers seeking to use radio are paying much more for oftentimes less. Investors are ecstatic. And there won't be any new radio stations either. Licenses are locked. Frequencies frozen. The divvy is done. The broadcast towers are taken.

Of course, this sort of thing is happening everywhere you look.

After my year of hiatus, I contracted with out-of-town ownership to operate and assist in the sale of WSPD/WLQR in Toledo. They had paid $15 million for the combo in 1986 at the peak of the "Go-Go-'Eighties" and couldn't peddle them for four. I was there almost a year. We got $6.5 million for the pair, and "Radio Business Report" mentioned that "The price kept going up because the stations prospered under Peter Cavanaugh."

I had increased market revenue share by over 60 percent in the first four months, and recorded the highest "rating to rating" morning-drive audience increase in Toledo radio history on WSPD. My last official act at the stations was to fire a dozen employees for new buyers, including a Sports Director who'd been there almost 30 years.

Eileen and I sold our home and moved into a lovely Perrysburg apartment within easy walking distance of a friendly bar. I knew that when the money went, there would be more. There always is. I've never felt concern about such things.

Now we've seen other towers fall.

These are troubled times.

Love your family.

Support local radio friends.

Play your music loud and hard.

And thank you for reading my little stories. All of them are true.

Trust yourself any time you choose.

Be Rock 'n Roll.

PETER C. PRESENTS
THE King Of ROCK n' ROLL
CHUCK
WITH THE
WOOLIES
BERRY
SILVER HAWK
SUNDAY FUNNIES
RUMOR
SPRINGWELL
THE MIKE QUATRO JAM BAND
AND MOOG SYNTHESISER AND OTHERS
Wednesday
Sept. 1rst
Admission
$4.00
SHERWOOD FOREST
IN DAVISON
3p.m.'til midnite
outdoors, lakeside.
twin Concert stages.
bring everybody.
Final Summer '71 Concert

Wednesday, July 14th

Admission $4.00

Peter C. PRESENTS

3p.m.'til midnite

Bring picnic lunches, blankets, and lots of friends.

A Summer Outdoor Rock 'n Roll Revival

TWIN CONCERT STAGES

at Sherwood Forest in Davison

with

EDGAR WINTER'S WHITE TRASH

SAVAGE GRACE

THIRD POWER

GUARDIAN ANGEL FEATURING SCOTT MORGAN

MISTER FLOOD'S PARTY

QUESTIONMARK & THE MYSTERIANS

AND OTHERS

PRESTON

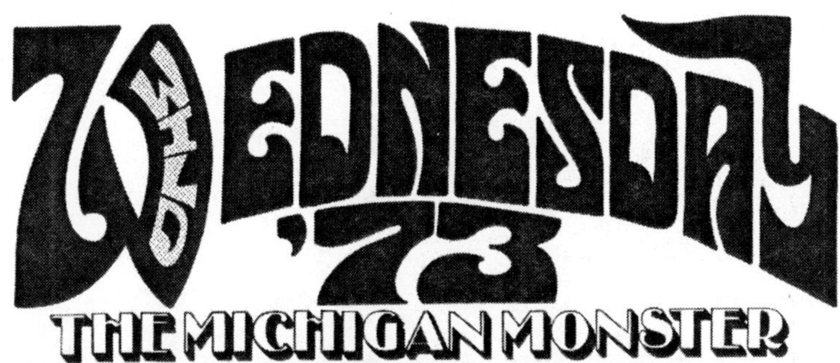

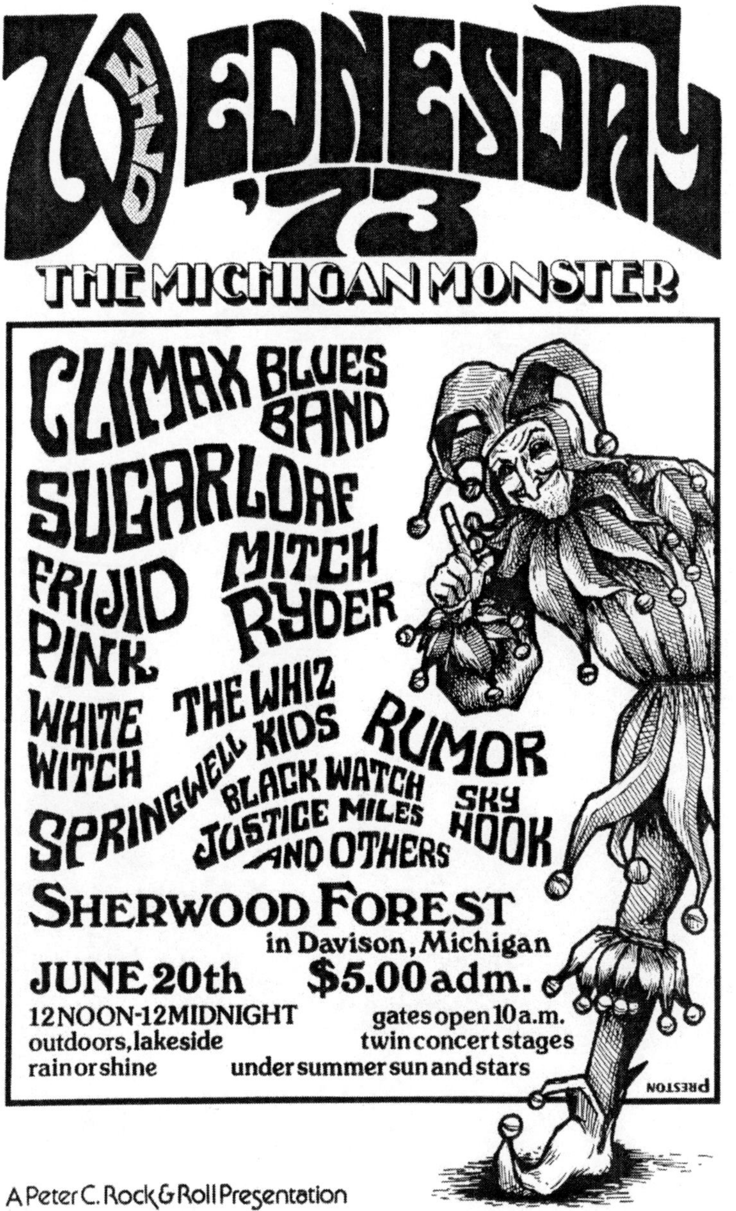
WWHND
WEDNESDAY
'73
THE MICHIGAN MONSTER
CLIMAX BLUES BAND
SUGARLOAF
FRIJID PINK
MITCH RYDER
WHITE WITCH
THE WHIZ KIDS
RUMOR
SPRINGWELL
BLACK WATCH
JUSTICE MILES
AND OTHERS
SKY HOOK
SHERWOOD FOREST
in Davison, Michigan
JUNE 20th
$5.00 adm.
12 NOON-12 MIDNIGHT
outdoors, lakeside
rain or shine
gates open 10 a.m.
twin concert stages
under summer sun and stars
PRESTON
A Peter C. Rock & Roll Presentation

freakout no. ten
PSYCHE
SUNDAY
THE MC5
THE UNIVERSAL FAMILY
SUNDAY APRIL 20 8-1
NO AGE LIMIT
TERRY SHARBACH
Grandmother's
3411 E. MICHIGAN 332-6565
$2.50 admission
AN S&S ENTERPRISES PRODUCTION

PETER C. presents
The 3rd ANNUAL
CHRISTMAS
CONCERT
DEC. 25
SAT.
BROWNSVILLE
STATION
AND
PLAIN BROWN
WRAPPER
SHERWOOD FOREST
Richfield rd.
in Davison
8-12
Preston

Peter C. presents **Under Autumn Sun & Stars** on Sept. 26

PETER C. presents THE
BIG ONE
TED NUGENT AND THE
AMBOY DUKES
IDES of MARCH
RASPBERRIES
SUNDAY FUNNIES
GUARDIAN ANGEL
WOOLIES
SALAMANDER
LIMOUSINE
SONAURA
THE DOGS
AND OTHERS
WED. AUG. 2
NOON-MIDNITE
Outdoors. Lakeside at
Sherwood Forest
In DAVISON. MICH.
ADMISSION
$5.00

PETER C.
presents
SUPER SUNDAY '72
THIS IS THE LAST OUTDOOR FESTIVAL OF THIS YEAR.
SUN. SEPT. 24th
TED NUGENT & THE AMBOY DUKES
FRIJID PINK
TEEGARDEN & VAN WINKLE
LIMOUSINE
FRUT
REGGIE ROBERTS & HOT ICE
SMACK DAB
RUMOR
AND OTHERS
ZAH ZAH!
PETE SAID THE GATES OPEN AT 10 A.M. BUT THE CONCERT LAST FROM 12 NOON TO 10 P.M.
OLE PEETEE SAY, THIS IS THE LAST ONE THIS YEAR.
OUTDOORS, LAKESIDE AT SHERWOOD FOREST IN DAVISON MICH.
IF I HAD $5.00 ID GO.

THE MICHIGAN MONSTER

Sherwood Forest June 26

Davison, Michigan Adm. $6.00

12 noon-12 midnite | gates open 10 am

OUTDOORS, LAKESIDE RAIN OR SHINE

A PETER C. ROCK & ROLL PRESENTATION

BVG